MICHAEL'S **G**UIDE

ECUADOR COLOMBIA VENEZUELA

Series editor
Michael Shichor

I *NBAL*
Travel Information Ltd.

Inbal Travel Information Ltd.
P.O.Box 39090 Tel Aviv Israel 61390

Intl. ISBN 965-288-086-8

Text: Michael Shichor
Cover photo: Avi Maromi
Photos: Moshe and Joana Frankfurter,
        Amos Kreiner, Miki Kreiner
        Avi Maromi

Distributed in the United Kingdom by:
Kuperard (London) Ltd.
9, Hampstead West
224 Iverson Road
West Hampstead
London NW6 2HL

U.K. ISBN 1-85733-032-3

*C*ONTENTS

*I*NTRODUCTION   13

A special place for tourists   **13**

Part One — Our First Steps   **15**
Making the decision to go   **15**
Who's going (15), How to go (16), When to visit and how long
to stay (21), How much does it cost (23), First Steps (24),
How to get there (33)

Part Two — Easing the Shock: Where Have We Landed?   **36**
Accommodation (36), Food and drink (37), Domestic
transportation (38), Personal security (40), Local currencies
(41), Altitude — how to cope with thin air (43), Discounts for
students and young travelers (44), Behaviour and manners
(44), Keeping in touch (45), Shopping and souvenirs (46),
Overland border crossings (47), Taxes and custom duties
(48), Working hours (48), Holidays and festivals (48)

*E*CUADOR   49

History (49), Geography and climate (53), Population,
education and culture (56), Economy (56), General
information (57)

C_OLOMBIA_ 139

History (140), Geography and climate (142), Population
(144), Economy (144), General information (145)

V_ENEZUELA_ 225

History (225), Geography and climate (228), Population and
Government (229), Economy (229), General Information
(231)

I _NDEX_ 261

T*ABLE OF MAPS*

Preface

Writing this guide, we have aimed at coming out with a comprehensive, in-depth companion for the tourist who wants to get to know the South American continent in a direct and personal way.

The modern traveler is interested in a significant, relevant, first-hand experience when touring foreign lands. He wants to get to know new and different worlds and is well aware of the effort involved. This book is written for this traveler — curious, intense, experienced and open-minded — the tourist who really and truly wishes to meet South America, face-to-face.

While writing this guide with special emphasis on enlarging upon and clarifying general areas, it was not done so at the expense of the plethora of practical details which are of vital import, if you are to fully succeed in your venture and truly enjoy the experiences awaiting you. An attempt has been made to create an information pool, which would combine material relevant to understanding the **what**, while contributing to the practicalities of the **how**.

Aware of the responsibility involved in being guide and companion to all who choose to see South America "through our looking glass," we have tried to compile as many facts and details as possible. From this pool of information, let each person take what fits best, what is most appropriate.

In the course of this work, we have labored to separate the wheat from the chaff and have tried to be as precise as possible. Naturally, many of the impressions and recommendations included in the guide are subjective. However, the guide do contain those elements which will fulfill the expectations of the kind of tourist mentioned, and will guide and assist you in making the most of your trip, in as enjoyable, comprehensive and pleasant a way as possible.

Michael Shichor

Using this guide

In order to reap maximum benefit from the information concentrated in this guide, it is advisable to read the following material carefully and act upon it.

Before setting out, it is important to read the Introduction in its entirety. The information contained there will supply you with details which will help you in making early decisions about your trip. Once you arrive at your destination you will already feel familiar and comfortable there, more so than would otherwise be the case.

In the chapters dealing with the individual countries you will find a broadly-based Introduction, whose first section deals with general topics, while the second part includes practical information about the country, its customs and ways.

The country's capital is the next section in the chapters. The information here — suggestions, recommendations and advice about the city — will guide and assist you from the time you arrive and until you leave.

From here on, the chapters are organized geographically: the different regions are presented in logical sequence, with each region surveyed along major touring routes. Following main sites noted, you will find suggestions for touring the areas around them — using the site as both your point of departure and return. In each of these touring sub-sections too, the sites are noted according to their geographical order rather than their importance, so as to make it easier to follow along the way.

As you read through, you will notice that similar information is mentioned in more than one place. This is meant to assist tourists who decide to start their tour from a particular place along the way, but have not arrived at this point via the route described or suggested in the guide, and with no prior knowledge. This allows for greater flexibility in planning your tour, without being tied to the geographical divisions or considerations of this guide.

For travelers crossing borders by land, you will find in each border town discussed a section on the procedures required for continuing into the neighboring country. Treat this as you would treat a plan to go from one site to another: read the material dealing with both places — the place from which you are coming and the one to which you are heading.

At the end of this guide we included a short vocabulary, and an alphabethic index of sites and places.

When mentioning information about transportation, accommodation, food, etc., we have tended to simplify and have preferred to give general guidelines, placing more emphasis on existing possibilities than on variable specifics. It is always disappointing to find that what you have counted on seeing or doing is not available once you finally get to the location. We have therefore tried to avoid giving specific details about subjects given to frequent change, preferring rather to advise you of those places where relevant, here-and-now information can be obtained once you are actually on the spot.

Therefore, an important rule of thumb should be to consult the local Tourist Office in each place you visit. Their addresses are mentioned in the text. They can advise you of the latest updated information for the specific time of your visit.

As for updating — this kind of guide to this part of the world cannot afford to march in place. A technical update from year to year is not enough, either. A finger on the continent's pulse is ever necessary. Up to the day this guide went to press, we attempted to confirm its relevance and up-to-dateness. However, it is only natural that due to frequent changes which occur, travelers will find certain time-related facts somewhat less than precise when they arrive at their destinations, and for this we apologize in advance.

To this end, cooperation and assistance from you who have enjoyed the information contained in this guide, is necessary and vital. It ensures, first and foremost, that those who travel in your wake will also enjoy and succeed in their ventures, as much as you have. For this purpose, we have included a short questionnaire at the end of the guide and we will be most grateful and appreciative to those of you who will take the time to complete it and send it to us.

Have a pleasant and exciting trip!

INTRODUCTION

A Special Place for Tourists

South America's exciting, exotic charm combines forces with the veteran tourist's natural curiosity. When these are reinforced by a significant drop in the costs of touring and by a constantly developing tourist infrastructure, it's no wonder that South America has become a new and captivating destination for travelers. Here is a continent that offers innumerable experiences, sights and impressions. On the one hand, it has incredible untamed scenery — canyons, deserts, mountains, jungles, rivers, and glaciers; on the other hand there's an astonishing and varied "human landscape" — a blend of cultures and races woven into a fragile and enchanting social fabric. Anyone seeking an encounter with rare worlds — a fascinating harmony of nature and scenery, man and animal, progress and antiquity — will find it here.

A trip to South America, whether for business or for pleasure, is wholly different from a trip anywhere else. Before we set out we must prepare, investigate, interpret, comprehend. As we travel, too, we engage in a process of learning, becoming acquainted and adjusting. Our ordinary ways of life and thought, attitudes to time, people, and things are simply not the same as those found in South America. Its languages, foods, clothing and customs are all quite remote from those we know. As we head for South America, we must disabuse ourselves of many biases; we must open ourselves up, both emotionally and intellectually, to wholly different messages and impressions. Though it's certainly true that the transitions are not so sharp between New York and Caracas or between Paris and Buenos Aires, the contradictions remain in full force. They accompany the tourist every step of the way, and place him in daily confrontation with his own values, opinions, and habits. The greatest return one can expect from a trip through South America is the knowledge of the existence of another world, one which lives, thinks and behaves differently, a world no better and no worse — merely different.

South America invites the tourist to share numerous experiences and ordeals — cosmopolitan cities, ancient villages that have not changed in centuries, untamed scenery of mighty grandeur, massive power projects, and all the rest. Here you'll find a fantastically wealthy elite beside shameful poverty, incomparably primitive scenes alongside technological wonders. Wonderful outings on foresaken trails will take you to Indian tribes who still go about naked, fish with harpoons, and hunt with bows and arrows. Other journeys will lead you to some of the world's best-known and most important archaeological sites.

South America has it all — for the family on their annual vacation, for the youth out to wander with a backpack, or for the retired couple on their second honeymoon. Each will find what he is seeking here. There's enough here for everyone, on every topic and in every field. On every itinerary, every form of travel, visitors are sure to find what they want — and more.

It is important to mention again that the substantial difference between "North" and "South", which accounts for Latin America's exotic splendor, requires fundamental and thorough preparation. The sharp transition obliges you to be open and tolerant, and to reinforce those qualities with advance study and suitable intellectual and emotional preparation. These guarantee a successful tour, out of which you'll get the most enjoyment; in their absence you're liable to encounter many difficulties which may well spoil your pleasure. Under all conditons and in any event it's worthwhile to behave with great patience and to accept South America for what it is — beautiful, wild, fascinating. This, after all, is the purpose of our visit, one unequalled anywhere on Earth.

*I*NTRODUCTION

Part One — Our First Steps

Before we set out we must consider a number of important points: deciding upon our route, destinations, and the like. The paragraphs that follow will guide you in these matters.

Making the decision to go

Who's going

Anyone can visit South America. Due to the great variety of sites, plentitude of things to see, and abundance of areas of interest on the way, there's almost no one who won't find what he's seeking. A great many **young tourists** spend several months exploring South America from one end to the other, wandering along the roads with backpacks and a few coins in their pockets. It's a nice "timeout" from the rat race, in addition to being an enjoyable and fascinating experience. These backpackers, known in local parlance as *mochileros*, come to know the continent perhaps better than most natives, and enjoy unrestricted mobility on all of South America's highways and byways.

More and more **middle aged** tourists have been frequenting South America in recent years, generally after having come to know both the United States and Europe. Now, in search of new and interesting places to visit, they've packed their bags and wandered to the faraway southern continent. Faraway? Not really. For the tourist, South America is closer today than it's ever been. It's no longer a backward continent, but rather a bustling and popular place, connected to the rest of the world by excellent air service.

There is no longer anything to fear about going to South America, as far as you arrange your immunizations before arrival and avoid focuses of disease. Sanitary conditions and the public services offered tourists are constantly improving, and today are not significantly inferior, in the large cities, to those we're used to in the West. Transportation services, hotels and restaurants have also conformed to a great degree to the new tourist's demands and, though difficulties still occur, the experienced tourist has no reason to refrain from visiting. Vacation and resort sites, too, are flourishing, and many people combine rest and recreation with their visit.

INTRODUCTION

As trade between Latin America and the rest of the world expands, a great many **business people** have been combining business and pleasure, enjoying the experience of getting to know different economic systems. The Latin American business world is lively and effervescent, and has adopted Western work patterns and behavior in the large cosmopolitan cities. Grand hotels, superb restaurants, and office, guide and rent-a-car services are available for the businessman and tourist of means. The South American ambience, the "flexibility" of the clock, and tendency to do things lightheartedly and at leisure leave their impact here, too, though when you get down to it, business is conducted strictly and thoroughly.

Bringing the children along requires special preparation. In many places — mainly in Andean countries such as Bolivia, Peru, Ecuador, and Colombia — it is difficult, for example, to obtain milk products. Sanitary conditions are not the best, and are liable to cause problems for adults as well. At the same time, do not hesitate to take children from the age of 7-8 years old to the large cities or the famous tourist sites. These are served by convenient access roads beside which you'll find visitors' facilities. There is no problem in touring with children in Argentina and Chile — quite the contrary.

How to go

The most comfortable way to go is, of course, with **organized group tours**. Many companies specialize in providing this kind of service — generally rather expensive — in a number of Latin American countries. Here you'll be assured that your trip will involve a minimum of difficulties and breakdowns, though you'll be deprived of personal contact with the natives, the ability to set your own timetable and itinerary, and more. It's nevertheless important to remember that there are few English speakers in South America, and visitors who don't speak Spanish or Portuguese are liable to find themselves in tight spots, especially when meandering in remote locations outside the cities.

South American group tours are varied and diverse, so that it is hard to relate to them as a single unit. Every visitor should draw up a list with a number of destinations and objectives, carefully examining the means by which he'll reach them with the greatest success and least expense.

Another way of going, of course, is the private, individual trip, where you're free to choose your own dates, destination, pace, budget, etc. Indeed, there's no greater freedom than that of a long, extended tour, where one has no obligation to preset an itinerary and timetable, but can suit these to the needs and desires of the moment.

*I*NTRODUCTION

Backpack tourism is especially popular among the young, and the young in spirit. Many spend several months in South America, making their way through the continent from country to country and site to site. It's a fascinating and pleasant way to travel. Most such visitors pick up some Spanish or Portuguese en route, get to know the natives, and get to interesting places that few visitors reach.

Backpack tourism is cheap, pleasant, and easy. The visitor should not expect many difficulties, and excluding a few countries where the police pick on tourists — such as Peru, Colombia and, to a certain extent, Argentina — it's highly improbable that you'll encounter any problems that will mar the pleasure of your trip.

Mochileros, with their packs on their backs, are usually received cordially. Tourists of all nationalities tend to meet anywhere on the continent and continue together.

Women, too, have nothing to fear in South America. Apart from several places which I wouldn't advise young women to enter alone, and apart from the fact that they shouldn't go about in dangerous urban areas late at night, I find no reason to be deterred. Traveling in pairs or small groups helps a great deal to solve these problems.

By traveling in this manner, you won't have to carry a lot of money; a few ten dollar bills per week will enable you to get along fine and in relative comfort. At the same time, bear in mind that such a journey does involve difficulties: the means of transportation you'll use aren't very good, the hotels will offer no more than the bare essentials, and so on. Hence, you'll need extra time, more strength, and lots of patience, openness, and good humor.

Well-off tourists, and those whose time is limited and who want to get in a lot of sites comfortably without wasting precious time on the road, can get the most out of their visit by careful advance planning and by making reservations. One should carefully select the sites you consider most important to visit, and draw up a timetable for your trip.

Reservations are not always essential, a fact which allows for greater flexibility en route. In this guide we've noted the places, routes, and dates that attract crowds. If you've placed these on your itinerary, be sure that you have a reliable travel agent make reservations before you set out. Make sure he obtains written confirmation since overbooking is a common phenomenon in South America and is liable to cause you great unpleasantness.

Business people would do well to arrange all matters

beforehand. The big cities frequently experience unexpected pressure on hotels, flights, and car-rental firms; though ordinary vacationers would hardly notice these problems, they are apt to cause delays and annoyance to a businessman on a tight schedule.

Where to go

In our opening paragraphs we noted that South America is rich in all kinds of places to visit. Therefore it is important to determine and locate the types of places that attract you in particular.

Mochileros setting out on an extended visit can expect to discover many of the beautiful continent's hidden secrets on the way, and will meet and enjoy its abundant treasures. Others, especially those whose time is limited, will prefer to designate one or several countries, and do them throughly. Both sorts of tourists might give preference to subjects in which they are particularly interested, and plan their trips so as to achieve the maximum in these spheres. We will survey below a number of categories in which we'll try to sketch out various directions of interest. Individual tourists will choose the categories that attract them, and draw up a plan that includes one or several.

The first possibility involves those **natural and scenic attractions** which are found throughout South America. They are divided into several types:

Glaciers and lakes are located chiefly in the continent's southern section, in southern Argentina and Chile. Here you'll find some of the world's most beautiful tour routes, enchanting scenery, friendly people. Many Andean peaks in the region feature well-developed ski areas, in top condition, because here the seasons are reversed. In Europe, holiday-makers are tanning themeselves on the beaches. North of Lima, Peru, in the vicinity of Huaraz, you'll find lovely hiking trails that demand good physical condition, the ability to adapt to unusual climatic conditions and a willingness to live primitively. All these routes require first-class camping gear.

For a pleasant stay on the **seashore** there's nothing like Brazil. Resort towns with pristine beaches abound along the Atlantic coast, especially between Vitoria and Puerto Alegre and in the Nordeste (North East). These are especially popular among Brazil's wealthy, and tourists frequent them primarily at Carnival time in February and March. Their great advantage — like that of the ski areas — is in the reversed season. Here you can swim and sunbathe from January to March, while most of Europe is buried in snow. The few coastal sites in Argentina and Chile serve mainly the local population. Peru and Ecuador have lovely beaches, though these lack a developed service infrastructure. There are developed beaches in Colombia and Venezuela, with the popular ones located along the Caribbean. Hotel occupancy and prices are high during the summer months (June-August), and it's important to make advance reservations.

A long strip of exclusive resort clubs has sprouted along the Caribbean coast, where you can spend a seaside vacation under ideal conditions, renting gear for fishing, sailing, diving, and more. Some of the beaches, especially those in the Caracas area, are rather neglected; their level of upkeep has deteriorated perceptibly.

About one-third of South America is covered with thick **jungle**. On the exceedingly popular jungle excursions tourists can encounter out-of-the-way cultures and get a first-hand impression of ancient ways of life that are rapidly disappearing. It's important to remember that jungle trips require special effort, organization, and experience. You can take such trips in Brazil, Bolivia, Peru, Ecuador, Colombia and Venezuela. Each of these countries has extensive jungle regions.

The jungle's harsh and unpleasant climate — an oppressive combination of high temperatures, high humidity, and frequent rainfall — explains to a large extent why the area has not been settled, though it also deserves credit for the lush wild vegetation. This flora, watered by giant rivers such as the Amazon, the Orinoco, and their tributaries, is of decisive importance in reducing air pollution and maintaining the natural environmental equilibrium in all of South America. An outing to the jungles must be planned carefully and with great caution. Though most of the jungle is free of malaria, it is recommended taking medication against that disease, along with water purification tablets and mosquito repellent.

Travelers visit the jungle cities of Peru and Brazil in great numbers, either on organized tours or on their own. Though the former are very expensive, it's worth remembering that the "unattached" visitor, too, will find a visit to these areas far from cheap. Prices in and around the jungle towns are far higher than elsewhere as goods must be imported from far away. Be prepared for this, and bring along a sufficient amount of the local currency.

The jungles in Ecuador's eastern region are home to a number of Indian tribes, and are accessible as a relatively "short hop" from the capital. The jungles in Ecuador offer a maximum return of enjoyment and interesting experiences while demanding minimum investment of time, effort, and expense.

*I*NTRODUCTION

Wildlife: Though the jungle might appear to be **the** place for observing wildlife in its natural habitat, this is in fact not the case. It is true that jungle tours can give you a glimpse of thousands of strange and varied species of birds, insects, butterflies, and even reptiles, monkeys, and wild boars, but you can't assume so. You must penetrate deep into the jungle, and there's no guarantee that you'll find what you've come for there, either.

By contrast, the Galapagos Islands off Ecuador are famous for their abundant wildlife, most of it unique. It is rather expensive to visit, and it's best to make reservations for a flight to the islands, and on the ships and boats that sail among them. The lovely nature reserve on the Paracas Islands off central Peru has thousands of birds and sea lions, and is far less expensive and more convenient to visit. Bolivia and Chile, too, have nature reserves with a multitude of wild animals, primarily of the llama family.

In Brazil, in the area of the Bolivian border, there are vast stretches of marshes known as the Pantanal, inhabited by an abundance of birds, alligators and other animals. The best time to visit here is during the dry season, between May and September, when one can really appreciate the variety and profusion of wildlife.

The Valdéz Peninsula in southern Argentina is another fascinating reserve, with penguins, whales, sea lions, and more. The best time for visiting it is October or November, when the animal population reaches its annual peak.

Another planning strategy places the emphasis on South America's **complex social structure**, concentrating on sites from **the continent's past**, as well as those which accent its special present.

Archaeology: The glory of pre-Columbian settlement in the southern half of the Americas is, of course, the Inca Empire and its center, the city of Cuzco, Peru. From these, the Inca (emperor) and his men dominated the tribes from Ecuador in the north as far as central Chile in the south. Few pre-Incan remains have survived in South America. Remains of what is thought to be the oldest settlement in all the Americas have been discovered at Puerto Varas (Southern Chile), and are being studied thoroughly. Pre-Incan civilizations existed primarily in Tihuanacu, Bolivia, around the village of San Agustin in southern Colombia, and in various locations in Peru. While the tourist will certainly want to visit San Agustin and Tihuanacu, the pinnacle of his archaeological experience will undoubtedly be a visit to the Inca sites, with the lost Inca city of Machu Picchu as the highpoint.

INTRODUCTION

Folklore and folk culture: Age-old Indian traditions have blended with the Spanish influence to produce a unique and extraordinary compendium of folklore and culture. All of South America, and the Andean countries in particular, excel in uncommonly beautiful handicrafts of unique character and style. Visiting these countries is like an extended shopping trip. This activity centers on the marketplaces — in large cities, country towns, and remote villages. In some, the barter system is still practiced. The markets of South America are colorful, effervescent, lively, and enchantingly beautiful. Most commerce is carried on by women, and they are most skillful at it. As you meander through the markets choose carefully, check quality, compare prices, and bargain, **always** bargain.

Most South American countries have a rich and varied folklore. Folk music varies from country to country: while quiet cowboy songs typify Argentina and Venezuela, Brazillian music is usually stormy and rhythmic. Music and dance in the Andean countries draw on Indian sources; typical musical instruments are the *charango*, the drum, and the reed flute. Music and dance dominate Latin American life. Numerous holidays and festivals are celebrated on the continent every year, and there's hardly a month when some part of the continent isn't gearing up for a festival. National festivities reach their peak with folk festivals, most in February or March. The largest and most famous is the Brazillian Carnival, unequalled anywhere in the world for beauty and joy. The most important festivals in Peru and Bolivia are held in February-March and June-July.

When to visit and how long to stay

Getting to know South America inside and out is a matter of month after month of intensive touring. The first condition for success is command — albeit of the most rudimentary nature — of Spanish (or, for Brazil, Portuguese). *Mochilero* touring of this sort usually lasts from three months up to more than a year, and allows you to visit most countries on the continent, exploring them exhaustively and comprehensively. Eight to ten months seems the optimal length for such a trip, broken down more or less as follows: two to three months in Argentina and Chile, three to five months in the Andean countries (Bolivia, Peru, Ecuador, and Colombia); two to four months in Brazil; and one more month for the remaining countries.

The tourist with this much time available can fix his original port of entry at whatever point is cheapest to reach, and move around in accordance with weather conditions and the various special events that take place throughout the year.

*I*NTRODUCTION

Argentina and Chile

The period from September to March is best; plan to visit the southernmost regions close to the middle of that period, when the weather there is best. Before September and after March the continent's southern reaches suffer harsh and unpleasant wintery weather, when touring is almost impossible. These countries' central and northern areas can be visited the year around.

Brazil and Venezuela

The period from October to June, the hot season, is recommended. Then you can go most places with ease, tan on the beach, roam the jungles, visit the cities, and so on. The desire to participate in the Carnival, celebrated annually in February or March determines for most tourists when they go to Brazil, and this is how it should be. Participating in the Carnival is undoubtedly an experience not to be missed; what's more, it's held at the best time of the year for a visit. Yet, this is the peak of the tourist season, and you better make reservations well in advance for hotel and other tourist services.

The Andean countries

These may be visited the year round, though the summer months (November-February) are the wettest, with showers liable to mar your enjoyment. During those months excursions to the mountains and jungle are difficult, so it's a good idea to make the effort to come during the winter (May-September), when although it's a bit cooler, the skies are clear and the weather excellent.

On the Galapagos Islands (Ecuador), as in the countries along the equator (Ecuador, Venezuela, and parts of Brazil, Colombia, and Peru), the weather is stable the year round, with no extreme differences among the seasons.

These climatic details describe somewhat generally the course of the season according to a rough division of the continent, and are meant for those traveling for extended periods. Those making shorter visits will find a more precise description of the climate in the chapters on each country; furthermore, a section dealing with local weather is included for each of the large cities.

Tourists who want to know as much as possible of South America within a limited time period, may opt for a number of different possibilities, according to their special interests. In all events, it seems that any visit to South America, even if you wish to focus on a certain region and a simple field, requires at least three to four weeks. It's most desirable that it be planned with enough flexibility to allow for possible changes in your intinerary.

None of this applies, for example, to those coming for a week-long organized tour of Brazil to attend the Carnival, or for ten days of sailing among the Galapagos Islands. But apart from such limited frameworks you should allow a longer period. The great distances, extreme variation from place to place, range of sites, and tour and holiday possibilities make this much time necessary. One must always bear in mind the chance of delays on the way, so that a packed and precise timetable — reminiscent of one's last visit to Switzerland — would be wholly inappropriate here.

How much does it cost?

Since the mid eighties, fierce competition among the various airlines has led to tremendous cuts in airfares to destinations in South America. Today they are not much higher than for flights of similar length to other destinations and we are the fortunate beneficiaries.

Another factor which played a role was the depreciation of the local currencies. The difficult economic situation of the Latin American countries finds expression in inflation and frequent devaluations of their currency against the dollar, which has gained greatly in strength in recent years even in comparison to stable European currencies — and all the more so in comparison to the South American currencies, which generally serve as legal tender in rickety economic systems that have been in a distressed state for some time.

From the tourist's point of view, of course, there's a distinct plus to this situation. Domestic price rises do not always keep up with the rate of devaluation, and sometimes people with dollars or a stable European currency to spend will find prices for meals, lodging and shopping which may appear ridiculous when judged by Western standards. However, local people, earning local incomes, can not always afford even minimal needs.

South America is, therefore, a better tourist bargain then ever before. On the one hand, airfare is cheaper than in the past; on the other, expenditures for transportation, accommodation, food, shopping and so forth are far lower than they used to be. The cost of living is not uniform everywhere, and prices, of course, vary from country to country. The cheapest countries to visit are the Andean ones, while the most expensive are Venezuela, Uruguay, and Paraguay. Even the last three, however, which in the not-too-distant past were expensive even by European and American standards, have become significantly cheaper, and a visit there today is no more expensive than an intermediate-priced tour in Europe or North America. Countries once considered prohibitive, such as Argentina, Chile, and Brazil, have become much less expensive, and the devalutation of their currencies gives you the chance to enjoy a tour of reasonable standards.

When dealing with luxury tourism, there's almost no gap with the West. The best hotels in Bogotá, Caracas, Lima, Rio, São Paulo, Buenos Aires and the like are rather expensive, especially at peak tourist season or at holiday or Carnival time. Car rental rates resemble those the world over, but first-class restaurants tend to be less expensive than their counterparts in the Western world.

In conclusion, it can be said that the range is broad; each of us must choose a path in accordance with our means. On every budget, though, tourists will find South America open, ready to meet them, and easy on the wallet.

First Steps

Once you've decided how, when and where to go, all that's left is to make practical preparations for the journey. The next section deals with these matters, spelling out everything that must be done before leaving home, in order to make the trip as successful, easy, comfortable and inexpensive as possible.

Documents and papers

Anyone going to South America requires a valid passport, except for citizens of certain South American countries who may cross into neighboring states with nothing more than an identity card. Some of the Latin American states require that your passport be valid for at least six months beyond your date of entry. It's best to get your passport some time prior to your trip, for some of these countries require you to obtain an entry visa in advance, and issuing this visa generally takes several days.

In our chapters on each country, we've spelled out the relevant regulations and documents you'll need; study them before you go. We should again mention that immigration regulations in the South American countries are in a constant state of flux; you **must** consult the embassy, consulate or tourist bureau of the country you intend to visit, shortly before your trip, in order to obtain up-to-date and reliable information.

Countries that require an entry visa have fixed procedures for issuing them. You'll need to present a passport, an entry and departure ticket, a photograph, and relevant travel documents (reservations, a letter from your place of work, etc.) The visa takes from one to three days to be issued, and usually involves no difficulties. All visa matters should be seen to in your own country, but if necessary, they can be obtained en route, in each of the countries you visit on the way.

A tourist card issued by airlines or distributed at frontier posts to those arriving by land has replaced visas in many cases. This card, which is free, must be filled out before you land or at the border station, and handed to the immigration officials along with your passport. A stamped copy will be attached to your passport, and returned when leaving the country.

We must stress that, as a rule, government clerks, police and military personnel check documents punctiliously, so keep them on you at all times, properly stamped and arranged. Many tourists have found that letters of reference (for example, a letter confirming that you were sent on business by your employer), various certificates (preferably with your photograph), and documents that have an official look to them are frequently of help in getting pesky clerks or policemen to leave you alone.

Due to frequent changes, find out before arrival which immunizations are required at your destination country, and how long before departing you need the vaccinations. This is specially true for cholera.

A tourist's national driver's license is accepted in most South American countries, on condition that a Spanish translation has been attached. Even so, we recommend that you obtain an International Driver's License and make sure that one of its languages is Spanish.

A Student Card is good for certain discounts and benefits. In Argentina and Chile students are granted discounts on public transportation, though foreign students may have to engage in lengthy bargaining to receive them. In Peru, significant discounts are given to students on tickets for museums, archaeological sites, and more. Venezuela discounts certain domestic flights. The essential condition for using your Student Card is that it be valid and bear your photograph.

One should not go to South America without an **insurance policy** covering health and baggage. Theft is a common occurrence throughout the continent, and the uninsured tourist is liable to suffer great financial damage. The matter of health insurance, however, is even more serious. Because disease is rife, and medical care and drugs are expensive, under no circumstances should one leave a matter as important as health insurance to chance or luck; no knowledgeable tourist would ever set out without being properly insured.

Though it can hardly be described as a document, you'll find in your travels that an MCO card is as important as if it were one. An MCO is a flight voucher issued by airlines that are members of IATA, and is honored by all other IATA members. At many border points where you'll be asked to show a departure card, and when you apply for a visa, an MCO will satisfy the requirement in most cases. It's important to check that its value is specified in dollars and in no other currency, for the voucher is calculated according to the value in the currency in which it was paid. At the end of your trip you can apply your MCO to pay for the flight ticket you want, or you can redeem it where it was issued or at the airline office.

Health

Most serious diseases have been totally eradicated in South America, and linger on only in the most remote jungles. Malaria no longer strikes in the cities and towns, though those wishing to penetrate deep into the jungles should bring malaria pills as a preventive measure.

Intestinal diseases are very widespread in South America, due to the poor sanitary conditions and inappropriate food storage methods. Be prepared for the near certainty that at some stage you'll come down with intestinal trouble. It's worth your while to bring along any medication you're used to taking. Don't hesitate to consult a doctor in serious cases, for common diseases such as hepatitis are liable to cause you great distress if not discovered in time. Bear in mind that in 1991 the colera attacked many countries in South America, especially in the Andean countries, where the epidemic killed thousands of people.

Avoid fresh vegetables (eat only boiled ones) and fruits. Drink bottled water only, and make sure that it wasn't opened before. Despite the fact that in most large cities the water undergoes filtration and purification, it's still contains pollutants and bacteria which not infrequently cause stomach aches and more serious ailments. Carbonated drinks and bottled water will help you overcome the problem (we're not referring to mineral water but to ordinary water that has been boiled and purified). When you're in the country or in places where bottled drinks are unavailable boil your drinking water and purify it with chlorine tablets.

Mosquitoes and other flying pests are especially common in tropical areas, and are a real menace. **Don't go there** without large quantities of mosquito repellent and — no less important

— ointment to spread on the bite when the repellent fails to work. A visit to Asuncion, Paraguay, or the jungles of eastern Ecuador cannot but end with dozens or hundreds of painful bites.

Every tourist must bring along a small kit with first-aid supplies and medicines. Many kinds of medication are hard to find in South America, and those which are available are expensive and not always usable due to their age or storage conditions. Before you set out, see your doctor in order to obtain an adequate stock of essential medications. A short list of essential drugs and medical items follows:

Medication for intestinal diseases.
Painkillers.
Fever pills.
Anti-malaria pills.
Chlorine tablets for water purification.
Antibiotic ointment.
Antiseptics.
Gauze pads, bandages and adhesive tape.
Medication for chronic illnesses.

The chronically ill, and heart and asthma patients, should consult their doctors concerning the treatment they may require in the climatic conditions and altitude of the lands they're going to visit. Asthmatics should be doubly cautious when going to high elevations, where even healthy people find it hard to adjust to the thin atmosphere.

Women should bring tampons and birth-control pills in sufficient quantity since these items are difficult to obtain in Latin America, except in some of the large cities.

Before setting out, it's best to have a thorough checkup to ascertain that your health permits you to take the trip. Medical care in South America is generally not of the highest quality, and it's best to try not to need it. See your dentist for preventive treatment to forestall problems that might arise during your tour. South American dental care is definitely not recommended, except in truly urgent cases.

For the trip itself, I'd recommend bringing an extra pair of eye glasses and the lense prescription. Contact lenses, though generally convenient to use, are liable to cause problems and discomfort in dry areas and at high elevation.

Thus far we've been speaking of the continent in general. It's obvious that in certain places — mainly cosmopolitan capital cities — the sanitary conditions are good and medical services advanced. Nevertheless, do yourself a favor and set out well-equipped and prepared for most eventualities.

*I*NTRODUCTION

Finances

The most popular and convenient currency to use and exchange in South America is the U.S. dollar, recognized and sought after everywhere; converting it presents no problem in the large cities. The Pound Sterling, Deutsch Mark, and Swiss Franc are also recognized, but exchanging them can involve problems, especially on the black market.

Currency laws vary from country to country. How much money to take and in what form depends to a great extent on the regulations in effect in the countries you decide to visit.

In most South American countries a black market in foreign currency is active. For cash dollars, moneychangers will give you local currency at higher rates than the banks offer. When visiting these countries, it's worthwhile to carry more cash and fewer travelers' checks. Credit card transactions and bank transfers involve the official exchange rate, since charge slips are calculated according to that rate and the transfers are paid in it — in local currency. Given that the difference between the official and "black" rates may reach 50% and more, it's only wise to avoid using these financial means.

The theft epidemic that has spread through some of the South American countries — especially Colombia, Peru, Brazil, and Venezuela — has led many banks to refuse to cash travelers' checks out of fear that they may be stolen, and, at times, tourists are put through an exhausting bureaucratic procedure. A letter of credit is not efficient either; getting it honored is a slow and complicated affair and here, too, and payment is made at the official rate.

Those traveling for short periods can make it easier on themselves by carrying cash, whereas long-term travelers would do well to divide their resources into a number of baskets, to minimize risk.

In certain countries — Uruguay, Venezuela, and at times Bolivia and Ecuador — travelers' checks can sometimes be converted into cash dollars for a fee, but the regulations in these matters are always changing and cannot be relied upon. This point is particularly important for tourists who want to stock up on cash en route to countries with black markets.

It's worth your while to bring a credit card. Their use is widespread throughout South America, and can be used to purchase goods, services, and for cash withdrawals. It's important to note that cash withdrawals involve a 4%-5% commission; you should consider whether this service is worth the price. In any case, using your credit card is worthwhile only in countries where there is no black market, so that your account will be debited at the same rate as that at which you would change money on the spot.

The alternative to carrying cash or using a credit card is travelers' checks. We recommend using small denominations — nothing over $50; hundred-dollar travelers' checks are harder to cash. In small towns, it is difficult to exchange travelers' checks in any case; not only is the exchange rate low, but there is a high commission as well. It's best to stick to travlers' checks issued by *Bank of America*, *Thomas Cook*, and *American Express*.

Always keep your money, credit cards, and documents **well-hidden** in your clothing. Guarding against theft here requires precautionary measures that we're not accustomed to in Europe and North America; nevertheless they are essential, and mustn't be scorned.

What to take

As a general rule, the less you take the better. The advantages of traveling light far outweigh the satisfaction of a few extra clothes — after all, you're going on a trip, not a fashion show. When all is said and done, a large portion of what you take never gets used in any case, and you quickly learn that most of what you took along was quite unnecessary.

Remember, whatever you need — you'll manage to find during the trip — perhaps not of the same type, model, or quality you are used to, but I have yet to meet a traveler wandering around the world. During the trip you'll be picking up many souvenirs and presents, so you should really take along the bare necessities — but plenty of resourcefulness.

Clothing depends on your destination and the season. Businessmen must be smartly dressed, although a jacket and tie are not usually necessary. In the large cities, appropriate evening dress is customary for both men and women, and sportswear for young people and children. *Mochileros* will feel most comfortable in jeans and casual wear, although they should also take along more festive wear for events that require this.

Lightweight and simple clothes are always appreciated, and are easy to wash and carry. Avoid taking elegant evening attire that requires careful transport and special care. It just isn't worth the effort.

I wouldn't suggest taking along more than one backpack or suitcase. These too should be at the most average in size. Baggage weighing more than 15 kg can be a real burden, and more than 20 kg can be even expensive. Many airlines are strict about the baggage limit, and travelers with overweight have to pay for it.

Comfortable walking shoes are perhaps the most important item. These are appropriate for any type of trip or travel. It is not an exaggeration to say that a bad pair of shoes can utterly ruin a trip. So make a point of getting good walking shoes and don't skimp.

Camping Gear

Those embarking on an extended tour and intending to explore the entire continent should put everything in a backpack, including camping gear. When buying camping gear, be sure that its quality is appropriate for your needs. Remember that it must serve you for long months, and that cheap equipment, saving you money at the time of purchase, is liable to prove a painful impediment when you're on the road.

A list of essential items follows:

A lightweight **backpack** with **internal** metal frame, lots of pockets, and laces to which a sleeping bag, mattress, and other gear can be tied.

A **sleeping bag:** Chose one appropriate for the season and the area to which you are headed. For a lengthy trip through a number of climatic zones you should get a warm sleeping bag (-5 or -20 degrees Centigrade) made of down. It must be of excellent quality, well sewn, and with a reliable zipper. Sleeping bags come in various sizes and shapes; be sure that yours matches your dimensions. The "mummy" style, wide at the shoulders and narrow around the legs, is the best of all. It holds body heat well and is easy to carry. Synthetic-filled sleeping bags are much cheaper, but are much larger, bulkier, and heavier. Remember that you'll have to carry it on your back — week after week and month after month — and the inconvenience will outweigh your savings. On the other hand, bear in mind that the down bag has one great disadvantage: when it gets wet, it loses its efficiency and special qualities; sleeping in it then is downright unpleasant.

A **mattress:** To soften the bed of rocks on which you'll spend many a night, we recommend — highly, if you've got a down sleeping bag — an easy-to-carry mattress. There are two common types: foam-rubber and inflatable (especially made for capming). The latter costs more, but provides comfort and ensures a good night's sleep, essential after a full day of walking.

A **tent:** We recommend a two-man, two-layer model with a floor. A one-man tent isn't enough, for you're unlikely to find yourself alone on outings into the country. A two-layer tent provides better protection against rain, retains heat, and repels moisture.

A **cooking stove:** This is essential on hikes through the countryside, and economical in town. Since gas for camping stoves is almost unavailable in South America and comes at great cost when it is at hand, we think it best to use a kerosene stove. The most popular models are made by Colman and the Optimus company of Sweden. They are reliable, safe, and easy to carry. Remember to exercise great caution when using them. Flammable materials may cause disaster if you don't treat them with the caution they deserve.

Utensils: Bring the minimum, but choose good ones. Metal or aluminium is best. Food should be kept in plastic or cloth bags, since cans take up more space in your pack.

Miscellaneous: Pocketknife, flashlight, rope, etc.

Buying equipment represents one of the largest expenditures of your trip. It's therefore worthwhile to do some comparison shopping and not buy hastily. At the same time, I must again stress that economy must not be at the expense of quality, for the "saving" is liable to cost you dearly on the road. It's also worth noting that camping equipment is in great demand in South America, so that at the end of your trip your gear can be sold for a reasonable price; not much lower than what you paid for it.

The traditional centers for buying camping gear are London and New York, where you'll find the widest selection and the most attractive prices. Though London has many stores that handle camping gear, the best, in my view, is the Youth Hostel Association store at 14 Southampton Street (Tel. 836-8541). This is a gigantic store where you'll find it all — from shoelaces to emergency dehydrated rations. A tourist could enter this store stark naked and come out a few hours later with everything needed for a trip around the world. YHA members receive a 10% discount on all purchases.

In New York you can pick up your gear at any of hundreds of camping and sporting goods stores. The largest, Paragon, offers a seemingly inexhaustible selection of merchandise, at prices suitable for all budgets.

Photography

One of the most enjoyable aspects of a trip is taking photographs. It is worth making your photographic preparations in advance, acquiring appropriate equipment, and learning at least the basics of how to use your camera.

Many tourists wander through South America with sophisticated and complicated photographic equipment. South America is a photographer's paradise, fertile ground for expression and creativity. Those who are familiar with the secrets of the art will come equipped with several cameras, lenses, and a range of film.

If, however, you wish to commemorate your trip without lugging a mobile studio around with you, it is recommended to take one camera with three lenses: a standard lens (50mm), a wide-angle lens, and a telephoto lens. A good lens that combines all three functions is the 35-210 zoom. Buy good and reliable equipment, and remember to wrap it well and to insure it. Avoid taking fancy and expensive equipment, since it is likely to get knocked about on the way. Such equipment can also attract thieves. Film is expensive in most South American countries, so take along plenty of film, since you can always sell what you don't use. As a general rule, use ASA 64 film, which is suitable for almost every type of light and weather conditions you'll encounter in South America. ASA 400 film is also worth taking, since it is hard to find, and particularly expensive when available. If you have to buy photographic supplies in South America itself, do so only in the large cities, since elsewhere, not only is film hard to come by and exorbitantly priced, most of it is also likely to have long since past its expiration date.

In South America film is developed in various sorts of laboratories, and it's not always worth taking the risk. As a rule, it's better to develop films in the United States or Europe. In some locations, such as Buenos Aires, São Paulo or La Paz, you can have your film developed with relative safety in Kodak laboratories. Slide film whose purchase price includes developing should be sent directly to the company laboratory, which will return it directly to your home address.

For those carrying video cameras, keep in mind that in some countries Betamax is more popular than VHS, and Video 8 is not always available, nor are the accessories (filters, batteries, etc.). Bring with you all the necessary equipment. When using rechargeable batteries, remember that some countries use 220V and others 110V. Bring along an adaptor with the proper amperage. Those who buy pre-recorded video-cassettes, pay attention to the fact that some countries use the NTSC (American) standard, while others use the more widespread PAL (German). Check the labels before you pay!

Language
You won't have any language problems in South America's large cities. Most people dealing principally with tourists have sufficient command of English to help you get what you want, and it can be assumed that shortly after your arrival you'll

pick up enough of the local conversational "code" to express basic needs. The problems begin when you venture outside the professional tourism framework, and even on its fringes — taxis and restaurants. Few taxi drivers or waiters speak English. Communication is in Spanish only, as are most restaurant menus.

It's even worse in outlying areas. English-speakers are few and far between in the towns, and in villages — nonexistent. On the roads, too, and even in tourist bureaus, airline offices, and banks, it's hard to find someone fluent in the language of Shakespeare, Keats and Milton, or even with enough English to understand a request for a glass of water.

Nor will a command of Spanish or Portuguese solve the problem altogether. In many places — Paraguay, northern Bolivia and the mountain towns of Peru, for example — ancient Indian languages are used. Although most locals speak Spanish at one level or another, it's hard to maintain verbal communication with them in the accepted sense of the term.

Those who've set their hearts on a long, thorough exploration of the secrets of the South American continent absolutely must acquire the basic linguistic skills before setting out. It's true that one picks up a language during a trip, and that within a month or two one is able to carry on a basic conversation with the locals, but advance preparation will make things much easier and increase your enjoyment. No less important is the fact that advance study will establish a correct grammatical foundation, to which a large vocabulary will be added as you go. On-the-road study, though easier, is built atop a shaky foundation, which will demand great efforts to repair afterwards.

How to get there

By air: Most European airlines maintain service between their respective capitals and various destinations in South America, as do the national airlines of the South American countries. The latter also fly to various destinations in the United States, as does *Eastern*.

A number of ticket options are available to and from South America; their terms and fares vary from airline to airline and from country to country. Excursion tickets, limited in time, are generally the cheapest, followed by youth and student tickets. The most expensive are ordinary tickets sold at IATA prices. A combined ticket, by which different sections of the route are flown on different airlines, is usually more expensive than flying all sections with the same airline.

*I*NTRODUCTION

Planning your flights requires thorough preparation and comprehensive market research. Careful investigation and resourcefulness can save lots of money and cut the price of your trip. The open market and fierce competition have led to a situation in which passengers aboard the same plane on the very same flight may well have paid completely different fares.

As a rule a round-trip ticket is worthwhile, unless you're making an extended trip and don't want to commit yourself about where and when it's going to end. Airline tickets bought in South America are subject to excise taxes at rates that vary from country to country; this makes them significantly more expensive. A round-trip ticket purchased outside the country from which you're returning is exempt from tax.

Those who want a one-way ticket should check which routes and combinations may make the trip cheaper. Such routes, for example, go via the Carribbean islands, Central America, and so on. Certain destinations are traditionally more expensive than others. Flights to São Paulo, Buenos Aires, Santiago, La Paz, and elsewhere are far more expensive than those to Lima, Rio de Janeiro, and Bogotá. Relatively low-cost flights reach the latter group of cities from London, Paris, and Miami. It's a good idea to inquire at travel agencies which specialize in these destinations about the cheapest and best way to get there.

Ordinary tickets are more expensive one-way than round-trip. Their great advantage lies in the fact that they are calculated on a mileage basis. Holders can change dates and arrange for stopovers on the way, so long as these remain within the permitted mileage. Thus, for example, a New York-Buenos Aires ticket gives one the right to stop over in Miami, Caracas, Belem, Rio, and São Paulo at no extra cost.

London and Miami are known as preferred ports of departure for Latin America; here you can usually find the cheapest tickets. A significant portion of these tickets are sold over-the-counter only, and travel agents in other countries are not permitted to sell them. A stopover in one of those cities and a visit to some of these agencies may be worth your while, even though you must remember that two days in London cost money too, as does a separate ticket to London. At times it may be cheaper to buy a slightly higher-priced ticket where you live, with the margin offset by the savings in time, stopover expense, and the effort involved in getting around a foreign city.

The national airlines of Venezuela (*Viasa*), Colombia (*Avianca*) and Peru (*Aero Peru*) are known for being less expensive than the other South American flag carriers. They fly to numerous destinations, but you must change planes in their respective capitals. European airlines such as *Air France, Iberia*, and the Portuguese *TAP* also offer seasonal packages worth taking advantage of. Never buy until you've checked and compared prices!

When buying discounted tickets, be very careful about their validity and reliability. Remember that any change involves additional payment, and it's best to know how much is in question in advance. Avail yourself of the services of reliable travel agents — there are charlatans in this field too. Best of all are travel agencies that specialize in tourism to South America, and have package deals with various airlines.

By land: An overland trip from North America via Central America is a unique experience. It can be done by car, bus, or train, and you'll need to do the Panama-Colombia stretch by sea or air. The highway there still isn't suitable for traffic, and is impassible several months out of the year. Due to political tensions in Central America, you should check exactly when and how to cross various countries, and, even more so, when and how not to. If you're driving, bring along plenty of spare parts, and have someone along with mechanical knowledge. Your car papers must be in good order, since they'll be inspected every time you turn a corner.

*I*NTRODUCTION

Part Two — Easing the Shock: Where Have We Landed?

Previous sections of this introduction have dealt with the preparations and arrangements necessary before the trip begins. Now we shall survey some relevant details concerning the trip itself, to make the experience of landing in this alien world a bit easier. The material we're about to present is meant first of all to facilitate your adjustment to South America, but reading it before you go may be of great importance in determining the form and nature of your tour. Here you'll find much **useful information** about all spheres of your trip which will help you overcome quickly, comfortably, and efficiently the range of problems liable to arise at the very beginning of your trip.

The paragraphs that follow offer some general advice, and in the chapters on each respective country, you'll find more specific information on those countries and their sites.

Accommodation
South America offers a wide variety of accommodation possibilities. All the large cities have luxury hotels, some of which belong to the world's great hotel chains; standards here equal those in the Western countries, with prices set accordingly. In the large cities you'll also find locally owned luxury hotels, whose prices are lower although the level of service is in no way inferior.

Intermediate-class and inexpensive hotels abound. Almost all hotels outside the cities charge intermediate or low rates, and many are very inexpensive. Lodging is significantly cheaper in the Andean countries than in the lowland countries (Brazil and Venezuela), but conditions there, too, are far worse.

Be careful when choosing a hotel that is not first-class. In many places these are not regulated in any way. At the same time we must note that the Ministries of Tourism in most South American countries are making an effort to enforce hotel regulations. In the large cities and major tourist centers you'll find that most hotels are clean, reliable, and altogether satisfactory.

Away from the big tourist centers and along the roads, there are always places to stay. Almost every village has a house that serves as a hotel, but don't expect much here — at best a creaky bed and rickety chair. Sanitation and cleanliness, too, are not the best.

Youth hostels aren't popular in South America, though you will find them in some places. On the other hand, it's customary to put up young travelers in churches, schools, youth clubs, and even fire stations — for no charge.

Camping grounds are rather rare. In some countries — mainly Argentina, Chile, and Brazil — they do exist and can serve the tourist public. They aren't organized along North American lines, and the tourist must provide his own tent and sleeping equipment. On many routes tourists spend their nights under the stars in improvised campgrounds and an informal atmosphere.

Food and drink

In the culinary field, too, we've landed in a very strange place. We've all heard the legends about Argentinian steaks and Brazilian coconuts, but we should also be ready for what comes along with them — guinea-pig (*cuy*) in Peru, eel in Chile, and similar terrors elsewhere.

The South American cuisine, like everything else on the continent, combines Indian tradition with Spanish influence, and its national character is determined by what's grown where. A lot of meat is eaten in Argentina, Uruguay, Paraguay and Venezuela; lots of fish and seafood in Chile and Peru; and tropical fruit in Brazil. Potatoes and rice are standard side-dishes in every restaurant; so is soup, a very popular item throughout the continent and many varieties are served.

Milk products are hard to get in the Andean countries, in contrast to Argentina, Chile, and Brazil where they are plentiful — and excellent. *Empanadas* (stuffed pastry), *mate* (South American tea), and many other delicacies are only some of the contents in the bursting menu of excellent food and drink enjoyed by the local populace. We'll cover them in detail and at length in our Introduction to each country.

South American restaurants are innumerable. Every second house serves as one, and every streetcorner has two more. In the cities, a variety of food is served at all levels of quality, while in towns and villages native and peasant cooking is the most common fare. Hygienic conditions aren't the best, but that's something you get used to as time and upset stomachs pass... Western manners and dress are customary in the better restaurants, while the more popular ones favor a free and informal atmosphere. Eating at streetside stands, kiosks, and market stalls is a common practice. It's a quick and cheap way to get a meal, and how most of the locals get their nourishment. Try it, but remember to check how clean, or perhaps how "undirty" the place is. Mealtimes vary from country to country, according to the climate.

Fruit and vegetable lovers will have problems in the Andean countries, where most produce may be tainted with various diseases. Even if they appear healthy to the eye, their insides are liable to be infested. You must therefore adopt an ironclad rule about fruit and vegetables: peel them, cook them, or throw them out. If you can't peel or cook it, **don't try it!**

Vegetarians will manage quite well. Although vegetarian restaurnts aren't very common, the major foods on which a vegetarian diet is based are available in abundance, and can be prepared yourself.

Domestic transportation

Airlines link the South American countries with one another. International flights are frequent and convenient, and prices resemble those of short international flights in the West. Domestic flights are another story. Here the range is broad, complications are rife, and confusion reigns.

In Brazil, Argentina, Peru, and Colombia the airlines offer an open ticket for unlimited flights during a predetermined time period. In these countries, where covering distances overland requires many days, this is an offer certainly worthy of consideration. To go from Rio de Janeiro to Manaus or from Buenos Aires to Bariloche takes days or weeks by land, and the cost of an individual flight is high. In addition, *Aerolineas Argentinas* has reduced-price night flights, which cost about the equivalent trips by bus. You must therefore weigh the alternatives well and decide accordingly. An unlimited-flight ticket may be bought only **outside** the country in which you intend to fly.

The armed forces of the South American countries also operate flights that carry civilian passengers. These are cheaper than their civilian counterparts, but take off at irregular intervals and generally involve antiquated aircraft.

Another typical problem of domestic flights is overbooking. Airlines are not reliable when issuing tickets, and frequently sell more tickets than the number of seats at their disposal. You must therefore get to the airport early; otherwise the flight is liable to fill up and leave you waiting for another. Cancellations, delays, and changes of routes are also common occurrences, for which the tourist must be prepared.

Be very sure to mark your gear, although even this doesn't guarantee that it will reach its destination. The care of passengers' luggage, especially in Peru, is negligent and contemptuous. Try to carry as much as possible, and relegate to the baggage compartment only the necessary minimum, **after** you've packed and marked it properly.

Driving a private or rented car is widespread in all South American countries. More and more tourists choose this way to get around, and avail themselves of the large international car-rental companies or local firms.

If you want to bring your own car, you should stock up on spare parts and make sure your documents are in order. Bureaucratic difficulties are especially frequent at border crossings, and garage services are rare in the hinterlands. Consult Auto Club experts in the United States or Europe before you set out for up-to-date material, including maps and the addresses of local Auto Clubs (which we've provided in the chapters pertaining to each country). Auto Clubs in South America are very active, and their personnel provide assistance and guidance to members of similar clubs abroad.

Your car must be in top mechanical condition before you set out. In the Andean countries many roads reach thousands of meters above sea level, where engines must be specially tuned. Note that the road networks of Colombia, Venezuela, Brazil, and Bolivia are undeveloped (apart from main highways) and difficult to drive on. It's better to avoid driving there, and find another way of getting around. When traveling off the main roads, be sure to have enough fuel for the return trip, plus spare parts — service stations are almost nowhere to be found. A breakdown here is both unpleasant and expensive.

Car-rental rates vary from country to country, but usually they are around an international average for mid-sized cars in the large agencies. Local agencies can sometimes be cheaper, but do not offer the same level of service. The minimum age for renting a car is 22 (25 in some countries), and the customer must leave a sizeable deposit or a credit card. It's important to ensure the car when you rent it.

River boats are a common means of transportation in a number of areas, especially the eastern portions of the Andean countries and northwest Brazil (the jungles). Here you'll find that the only way to get from one settlement to another is by boat or ship along the river, and not infrequently you'll have to rent your own to reach your destination. Rental fees are high, but energetic bargaining will drive them down to something almost reasonable.

The major means of **public transportation** include trains, buses, trucks, and taxis. **Trains** operate only in some of the countries, and most are old, slow, and uncomfortable. They are not as common a way of getting around as they are in Europe, so don't plan a tour based on the railways. **Buses**, by contrast, are the most popular form of transportation, and connect all places of settlement. In several countries — Brazil, Chile, Colombia and Argentina, for example — the buses are modern and comfortable; in others they're motorized crates. Differences in quality and service are extreme, precluding a uniform and precise description. On some routes, you'll find smiling stewardesses; elsewhere you'll find terrible overcrowding and rampant theft. In any case, the bus remains the cheapest and most efficient way of getting around on land. **Shared taxis and minibuses** run on many intercity routes. Their fares are higher than the buses, but their advantage lies in far greater speed, comfort and safety. **Trucks** (*camiones*) carry passengers mainly in the poorer countries, where they ply remote dirt roads with their loads of shoulder-to-shoulder animals and people, the latter seated on piles of freight and clinging to their baggage lest it tumble off. It's a unique experience by all accounts — a cheap way (sometimes the only way) of reaching many remote places.

Hitchhiking is common in Chile and Argentina, chiefly in their southern regions. Hitchhikers there — especially women — get lifts easily, and vast distances can be covered quickly and cheaply. In the Andean countries, an accepted practice is to demand payment from a passenger, even if he thought he was getting a free ride. In Brazil and Colombia tourists have been attacked and their gear stolen: avoid hitchhiking in these countries by no means!

Urban transportation is efficient in most large cities. Bus lines, subways, taxis, and *colectivos* (shared taxi service) contribute to mobility in densely-populated urban areas and are usually rapid and reliable. In many countries, particularly the Andean ones, taxis have no meters and the fare must be agreed upon with the driver — **before starting out.**

Personal security

One of the most severe problems that visitors to South America are liable to encounter is protecting themselves and their belongings. A combination of social and political ferment, plus the desperate poverty, makes violent outbursts all too common. Sometimes these are directed at the authorities, in the form of hostile underground activity, and sometimes aimed at the tourist, whose valuable baggage attracts thieves. The problems are especially serious in Colombia, Peru, Brazil, and Venezuela — in that order. In the Introduction to each of those countries, we have included guidelines on appropriate behavior and preventive measures. Argentina, Uruguay, Paraguay, Chile, Bolivia, and Ecuador are considered to be tranquil and relaxed; have no fears about touring there.

Local currencies

The various South American currencies are noted for their worrisome instability. In recent years they've been considerably devalued against the dollar; for the tourists, this has lowered the cost of a stay there significantly. If on an extended visit, you'll find that for every dollar you change on your last day you'll receive more local currency than you got when you arrived. Accordingly, it's worthwhile to change money only to cover your immediate needs since within a few days you are likely to get more for your dollars.

Banks and moneychangers (*Casa de Cambio*) change currency; the latter usually offer a slightly higher rate and far less bureaucratic red-tape than the former. Though several countries do not allow private dealing in foreign currency, and restrict activity to the major banks, black-market moneychangers will always find a way to offer you a more attractive rate. Be extremely careful about dealing with them — verify their reliability and be sure to count what they give you.

Most airports also have some arrangements for converting foreign currency. If you've arrived on a weekend or holiday, change enough to cover your needs until the next business day. In the city itself you probably won't find a bank open, and may be forced to change money at a poor rate. Cash dollars are always preferred, but it's best to hold onto these for countries where a black market operates, and use travelers' checks elsewhere.

When entering a new country by land, don't change more money at the border checkpost than you'll need to reach the nearest large city, where you can expect to get a better rate. In any event, check and compare rates carefully with a number of moneychangers before you decide; differences among them are by no means small. Count the money you're given very carefully, making sure you get what you paid for.

Many moneychangers will try to exploit your innocence by holding back a few bills from the stack they hand you.

When leaving a country, get rid of any remaining local currency; it's worth considerably less in other countries, even those right across the border, and sometimes in the country itself, if you are back the next day.

Tourist services

A well-arranged and efficient system of services awaits the tourist in most South American countries. As tourism increases, governments become more aware of its tremendous economic impact. They have begun investing in expanding and improving the infrastructure and services which will help tourists get oriented and acclimated. This infrastructure includes not only hotels and restaurants, but also information centers, transportation services, guides, various publications, and more. Major airports will greet you the moment you touch down with counters to provide information, hotel reservations, car rental, and baggage checking. The bus and taxi fares from the airport into town are usually fixed by the government.

Almost every city has a tourist information bureau which offers guidance, maps, and other material. One of the noticeable drawbacks of these bureaus is the lamentable fact that their personnel often speak only Spanish, so that a tourist who cannot get along in that language will find it hard to avail himself of their services.

In addition to the tourist bureaus, several other organizations offer tourists information and assistance. The most important are the various Auto Clubs (*Automóvil Club*), which will keep you updated in matters of transportation and tour routes. There are also the military geographical institutes (*Instituto Geográfico Militar*), where you can obtain maps for hiking tours, the nature reserve authorities, etc.

Medical and health services

The most common health problems that a tourist to South America is liable to suffer are intestinal problems and difficulties in adjusting to the thin air at high altitudes. In both cases you'll probably need nothing more than short and routine treatment, which can be obtained at any regional clinic.

For more serious problems you'll have to go to a hospital. In national capitals and other large cities there are British or American hospitals, to which tourists should turn in case of need. In other cases, it's best to turn to English-speaking private physicians to whom you can describe your ailments, though you must be cautious about accepting treatment which seems inappropriate to you.

First-aid services in South America aren't the best, and still can't treat many health problems. You must therefore be doubly careful, and seek out qualified medical help in any case of suspected illness.

Dental treatment that can be put off should be put off. When that is impossible, visit a qualified dentist who has modern equipment.

Altitude — how to cope with thin air

The high elevation of South America's mountains requires one to take appropriate measures. Remember that the atmosphere is thin at these altitudes. The amount of oxygen is less than at sea level, upsetting the body's equilibrium. If you breathe at your normal rate you'll simply take in less oxygen, and consequently suffer from asthma-like sensations of choking and weakness. A certain amount of attention or caution may alleviate the problem and lessen its impact. Common side-effects are dizziness, nausea, headaches, and at times fainting. To avoid these reactions — which involve a certain discomfort even if they are not dangerous — you must take a number of precautionary measures.

First, it's best to reach the mountains by an overland route, in order to moderate the rate of ascent and give your body a longer period of time to acclimatize. If you arrive by air, there will be a sharp transition which results in a quicker and stronger impact. In any event, be sure to set aside the first twenty-four hours for rest, relaxation, and reduced food intake. This will grant your body a suitable interval to adapt to the lower percentage of oxygen in the atmosphere.

At high elevations you should refrain from physical effort, including that considered insignificant under normal conditions. Walk slowly, do not run or carry heavy loads, slow down even more when walking uphill or climbing stairs, and take frequent rest stops. Keep physical activity to a minimum: don't smoke, and avoid large, heavy meals. If necessary, you can buy special medication in drugstores which expand the blood vessels, thus increasing the amount of oxygen supplied to the body. Asthmatics, heart patients, and pregnant women tend to suffer more at high altitudes and it's recommended that they stay away from these areas as much as possible.

In most cases, as we have said, rest will help but sometimes this may have to be augmented by medical care and short periods of oxygen treatment. Hospitals, clinics, and even ordinary institutions recognize the problem, are experienced at treating it, and will be glad to help. As time passes, the body grows accustomed to the new situation and can resume normal activity — if more slowly and cautiously, and less strenuously.

Discounts for students and young travelers

In South America students are eligible for discounts on public transportation and admission to various sites. The discounts are not offered on all occasions, and certainly not automatically. For details, consult the section on documents, and the text, where you will find these discounts mentioned wherever they are offered.

In regard to accommodation, few places offer reduced youth rates and those which do, are mentioned in the relevant chapters.

Behavior and manners

The rules of manners accepted in the West apply here as well. The "dress code" is similar, though less formal. Both men and women wear sporty evening wear for official events, concerts or dinner in an elegant restaurant. In the daytime, light and airy clothing is wholly acceptable. For men, shorts are out of place except on the beach. In certain places, such as Caracas, the police can fine anyone who's improperly dressed in public. In Brazil, seashore dress is acceptable, but only in town and not on an intercity bus, for example. Women should dress modestly and avoid revealing garments. At holy places, those improperly attired are not allowed to enter.

Behavior toward women is somewhat archaic here, a matter which carries with it a certain grace and charm. Among descendants of the Indians as well, whose women bear the brunt of the physical burden, women are accorded respect and are treated with great consideration.

Latin Americans are friendly and hospitable. Many tourists are warmly welcomed into local homes, where they are made to feel at ease.

Among the European communities in Argentina and other countries it is customary to greet guests with a friendly kiss on the cheek. It's a gesture of friendship, and expresses no intimacy of any kind. The South American way of life is conservative and restrained; conspicuous permissiveness is nonexistent here.

In Spanish it is accepted practice to address people with the formal *usted* rather than the familiar *tu*. This serves to express respect and esteem rather than distance and estrangement.

It's customary to tip restaurant waiters (10%-15% of the bill) and service personnel (a small amount). Taxi drivers with whom you've negotiated a fare at the beginning of your trip do not expect a tip.

Keeping in touch

Postal and telephone services in Latin America are far from efficient. They are slow and clumsy, unreliable, and some are even expensive. An airmail letter sent to South America is liable to spend an extended period (up to several weeks) en route, perhaps not arriving at all.

Poste Restante (General Delivery) service is available in national capitals, but one shouldn't rely on it too much. Mail which arrives for you at the post office will only be kept for one month. *American Express* offices accept mail for their customers, and we recommend this method: have your correspondents send letters to an *American Express* office, where they will be kept for you until you get there.

Sending postal items from South America also requires attention. Mail letters only at post offices; use airmail, preferably registered. Film and important items should be sent registered, and only from main post offices. Avoid stamps in favor of a post-office cachet, since stamps not infrequently catch the eye of the sorter, who appropriates them for himself; more seriously, he destroys the contents. Letters encounter prolonged delays on the way, and if your tour lasts for two or three weeks your letters are likely to reach friends and family when you're already back at home, planning your next vacation.

Sending parcels involves much effort, time, and trouble. Parcels must be of fixed weight, and need to be boxed and wrapped. Those weighing more than one kilogram require inspection by a customs clerk, who sits — of course — somewhere other than the post office. The parcel has to be left open for inspection; only then can you seal it. Parcels may be sent by air or surface mail. The former is fast and sure, but is immeasurably more expensive than surface mail. Though surface is cheaper, it is far slower, and your parcel may spend many months in transit. It also happens that surface-mail parcels "get lost" and do not arrive at all. Surface mail is considered reliable from Argentina,

INTRODUCTION

Chile, Ecuador, and the Brazilian coastal cities, but not from Peru, Colombia, or Bolivia.

South America has telephone links to the rest of the world. International phone service is slow and expensive, but the connections are usually of satisfactory quality. Placing an international call from your hotel is liable to involve a wait of several hours. It's therefore wise to make most such calls from the telephone exchange found downtown in the large cities. These have several booths to which callers are summoned, each in his turn. The minimum length for such a call is three minutes. Collect calls are not always possible; it depends on where you are and to where you're calling. (This is not the case in Brazil, where the International phone service is quick and efficient, and one can make collect calls from any public phone.)

Shopping and souvenirs

Any tour of South America will add many kilograms of souvenirs and purchases to your luggage. Whether it's a Dior suit from Buenos Aires, a poncho from La Paz or jewelry from Brazil. Every traveler, even the most frugal, will end up buying at least a few of the innumerable souvenirs encountered on the way. And this acquisitiveness is perfectly justified.

In South America you'll find an amazing concentration of crafts and other artifacts, called *artesanía*, most hand-made — the glory of local craftsmen and artists. Their beauty and the special character of these items will have you digging into your wallets time and again.

Those touring only one or two countries will find information on the characteristic wares of each country in the relevant chapters, and will soon discover the wealth of possibilities. Keep in mind a number of important rules so as to avoid later problems with budget and weight (or rather excess weight).

Firstly, remember that all of South America resembles one gigantic market. It's hard to find a product exclusive to a single place, though there are, of course, differences in quality, types, and the like. Accordingly you'll be able to compare styles, prices, and quality, to ponder the various options... and to bargain! Bargaining is essential here; if you accept the stated price, not only will you pay more than you should but you'll also hurt the vendors' feelings, for they look forward to this give-and-take with their customers.

Each of the South American countries has its own characteristic forms of *artesanía*. These give artistic expression to the economic condition of the country in question and the sources of its treasures. Thus Chile abounds in metalcrafts, Argentina in clothing, Brazil in precious stones, and the Andean countries in woollen fabrics and woodcrafts.

Andean *artesanía* is noted for its strong Indian influence. In this region you'll find lovely woollen products, musical instruments, pottery, and astonishingly beautiful woodcarvings. Wall hangings, various garments, and antique fabrics are only some of the local treasures, and it's only natural that we'll cram them into our suitcases in considerable quantities. If you are travelling many months, it's best to send these home by mail (see above), for otherwise they're liable to interfere with the rest of your trip, getting in your way and causing problems.

In the cities you'll find tourist shops that offer top-quality merchandise at prices to match. As you travel you're bound to find these where they're made, closer to their natural environment and at their natural prices.

Overland border crossings

To explore South America properly, we must cross borders rather frequently. Whether during a combined tour of Argentina and Chile, a journey from Colombia to Ecuador, or on any other route, we'll encounter a number of traits common to all these inspection points.

All frontier stations are staffed by immigration officers in charge of the gates to their respective countries. They allow traffic to pass only during certain hours, which vary from station to station. In most cases border crossings are open from morning to nightfall, sometimes closing for an afternoon *siesta*. Some stations are open for only half a day on weekends. Check out the situation thoroughly before you reach the border, so as not to lose a full day's touring.

The main crossing points have separate lines for tourists and local citizens; crossing procedures here are simpler and quicker. In most countries you'll have to fill out a tourist card, stamped by the immigration clerk, which indicates how long you are permitted to stay. Always be sure to request the maximum time allowed — generally 90 days. Though getting an extension once you're in the country is possible, it can be very time-consuming.

Moneychangers congregate near crossing points. When changing money with them beware of being misled as to the exchange rates or in counting the bills.

Border posts can be reached by taxi or local bus. Direct bus routes from one border town to its counterpart on the other side are more expensive. It's therefore best to get to the border, cross on foot, and continue by vehicle on the other side after having taken care of the formalities.

Taxes and custom duties

Tourists must pay duty only on valuable items brought in as gifts, cigarettes and alcohol in excessive quantities, or commercial samples. These excluded, tourists can bring in personal belongings, including all required gear.

Among the many taxes imposed in South America, tourists are obliged to pay two: a port tax when leaving the country, and in some countries an excise tax on air tickets purchased there. Port taxes vary from country to country, as do the rates of the air ticket tax. When planning your return trip, it's therefore convenient to find out where to end it according to the tax you will have to pay. Sometimes these taxes can add more than 10% to the price of the ticket.

Working hours

The afternoon *siesta* is almost the Latin American trademark. In every country, businesses, shops, and offices close for two or three hours in the afternoon; during that time it's hard to find a seat in a restaurant, and even the streets seem more crowded.

Most businesses open early in the morning and stay open until evening. Office reception hours are usually only before noon. On weekends most businesses and offices are closed. Shops are open half-day on Saturdays, and are closed Sundays. Many museums are closed on Mondays.

Holidays and festivals

South America's holiday season, on a continent-wide basis, lasts the entire year, though most special occasions tend to be concentrated in February-March, June-July, and December, when you can celebrate the carnivals in Rio and elsewhere, *Inti Raimi* (the Sun Festival) in Cuzeo, Peru, and Christmas everywhere. During those seasons, much of the local population are themselves on vacation, and the general ambience isn't conducive to business. On national holidays, most services and many institutions are closed. When planning your tour, be sure to keep the dates of holidays in mind, and arrange matters so that your visit won't suffer on their account.

E CUADOR

Ecuador, among the smallest of South American countries, owes its name to its geographic location — astride the equator. The country is divided into three regions: the western coastal strip, the central Andes and the jungles to the east.

Though not large in area or population, Ecuador's charm and national character lend it a special grace. The Ecuadorians' warm nature, a relaxed political atmosphere and the gorgeous scenery, impart to Ecuador a splendor that captivates the hearts of multitudes. A visit to Ecuador may be nothing more than a flying tour of the capital, Quito — a quiet and pleasant city in its own right — or it can last many weeks, allowing time to really discover and get to know the people and places of this special land.

Ecuador is undoubtedly one of those countries which shouldn't be missed. Trapped between Peru to the south and Colombia to the north, Ecuador exudes an unmistakable atmosphere of calm and tranquility — so different from the tension which reigns across its borders. In Ecuador there are few thieves; robbery is truly rare.

The Ecuadorians are hearty, unprejudiced, generous and guileless. Given these national traits, a visit here is everything a tourist could wish. Those who spend their vacations here, or simply traverse the country, are bound to leave with feelings of pleasure and affection.

History

Because of its particular geographic situation — sandwiched between two huge neighbors — Ecuador has been pushed aside in the Latin American political game. Even before the Spanish came, when quiet and unassuming Indian tribes peopled its territory, Ecuador aroused little interest. The Incas from Peru bestirred themselves to conquer its central mountain region only during the fifteenth century; they did not enjoy a very long stay. The war between the two brothers Atahualpa and Huascar, heirs to the Incan ruler Huayna Capác, weakened the empire. When Francisco Pizarro reached Peru in 1533, he had little more than a mopping-up operation to perform.

E<u>CUADOR</u>

Ecuador was a bone of contention between the Spanish territories of Peru and Colombia. Eventually it fell under Peruvian control. For almost three hundred years its people enjoyed quiet and serenity. This period witnessed the development of agriculture in the coastal region and the consolidation of social classes, whose internal conflicts continue to be an issue to this day. With Bogota and Lima the great centers of Colonial activity, Ecuador was considered to be an insignificant backwater.

Only at the beginning of the nineteenth century, when the tide of nationalism washed over Spain's South American colonies, did significant political developments take place in Ecuador as well.

An unsuccessful revolt was mounted in 1809, while the Napoleonic Wars raged in Europe and King Ferdinand of Spain's power was wavering. But it was only thirteen years later (May 24, 1822) that General Antonio José de Sucre, supported by the forces of the Venezuelan Simón Bolívar, drew Ecuador out of the Spanish orbit for good.

The newly-liberated country was annexed into "Greater Colombia", the federation of Colombia, Venezuela and Ecuador that was Bolívar's dream. However, once Venezuela seceded from the forced union in 1829, Ecuador's ties unravelled as well and on August 10, 1830 Ecuadorian independence was declared.

It took Ecuador another hundred years to achieve political stability. This era of domestic and external strife, some of it violent, ruined any chance of economic development.

A border dispute with Colombia (Ecuador regarded that country's southern region as a natural extension of its own north) ended in compromise only in the early years of the 20th century, while disagreements with Peru over extensive jungle areas in eastern Ecuador have lasted to this very day, turning violent at times. The fiercest struggle, however, was the domestic one between the *Flores* of Quito and the Andes, and the *Rocafuerte* of Guayaquil and the coastal strip.

Quito has served as Ecuador's administrative hub — the seat of government bureaucracy and home of the conservative landholding aristocracy — since the Spanish conquest. Guayaquil, by contrast, developed into a cosmopolitan port city subject to the influence of well-to-do merchants with a liberal world view. The two groups clashed ideologically and fought for control of the state, with the army alternating in its allegiance between the rival blocs.

At the peak of the strife, between 1830 and 1845, Ecuador was plunged into political chaos. Only in 1861, when García

Moreno rose to power, did the situation change. Though a liberal, Moreno ruled dictatorially, restricting freedom of speech and assembly, exiling opponents and strengthening the status of the Catholic Church. Economic development began during his years in power: major highways were paved, the foundations of a Quito-Guayaquil railway were laid, schools and hospitals were built and steps were taken to promote agriculture and expand cultivated land.

In 1875, fifteen years after taking power, Gracía Moreno was assassinated. His death sparked renewed Liberal-Conservative strife and the period of relative calm ended. The Liberals, led by General Alfaro, seized power once again at the end of the nineteenth century. Among the legal reforms they introduced, the most important was the removal of public education from Church control. Alfaro's regime, however, was not substantially different from his predecessors: Ecuador was run by a handful of plutocrats and special-interest groups. Alfaro was deposed and jailed in 1911 and was lynched several months later by a mob in the streets of Quito.

The world economic crisis of the 1920's hit Ecuador grievously, for its cocoa exports fell even as food prices rose. The economic hardship and social unrest it entailed brought a military junta to power; this regime, however, was no more successful than the previous one at relieving the distress. Between 1925 and 1948, Ecuador suffered slow economic development, political anarchy resulting in sporadic outbreaks of violence and continued social tension.

In 1941 Peru exploited Ecuador's weakness and sent its army into large sections of the uninhabited Amazon Basin in eastern Ecuador. Though a temporary arrangement — reached under United States mediation — left most of the disputed territory in Peruvian hands, Ecuador has never accepted the decision and continues to consider those regions as occupied territories which must be returned. The border areas remain tense to this day. Armed clashes between the two countries erupt from time to time, with the Government using the controversy to divert public attention from sensitive domestic problems.

Post-World War II Ecuador has enjoyed relative stability, founded on reforms instigating a constitutional government which is elected every five years. Though the army has aborted the democratic process on several occasions by seizing power, the takeovers have been short-lived and have ended with the return of power to an elected civilian president. Until 1972 the charismatic President Dr. José María Velyco Ibarra left his imprint on affairs, and despite his own involvement in recurrent

E _CUADOR_

scandals, contributed greatly to stabilizing the rule of law and order.

A new constitution was approved by plebiscite in 1978. Among its provisions are the guarantee of civil rights, extension of suffrage to all literate adults, expanded presidential powers and a one-term limit for presidents.

Excluding temporary aberrations, the spirit of this constitution has been preserved; today Ecuador is experiencing a political tranquility it has rarely known. The main thrust is now directed at developing agriculture and the economy, expanding the educational system and introducing moderate social reforms.

Geography and climate

Ecuador has a diverse geographic structure, with wide variations in scenery and climate. Its estimated area of 284,000 km2 can be divided into a western coastal strip, a central mountain range and the eastern jungles. The country is bounded by the Pacific Ocean in the west, Colombia in the north and Peru to the east and south.

Since Ecuador straddles the equator, we would expect its climate to be tropical. Due to its diverse topography, however, the decisive climatic factors are elevation and terrain. Certain regions, especially the mountain strip, enjoy a temperate and pleasant climate. Ecuador's location on the equator has an interesting advantage: sovereignty over the Galápagos Islands, a unique archipelago that lies about 1000 km west of the Ecuadorian coast. Here biological time appears to have frozen, leaving behind flora and fauna which seem to have undergone no change since Creation.

Most of Ecuador's soil is volcanic; earthquakes and eruptions have always been part of the country's life. Dozens of volcanoes, some of them active, jut above and constitute a constant threat to their placid surroundings. The tallest of these is Chimborazo (6310 m), but it hasn't given cause for alarm in many years.

The coastal strip (_Costa_) between the Pacific Ocean to the west and the Andes to the east (with a maximum width of 100 km) is the nation's traditional breadbasket and a number of cities have sprouted there. The most important of these, Guayaquil, serves as Ecuador's major port and the commercial and economic center of the country.

The coastal strip itself is not uniform. Its northern section, bordering Colombia, is very wet and covered with thick vegetation and forest. In the south, close to Peru, the land is arid and requires irrigation if agriculture is to be at all possible.

ECUADOR

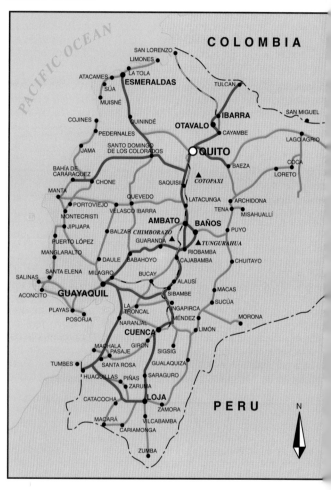

The inhabitants of the northern coastal strip are black or mulatto
descended mainly from African slaves brought there to wor
the plantations, while descendants of the Indians dwell in the
south. In Guayaquil and environs you'll find mostly *mestizos o*

mixed white/Indian blood, who deal mainly in commerce and in transporting produce from the farm to the major harbors.

The climate here is tropical, though the chilly Humboldt Current holds temperatures down to 23-24°C (73°F). Day-night temperature differences are considerable, though there are no extremes between seasons. From December until April it is warmer and from late May to late November it's really quite pleasant.

Nearly half of Ecuador's population lives in the coastal area and produces most of the country's agricultural yield. Bananas, cocoa, sugar, rice and even cotton, familiar crops in this vicinity, amount to about half the country's exports. The lowlands near Guayaquil consist mostly of very fertile sedimentary soil. The region enjoys abundant rainfall, high humidity and plentiful river water. The yields have improved progressively in recent years.

The mountains (*Sierra*): The Andes divide into two parallel chains in Ecuador — the western (*Cordillera Occidental*) and the eastern (*Cordillera Oriental*), which run like twin spinal columns from north to south. The valley in which most Ecuadorians live, and where most of the mountain area's agricultural produce is grown, runs for about four hundred kilometers in between. Some thirty volcanos serve to fence in the valley from either side, thrusting proudly to a height of 6000 m and more. Some peaks are perpetually snow-clad and extremely beautiful. The mountain chains are broken by several rivers, each with its own isolated arable valley. The deep river valleys (*hoyas*) are home to agricultural communities whose way of life seems to have remained unchanged for centuries.

The climate of the mountain zone varies according to elevation, but is comfortable and pleasant for the most part. Rain falls chiefly from November to May, mostly in the evening and at night. The highlands are wintry and cold throughout most of the year, while the lower parts are tropically hot and humid. The valleys are noted for a comfortable, healthy climate and the Indian population for its longevity.

Most sierra-dwellers are of Indian descent and engage in agriculture and traditional vocations such as a variety of handicrafts.

The eastern region (*Oriente*) includes the lower, eastern Andes and the upper Amazon Basin. Its elevation is about 1500 m and its climate is tropical: hot, humid (up to 90%) and rainy (as much as 5000 mm (5m!) or more annually). The region is densely forested and carved by rivers great and small; most of its territory is uninhabited and unexplored.

ECUADOR

Though it accounts for about one-half of Ecuador's land area, only more than 1% of the population lives here, mostly in towns and villages. In recent years oil fields have been found in the area and economic development has accelerated with the urge to exploit them and find new drilling sites. This is taking a rapid toll on the region's special character: obscure Indian tribes are becoming more exposed to westernization with each passing year.

The Galápagos Islands undoubtedly belong to a separate geographic category by virtue of both their nature and their location. We'll discuss them in a separate section.

Population

Ecuador has about 12 million inhabitants, of whom more than a third are Indians, another third are *mestizos* and the remainder are Caucasions, Blacks and Orientals. The population density is of the highest in South America — almost 40 people per square kilometer in continental Ecuador. Though most of the population is agrarian and rural, the accelerated organization process typical of the Third World in recent decades has not skipped over Ecuador and its major cities are steadily growing. Today about 50% of Ecuador's people live in agricultural regions, while the urban sector is engaged in commerce and industry.

While the eastern jungle area is almost uninhabited, the population is divided almost equally between the mountain region and the coastal strip. The school system is constantly expanding, and this is perhaps one of the greatest achievements in the last years; the illiteracy rate had dropped dramatically in the last decade. Officials claim that there is still a long way to go but they must find the way to educate people in Spanish, when their mother tongue is Quechua. Nevertheless, at the beginning of the eighties more than one fourth of the Ecuadorians were illiterate, and ten years later only 10%, and the figures are constantly decreasing.

Most Ecuadorians speak Spanish, the national language, but the Indians often continue to use their original tongue, Quechua for some, it's their only language. An overwhelming majority of Ecuadorians — 95% — are Catholic.

Economy

Though only 15% of Ecuador's territory is used for agriculture, the national economy is based first and foremost on the fruit of the land. Until the early 1970's, when oil revenues from the east began to swell the national treasury, farm produce accounted for 90% of export income. Ecuador, fourth in the world in banana production, and sixth in cocoa beans, was subject to sharp economic fluctuations as world market prices for these commodities rose and fell.

Though agricultural produce is still a highly important factor in the national economy, oil has taken over the first place; and despite the fall in oil consumption and price, petroleum revenues are still the mainstay of the economy. About half the workforce is agrarian, but primitive agricultural methods, plus the geographic and transportational obstacles, cause Ecuadorian produce to sell at high prices which nevertheless return low profits. An agricultural reform that the Government sought to introduce during the 1970's enjoyed no conspicuous success. Its main contribution lay in its development efforts and the attempt to diversify the agricultural economy and expand it into previously unexploited areas.

Only 20% of Ecuador's working population engages in industry. This activity, mostly small scale, is concentrated mainly around the large cities, Guayaquil and Quito, and is not sufficient to supply the growing demand in the national economy. As a result of rising oil revenues, the government invested considerable sums in extensive development programs which were nipped in the bud, however, when prices and sales volume fell sharply. Per capita income has risen significantly: among South America's lowest more than ten years ago, today it amounts to around $1000 annually.

Ecuador has run up a high foreign debt and has begun to encounter difficulty in repaying it. The government has slowed the pace of investments and devalued the currency, but symptoms that arouse the concern of the world financial community are still discernable. Ecuador's membership in the Organization of Andean States, whose aim is free trade among all Andean nations, helped establish a number of industrial plants, which, together with a revitalized oil market, are expected to extricate Ecuador from its woes.

As for minerals, there are indications of some progress in the exploitation of existing mines and the development of new ones, though not at a pace that can guarantee significant momentum in the near future. Traces of gold, copper, silver and sulfur have been found in various locations, but they do not yet amount to anything significant at a national level.

General information

How to get there
By air: Ecuador has convenient plane connections with the

rest of South America, Europe and the United States. *Iberia, Air France, KLM* and *Lufthansa* fly from Europe to Quito and Guayaquil, while *Avianca, Viasa* and other South American airlines provide connecting flights to their respective countries. Young tourists who wish to hold down costs may find it best to fly to Lima, Peru, to which service is cheaper and more frequent; and from there, continue by bus to Ecuador. *Ecuatoriana,* the national airline, flies from Mexico City, Miami Chicago and New York, as do *AeroPerú, Air Panama* and others. South American countries — apart from Uruguay and Paraguay — enjoy regular air service to and from Ecuador.

By land: Since no railroad links Ecuador to its neighbors, the only means of reaching it overland is by bus or private car. The Pan-Amercian Highway passes through Ecuador, from its northern border with Colombia to the Peruvian border in the south. A number of bus companies provide service between Ecuador and the cities of Bogota and Lima and to even more remote destinations. However, we recommend that you do not rely on them. Rather, take the trip in stages: first to the border; then cross over by yourself and continue on a local company's bus or minibus.

Doing your own driving isn't hard as long as you stay on the main roads. On the lesser-traveled tracks you may find the going difficult. The unpaved roads are regularly damaged by floods and natural disasters. The authorities, unfortunately, don't always get around to repairing them. Hitchhiking is convenient and safe almost everywhere in Ecuador.

Documents and taxes

A passport valid for at least six months is a prerequisite for entering Ecuador. Tourist cards are distributed free-of-charge, either aboard the airplane or at frontier stations for overland travelers. Fill them out carefully and make sure they are properly stamped. Such a card is good for a ninety day stay, on condition that the immigration clerk has indeed approved this period of time. Tourists have often been called upon to present a departure ticket or, alternatively, to prove they have means of support sufficient for the duration of their stay. The border police will usually be satisfied if you display an MCO and several hundred dollars.

American and European citizens do not need a visa to Ecuador. Only visitors who wish to remain in Ecuador for more than ninety days during a single year require a visa. If a stay of less than ninety days' duration was approved for you at the border station and you wish to extend it, you can do so without difficulty at any of the immigration offices located in the large cities.

Airline tickets purchased in Ecuador are subject to a 10% excise tax.

A final warning: carry identification at all times! Police and army checkposts demand I.D. regularly — even within the cities — and react harshly against those who can't produce the required documents.

When to visit, national holidays

The best time to visit Ecuador is between June and September, the dry season. The weather is comfortable the rest of the year too, though the nearly daily rains between December and March are a nuisance. The coastal area swelters in heat and humidity between December and April-May.

Important holidays: January 1, May 1, May 24 (Battle of Pichincha Day), July 24 (Simón Bolívar's Birthday), August 10 (Independence Day), October 12 (Columbus Day), November 1 (All Saints' Day) and December 25.

Accommodation

Hotels, hostels and pensions are rather inexpensive; most are clean and tidy. First-class hotels are located only in the major cities; add 10-15% in taxes and service charges to their rates. Reservations are needed generally only at holiday time or for a short, rushed business visit. The smaller cities have very low-priced pensions and hostels (*residenciales*), most of which are clean and pleasant. Guest homes — some with attached showers, fans and other "luxuries" — have come into being in recent years.

Food and drink

Ecuador abounds with clean, reasonably priced restaurants that serve diverse types of cuisine. In the large cities you'll find a wide variety — Chinese, French, Middle Eastern, etc. — and the large hotel restaurants will satiate you on Continental fare. Menus in smaller cities and villages are characterized by the popular local dishes, and along the coast by a wealth of fish and seafood.

Breakfast in Ecuador is a light meal taken before 8am. The main meal is lunch, eaten at about 1pm, while supper may be as early as 7:30 pm. In the cities, five o'clock is tea-time.

The national dishes are similar to those of Peru and Colombia, Ecuador's neighbors. Among them: *cebiche* (fish and seafood marinated in tomato sauce with lemon, orange juice and sugar), a corn bread called *tostado*, cream of potato soup (*locro*) and others. Main courses: *churrasco* and *fritada*, chunks of pork fried in oil and served with corn bread and fried bananas (*maqueños fritos*).

Currency

Ecuador's currency, the *sucre*, is linked to the dollar at a rate set by the government. Ecuador has neither a black market nor any restrictions on the import and export of foreign currency. Dollar travelers' checks can be cashed almost anywhere for a small commission; this is recommended, especially for those heading for countries where there is a black market for hard American currency. Money sent to an Ecuadorian bank in dollars is paid out in dollars as well, an undoubtedly refreshing service in comparison with most South American countries, where you're given local currency.

Credit cards, especially *Visa* and *Diners Club*, are very common; you can also use them to withdraw funds in U.S. dollars. Before leaving the major cities it's worthwhile to obtain enough local currency, as it is difficult to exchange dollars in remote villages and towns. Even when you can do so, the rate you'll get for them there will be significantly lower. Before you leave Ecuador, buy the currency of the countries to which you're heading, or convert your remaining *sucres* into dollars.

Moneychanging is handled in banks or by moneychangers, without delay or hassle.

Business hours

Most offices and businesses open every morning at 8:30, close for a two-hour *siesta* at 12:30pm, and then reopen on weekdays until 6:30pm. On Saturdays they're open only in the mornings and are closed Sundays.

Government offices and quite a few private offices are closed Saturdays. Most banks are open on weekdays between 9am and 1:30pm.

Domestic transportation

Buses: The most convenient way of touring Ecuador, apart from airplane, is by bus. Many companies operate bus and minibus lines throughout the country: most are reliable, frequent, fast, inexpensive and quite comfortable. Almost all cities and villages are served by several companies that link them to their neighbors and it's worth your while to use them.

Trains: Travel by rail, by contrast, is miserable, slow and uncomfortable. There is really only one major line in Ecuador, between Guayaquil and Quito. Still, the route between coast and mountains is interesting and quite exceptional.

Airplane: The military airline *Tame* provides frequent air service between important cities in all parts of Ecuador, together with small airlines that serve local destinations. *Tame* has a monopoly on flights to the Galápagos Islands and flies there several times a week (see "Galápagos"). Air service between Quito and Guayaquil is frequent; the flight takes about forty-five minutes. It's important to note that you must reach the airport early, for the airlines have a strange tendency to issue more boarding cards than there are seats and to leave them unmarked.

In-town-travel: Buses and minibuses are very inexpensive, though most are rather crowded and do not run as frequently as one would like. Taxis abound and fares are not high.

Hertz, Budget and *Avis* rent out cars in the major cities.

Measurements, electricity, time
The metric system is customary in commerce and obligatory for official documents. Electricity is 110V. Time is GMT -5 in Ecuador and GMT -6 in the Galápagos Islands.

A suggested itinerary for your visit to Ecuador
The route we're about to present aims at taking in most of the areas worth visiting in Ecuador; it would take at least several weeks to cover in its entirety. Accordingly, visitors must select the route most suitable to their taste, based on fields of interest, time, budget and general direction of their trips. Quito will serve as a departure point for most of the excursions; you can reach it either from Peru via Guayaquil, or from Colombia via Tulcán. Sites are noted in a northbound direction, as follows:

From the Peruvian border to Guayaquil.
From Guayaquil to the Galápagos Islands and back.
Up the mountains to Quito via Riobamba and Baños.
From Quito to the eastern jungles and back.
From Quito to Esmeraldas (on the northern coastal strip) and back.
North to Otavalo, San Antonio de Ibarra, Tulcán and Colombia.

One can, of course, combine routes so as to eliminate the need to double back on any single section. One example: combining routes 3 and 4 and continuing from Baños to the eastern jungles, returning to Quito. Another possibility: combining routes 5 and 6 and going on to Colombia along the coast (less recommended).

ECUADOR

Quito

Ecuador's capital and its immediate surroundings rest a few kilometers from the equator at 2860 m above sea level. Its population (app. 1,500,000) enjoys crisp air, and a comfortable climate, and the ambience is serene, tranquil and slow-paced. Quito is altogether different from most South American capitals: smaller, cleaner and infused with a pervasive inner peace. Its residents are pleasant and forthcoming, their manners simple and honest. Their way of life seems to have been created with the express purpose of blending in with the surrounding green and placid mountains.

Quito is ensconced in a long, narrow valley running from north to south. A range of hills runs to the east, and Pichincha, an active volcano, casts it shadow to the west, its distant cone belching clouds of white smoke.

Quito was founded in 1534 by Sebastián de Benalcázar, who came to South America with Pizarro, conqueror of Peru. The original quarter is in the southwest part of town. The northern section is newer and there we find elegant residential quarters, parks and public institutions. Tranquility and security reign in both parts of town. Quito is not a violent city and has been spared the all too common blights of most South American cities — poverty, hunger, illiteracy, drugs and crime.

Everything moves slowly here — no one is in a rush. The city closes down at night; only a few people wander the streets or frequent the entertainment spots. Most folks in Quito prefer to spend their nights at home with their families.

Quito is the ideal starting point for the tourist who wants to get to know Ecuador. From here its easy to go just about anywhere, whether eastward to the jungles, northward toward Colombia, or westward to the lovely coastal areas. For tourists, Quito is bound to be a case of love at first sight and the feeling will grow stronger the longer they stay there and come to know its sites and attractions.

How to get there
By air: Quito's Sucre Airport, a somewhat antiquated facility situated not far from downtown, is a very busy place. Planes arrive from many points in South America and from other cities in

ECUADOR

Old Quito and the Panecillo Hill

.cuador itself. The airport is rather small, the service courteous
.nd efficient. You'll find a bank for changing money, several
hops and a small restaurant. You can reach town from the
irport by taxi or by bus. It's customary to modestly tip the
lue-uniformed skycaps.

Ry land: Buses and minibuses are Ecuador's most common
neans of getting around. They are run by many companies,
ach serving different destinations, and set out from the various
ompany offices scattered around town. Fares are low; the
ervice is reliable. Buy your tickets two or three days in advance,
et to the terminal somewhat early and be sure to lock and
ecure your gear before stowing it in the luggage compartment.
he bus ride to Peru and Colombia is best done in stages: take
ne bus to the border point, cross over yourself and continue
n a Peruvian or Colombian bus. This is bound to save you
noney, and often time as well. Buses that stop in Quito let
assengers off in various places throughout town and from
ere you can continue by city bus or taxi.

he **train** runs between Quito and Guayaquil, stopping on the
ay in Riobamba, Ambato and other cities. It's exceptionally
teresting train ride. The train passes through breathtaking
cenery, climbing over 3500 m on its 460 km course. There's

nothing like it for bringing Ecuador's scenery and variety to life
The climb from Guayaquil up the mountains to Quito is slow
and somewhat fatiguing, but the downhill trip is quite nice. The
trains are generally packed; tickets must be purchased several
days in advance. The railroad station is on Calle Maldonado, no
far from the city center. The cars are not modern and nighttime
trips can be very chilly.

Where to stay

Colón Internacional: Amazonas (corner of Patria), Tel. 561-333
Fax 563-903. One of the grandest and best in town, near Parqu
El Ejido.

Quito: Gonzáles Suárez 2500, Tel. 230-300, 544-600, Fax 567
284. Another luxury hotel, good restaurant (*Techo del Mundo*
and cafeteria (*Cayambe*), swimming pool and sauna.

Inca Imperial: Bogotá 219, Tel. 524-800. Good, inexpensive
located near Old Quito.

Embassy: Calle Pres. Wilson 441, Tel. 561-990, Fax 563-192
Convenient location, inexpensive.

Zumag: Av. 10 de Agosto (corner of Mariana de Jesús), Te
552-400, Fax 504-076. Inexpensive, basic services.

Residencial Italia: Av. 9 de Octubre 237. A recommended chea
lodge.

Gran Casino Hotel: García Moreno 330 (near Ambato), Tel. 516
368. Dirty, noisy, unsafe, unreliable, with a very low standard
and yet very popular amongst young travelers who come t
Quito. Located not far from El Panecillo and from Plaza Sant
Domingo, in Colonial Quito.

What and where to eat

Have a light breakfast at one of the cafés, diners, or kiosk
situated around town, especially along major streets. For lunc
and supper it's best to look elsewhere for a place to satisfy yo
appetite. The Old City abounds in small, inexpensive restauran
that usually serve tasty and fresh Ecuadorian foods which ar
certainly recommended. The restaurants, like the entire are
empty after nightfall: come early for supper, for it's hard to fir
anything open after 9:30pm.

Quito's streets present you with a large selection of eaterie
of diverse type and quality. In the markets and along maj
streets you can eat simply and well, but avoid dirty place
where hygiene is dubious. Hotel and luxury restaurant menu
by contrast, are far more sophisticated, though not necessari
expensive.

Some of the best restaurants in town are situated in the hote
On the *Quito*'s roof, *El Techo del Mundo* ("Roof of the World

specializes in a Continental menu served against a background of music and a gorgeous view of the city and the valley. The *Hotel Colón* too, serves excellent food in its cafeteria, coffee shop and elegant *El Conquistador Grill. Chalet Suisse* (Calle Calama 312) serves excellent, expensive steaks, and *Moby Dick* (Av. Amazonas 272) offers superb fish and seafood. The excellent French restaurant *Rincón de Francia* (Calle Roca, corner of 9 de Octubre) offers its patrons the finest French cuisine; *Costa Vasca* (Calle Reina Victoria 836) specializes in Spanish food.

Casa China (Ave. Amazonas, corner of Mariana de Jesus) for Chinese food, and *Pizza Nostra* for its fare (Calle Reina Victoria, corner of 18 de Septiembre). A Lebanese restaurant specializing in excellent Middle Eastern food is located next to the airport.

If you'd like to sample local delicacies, we can recommend *La Choza* (12 de Octubre corner of Cordero). There you'll dine in a pleasant atmosphere at reasonable prices, enjoying some of the finest Ecuadorian dishes.

Transportation

Getting around Quito and its suburbs is simple and easy. The streets in residential areas are broad enough to handle traffic; congestion is rare. On the other hand, downtown streets — especially in the Old City — are narrow, allowing little if any room for parking. Add mediocre street signs and the chances of losing your way and you'll find yourself refraining from driving and favoring public transit whenever possible. A great many buses and minibuses rumble up and down the streets, taking everyone everywhere. You'll hardly ever have to change buses to reach your destination and the journey will usually not involve prolonged waiting or inconvenience of any kind. At the same time, remember that public transit leaves one vulnerable to pickpockets: keep an eye on your handbags.

You can, of course, avail yourself of taxis if you so wish and have loose change to spare. Hundreds of them cruise the town and are easy to hail even in relatively distant suburbs. Drivers set fares in advance (bargaining with them is definitely acceptable) according to the destination and time of day. Expect higher fares at night and on weekends.

Tourist service

There's a Ministry of Tourism branch office in the arrival hall at the airport. If luck is with you and you haven't found the place closed, it will equip you with maps and pamphlets about the city and its attractions. The Ministry also has two offices

QUITO

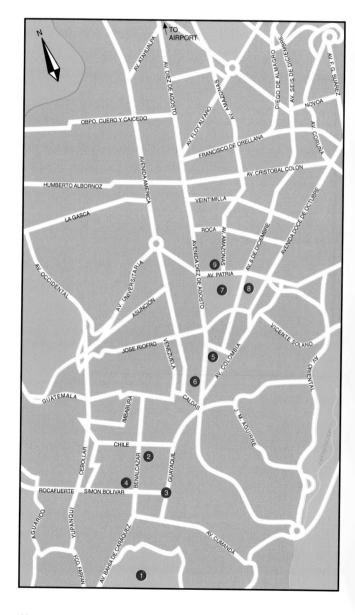

downtown, one on Calle Reina Victoria 514, corner of Roca (Tel. 239-044) and the other at City Hall — *Palacio Municipal* — on Plaza Independencia (Tel. 527-002). In the first you can watch video movies on various tourist sites in Ecuador, produced by the Ministry of Tourism. In order to do this come with at least 5 people to the branch office.

Additional maps, especially of distant sites, mountain hikes, jungle excursions and the like, are available at the **Instituto Geográfico Militar** (Calle Paz corner of Niño), or at the *Libri Mundi* bookstore, (see "Literature").

Cars are available from *Avis* and *Hertz* at the airport, or from *Expo* on Av. América 1116, Tel. 267-891, or *Budget*, on Av. Colón 11-40, Tel. 237-026. *Expo* also provides drivers. When renting a car, be sure to ascertain that the insurance is comprehensive; otherwise, breakdowns and minor accidents are liable to be expensive. It's important to compare prices and to check the car's condition from top to bottom.

Almost all Quito travel agencies are somehow involved in organizing tours to the Galápagos Islands; check on various possibilities concerning types and prices of excursions (see "Galápagos Islands").

South American Explorers Club is an American non-profit organization which provides very detailed and up-to-date information for travelers to South America. They also sell good maps and guidebooks and will provide information about unfrequented places like jungles and mountains.

The Ecuadorian branch of the Club is in Quito, Toledo 1254, Tel. 566-076. The head office is at 126 Indian Creek Road, Ithaca, New York, U.S.A. (Tel. (607) 277-0448).

Spanish schools
Many travelers choose to spend from a few days to a few weeks in studying and practicing Spanish in Quito. Numerous

schools offer their services for relatively very low prices, and it will surely be found extremely usefull and enjoyable to know the local language while traveling.

Most schools offer itineraries of 2-4 weeks of classes (some offer individual classes), and they may arrange a full board accommodation with local families — reasonable prices and an experience by itself.

You can ask for details of different schools at the Tourist Office. Two worth mentioning are the *Academia de Español Quito*, at Marchena 130 and 10 de Agosto (Tel. 443-647), and *Instituto Superior de Español*, Ulloa 220 and Carrión (Tel. 230-701).

Tourist sites

In addition to a comfortable, hospitable climate, nature has graced the Ecuadorian capital with an enchantingly beautiful location. It also enjoys a rare combination of Colonial grace and urban modernization. Quito lies in a long, narrow valley stretching from north to south between the green slopes of the soaring Andes. At almost every turn you will be greeted by a view of the mountains, which seem to shelter the city from the surrounding world. Quito has always been an isolated, cut-off city: expansion east or west is difficult, due to the obstacles posed by the mountain ridges. Thus the city developed lengthwise, chiefly northward, leaving its flanks uninhabited. Today's visitor to Quito will discern the substantial difference between north and south, which expresses centuries of social development, architectural perspective and a multifaceted national identity. It seems that a walk through Quito from south to north is a journey through both space and time: the sixteenth and seventeenth centuries in the south, the eighteenth and nineteenth centuries in the middle and the twentieth century in the north.

Visitors to Quito should take their time. Amble along the broad boulevards in the city's north; stroll through the alleys in its south; dine and shop along Avenida Amazonas, visit the museums and linger in the gardens and plazas, etc. Pleasant excursions await you close to town: mountain hikes, interesting lookout points, an enjoyable picnic. The most famous site is *La Mitad del Mundo* (Center of the World), a monument sitting precisely "on" the equator.

We shall survey Quito geographically, from north to south, focusing on the more unusual and interesting sites. We will conclude with a survey of the sites located outside the town. Avenida 10 de Agosto, which runs spine-like through the entire city (apart from the southern extremity) will serve us as a main artery.

ECUADOR

North Quito

Though the Old Quarter in South Quito is conventionally thought of as the city's most ancient section, it was actually in the north — the Cotocollao area — that human settlement in Quito began, five millenia ago. Here, in what today is a wholly modern area, was the Cotocollao Kingdom, one of the most advanced of that period's civilizations. Its survivors intermarried with the Indian invaders who, in turn, were subsequently annihilated by the conquistadores.

Nothing of that bygone era has survived in this area, now an exclusive residential neighborhood. The whole north end of Quito has been built up and is constantly developing; new buildings, streets and neighborhoods spring up year after year.

Even the Sucre International Airport, which seemed so far from town only a short time ago, is trapped today in the heart of well-tended residential quarters and constitutes a nuisance to their residents.

This rapid expansion has led to the development of a special Quito building style, which allows wealthy residents — those who populate the northern quarters — ample room, spacious apartments, public parks, streets, boulevards and so on. Some diplomatic missions and prestigious estates are situated here today, as are a number of modern office buildings and important shopping centers.

North Quito has no "tourist sites" in the conventional sense of the term, but those seeking to form an impression of today's Quito should nonetheless visit it.

The New City

While the north is Quito's prestigious residential district, the center — between those exclusive neighborhoods and the Old City — is a most interesting part of town, where traces of the 19th century mingle with the beginning of the 20th in a graceful manner. Here are many of the city's offices, shops, entertainment spots, restaurants and so on.

We shall tour the area between Parque El Alameda in the south and Avenida Naciones Unidas, bordering Parque Carolina, to the north.

Before entering Parque El Alameda, you should be sure to visit the **Museo del Banco Central** (Central Bank Museum), located on the fifth and sixth floors of the Bank building at Avenida 10 de Agosto, corner of Brinceno — right across from Bolivar's statue at the park entrance. It's open Tues.-Fri. 9.30am-4pm; Sat.-Sun. 10.30am-3pm; closed Mon. It's one of South America's

Colonial Quito

most interesting and important museums; don't miss it. The fifth floor is devoted to a display of thousands of archaeological finds from all over Ecuador, while the sixth floor presents a selection of paintings and furniture dating from the Golden Age of Spanish rule. The museum, through well thought out and tasteful displays, thoroughly and extensively covers the history of human settlement in Ecuador, beginning thousands of years before the Spanish arrived. Though the exhibits are documented in detail, we recommend that you join one of the English-language guided tours offered several times daily. On Sundays, admission to the museum is free of charge.

La Alameda Park stretches opposite the Bank. Here you can rest on a park bench, contemplate passersby, or visit the small planetarium located in the center. La Alameda Park is, in fact, a transition point between New and Old Quito. North of here, the streets become wider and the building style and types of businesses change. Continuing along Avenida 10 de Agosto, we arrive shortly at one of the best-known parks in Quito — **Parque El Ejido**.

This large park is divided into two sections by Avenida 6 de Diciembre. Its east is home to Quito's cultural center, **Casa de la Cultura**, with a display of paintings, works of art, books and musical instruments. It also has a movie theater that screens quality films.

The area around the park contains some of Ecuador's important institutions. The most important are the **Palacio Legislativo**, (Legislature) and **Palacio de Justicia** (Hall of Justice), both on Avenida 6 de Deciembre between La Alameda and El Ejido Parks. On the other side, in the northeastern corner, the **American Embassy** overlooks the park and Plaza Mantilla. A few blocks down Avenida 12 de Octubre, continuing from the American Embassy, we reach the **Catholic University**, one of Ecuador's most esteemed academic institutions. The University Library houses an interesting archaeological collection from the estate of the late researcher Caamaño. The artifacts included in this display thoroughly and comprehensively analyze and explain ancient Ecuadorian cultures. The University's museum houses a rather mediocre display of uniforms and paintings. Open Tues.-Fri., 9am-12.30pm; Weds. and Fri. also 3-5pm.

We will continue our tour from Ejido Park northward along Avenida Amazonas, Quito's most popular shopping and entertainment street.

Avenida Amazonas is one of Quito's longest, extending from Ejido Park to Plaza Olmedo behind the airport. Its bustling, famous section runs from Avenida Patria, on the edge of Ejido

Park, as far as Carolina Park. At its beginning is the grand *Hotel Colón*, which is not only a shelter for affluent tourists, but also an exclusive social institution in town. From here we'll head north along the attractive boulevard, peer into the shop windows, review the cars creeping along, pass tourist agencies and airline offices, restaurants, boutiques with some lovely leather goods and more. Avenida Amazonas is surrounded by small streets lined with hundreds of attractive businesses offering the best Ecuadorian wares — from typical *artesanía* (handicrafts) of the Indians in Otavalo (see "North of Quito"), to office services, banking, art galleries and the like. It's a lovely area, bound to capture any tourist's heart. Here, on the pedestrian section of Avenida Amazonas and in the small buildings crowded along the adjacent streets, you can find shops in line with your budget, restaurants for your palate, or bars in which to "let your hair down".

Several blocks west of Av. Amazonas, on Avenida 10 de Agosto, are the Treasury and the Foreign Ministries, in a quiet residential area.

The boulevard is busy and noisy as far as Avenida Cristóbal Colón (that's Christopher Columbus in Spanish). From here onward we may either continue northward to **Carolina Park**, where we'll find Quito's largest **Hippodrome** (race track), or turn left toward the University. If we go straight, to the north, we'll first pass the park and then encounter the *Iñaquito* commercial center — a shopping complex — along Avenida Amazonas. Past *Iñaquito*, a right turn from Avenida Amazonas onto Avenida Naciones Unidas brings us to **Atahualpa Stadium**, one of the city's most active sports centers. Almost every Sunday, many thousands of spectators attend the soccer matches (the official season runs from June to November).

Turn left onto Avenida Colón from Avenida Amazonas and walk several blocks (crossing Avenida 10 de Agosto as well) to reach **Ciudadela Universitaria** (University Campus) — site of the city's general university. The modern campus serves more than 15,000 students, with a stadium, cinema, and more. It's an interesting place to encounter the active and lively Ecuadorian youth.

The Old City
Quito's southern section, bounded by Alameda Park and Panecillo Hill, which juts 180 m above the city, is undoubtedly the most charming and interesting in town. Almost every house along the alleyways has a fascinating story to tell, from the expeditions of the Spanish founding fathers to the efforts today's city leaders are making to preserve the antiquities for posterity.

At the center of the Old City is **Plaza Independencia**, considered the heart of San Francisco de Quito since its founding. Were they able to talk, the surrounding buildings would relate stories of most of the important happenings in the annals of the town. The well-tended, troe-adorned plaza preserves the charm of bygone days with a rare grace; it continues to cast a spell of pleasant serenity on all its visitors. On its southern side stands the well-known Cathedral of Quito, one of more than eighty churches and chapels throughout the city. The **White Cathedral**, which has clearly known better days, houses an important art collection including the masterpieces of the most famous Ecuadorian artists, as well as the tomb of Sucre, the famous military leader. Open Mon.-Sat. 8-10am and 2-4pm. Open Mon.-Sat., 8-10am and 2-4pm.

Opposite the cathedral is the **Archbishop's Palace**, once the prelate's home and today packed with little shops offering a range of goods. The old **City Hall** building is also located on the square, at its northeastern corner. The handsome colonial **Government Palace**, on the plaza's northwestern side, serves the President (his office is on the second floor) and the highest functionaries of the Government. A splendid mosaic graces its first floor. To its left is a small lane running between the **Municipal Library** and the **Central Post Office**.

From here onward, a casual stroll through the alleys and a visit to some of the lovely sites is recommended. All the streets are narrow, paved with timeworn cobblestones and lined on both sides with little two-story houses in which people still live and work. Within the radius of a few blocks down, you'll find a concentration of churches and monasteries, which display an architectural beauty rarely seen with art collections to match.

We'll set out on a circular route from Plaza Independencia, passing the Quarter's important and famous sites. First we'll turn east onto Calle Chile and cross Calles Venezuela and Guayaquil, Quito's busiest commercial streets. This is where the locals do most of their shopping, as the piles of merchandise and crowds of people along the sidewalks attest.

Between Calles Venezuela and Guayaquil there is a conspicuous concrete structure to our right. It's the new **City Hall**, built in the late 1970's to replace the old Municipality Building on Plaza Independencia. After Calle Guayaquil we come to our first stop: the **San Agustín Monastery**. Here many heroes of the War of Independence are buried, and here Ecuador's Declaration of Independence (from Spain) was signed.

Now we turn right onto Calle Flores. Crossing Calle Espejo, we notice the Church of Santa Catalina to our left. Another two

QUITO — THE OLD CITY

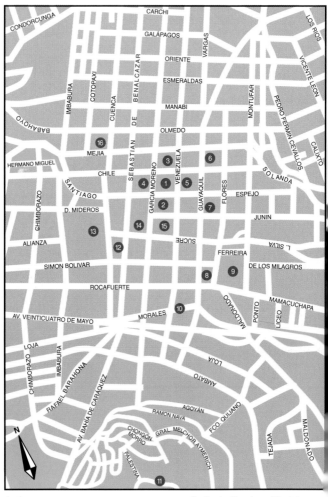

Index

A colonial street

blocks brings us to **Plaza Santo Domingo**, where a monastery and church of the same name are located. The center of the square features a statue of General Sucre, who appears to be gesturing proudly toward the slopes of Pichincha where he defeated the Spanish Royalists in battle. The monastery and church are decorated with unique woodcarvings and there is an art collection inside.

From here we turn left onto Calle Guayaquil and take a right a few meters later onto Calle Morales, known as **La Ronda**. The quarter's oldest street, it is lined with little houses renowned for their beauty. Walk down the narrow street until it ends at Avenida 24 de Mayo. This boulevard was once known as the gathering place for Indian traders, who sold and marketed innumerable products of diverse types. Severe restrictions have been placed on commerce along the boulevard in recent years and many of the traders have relocated to a covered market built especially for them. Though others still continue in their forefathers' footsteps along the boulevard, its special character has undoubtedly changed beyond recognition.

We may now head south, toward **Panecillo Hill**. Its summit affords us an enchanting view of all of Quito and especially the Old City. The climb, on paths and steps, is not difficult at all and takes no longer than half an hour. For a rather low fare, a taxi will whisk you in a few seconds to the picnic area at the top. The hilltop has a good restaurant where you can eat to your heart's content. A statue of The Virgin can be seen nearby.

A right turn from Avenida 24 de Mayo onto Calle Benalcázar and about two blocks' walking, will bring us to **Plaza San Francisco** (also called **Bolívar**). The church and monastery of that name — South America's most ancient Christian institutions — are on its western side. The **Church of San Francisco** was founded in 1535 by the Belgian Jaboco Ricke and is Quito's largest church. Its beautiful towers are not the original ones, having been reconstructed after the earthquake of 1868. Inside we find an altar of gold and a unique wooden ceiling, the epitome of human creativity. On the site is a **museum** (entrance from Cuenca 477) with a large and important collection of religious art. The church and museum are open to visitors Mon.-Fri. 9-11am and 3-5pm.

Two blocks east of Plaza San Francisco, on Calle Sucre at the corner of García Moreno, stands the **La Compañia Church** — undoubtedly Quito's most beautiful and one of the most impressive in all of Latin America. Its magnificent facade gives only a foretaste of its rich interior, covered with superb carvings in wood and gold. The beauty here will certainly excite even those who don't normally enjoy churches and religious art. It is open 9.30-11am and 4-6pm (unfortunately women are not allowed inside).

A short walk from here takes us to **General Sucre's Home**, at the corner of Venezuela and Sucre. The building has been reconstructed with great authenticity regarding its appearance in colonial times. Open daily 9am-noon and 3-6pm.

If you want an additional glimpse of the colonial art treasures with which Quito has been blessed, you'll certainly be delighted by a visit to the **Museum of Colonial Art** on Calle Cuenca, corner of Mejía, behind the La Merced Church.

Excursions

La Mitad del Mundo ("Middle of the World")

The equator — 0 degrees latitude — runs 23 km north of Quito. Since it gives the country its name, we should not wonder that the Ecuadorians attribute great significance to this imaginary line — greater than if it were real. Most tourists to Quito take the trouble to visit the spot where the imaginary line splits the world in half, and where an attractive monument, a restaurant and souvenir stands are also located.

La Mitad del Mundo is reached by a close-to-an-hour ride on a bus departing from Parque Hermano Miguel, marked with its name, through lovely mountain scenery. The park, which includes the monument, shops and a small museum of Indian Arts, open Tues.-Fri. 9am-3pm and during the weekends 10am-4pm. All told, crossing from the Southern into the Northern Hemisphere is an entertaining experience, definitely worth the effort. Though globe-shaped markers grace a number of sites in Ecuador, La Mitad del Mundo is the most famous, most beautiful and best displayed of them all.

Calderón

The pleasant Indian village of Calderón is about 30 km north of Quito. It has many *artesanía* shops where you find mostly the village speciality — little figurines made of dough. Many such miniatures are found also at Quito's shops, but prices here are much lower, and on weekdays one can see them being made.

The local bus to Calderón is at the corner of Av. Colón and 10 de Agosto, and is marked Colón/Canal.

Mt. Pichincha

West of Quito, volcanic Pichincha towers to 4735 m above sea level, and the city is built along its green slopes. Local residents love to wander about on the mountainside; many spend their weekends there when weather permits. Splendid sunsets can be seen from the mountain, whose distant peak often wears a mantle of gleaming snow. The view of Quito spread out below it is quite exquisite.

There are several routes to climb the volcano from different directions. The most recommended one is the route which starts at the village of Lloa. The taxi drive takes about 1/2 hour. From Lloa walk 5-6 hours to the *refugio* which is close to the crater. Stay the night here (bring your camping gear and food). In the morning there are fine views. A rough and steep path descends into the crater. It takes about 2 hours to descend, and another

La Mitad del Mundo

one hour brings you to thermal springs. Return to Quito by the same way.

Warning: if you are not an experienced climber do not attempt the climb by yourself. Join a group which is organized by one of the many climbers' clubs in Quito. They arrange everything — information, transport, guides and equipment.

Mt. Cotopaxi

A trip to the Nature Reserve on Cotopaxi, the world's highest active volcano, is a "must" for nature-lovers. The Pan-American Highway leading south of Quito will take you to the park entrance where there is a Nature Reserve to protect rare animals, whose continued existence is endangered because "civilization" is encroaching on their natural habitats. You should register when entering the Reserve. One day suffices for the excursion, during which you'll encounter wild animals which roam freely through an alternating landscape of forest and lava.

Many meet the challenge of climbing to the snow-capped peak of Mt. Cotopaxi which looms 5896 m above sea level. The trip takes about 3 days. On the first day one must reach the *refugio* (hut), which is also accessible by car. The second day is the climb to the summit which takes about 6 hours. One must leave at daybreak, not later than 4am, in order to complete

Mt. Pichincha — the crater

the climb before the snow, which hardens overnight, softens. The climb is exhausting with prolonged walking through snow and icy patches. One must be equipped with accurate route information and basic climbing gear. On the third day one makes the descent to the main base and from there back to Quito.

General information

Entertainment and culture

Quito is no entertainment "hot-spot". It's a city where nightfall brings quiet and tranquility, inducing the locals to head home. The people of Quito are early-to-bed types, rarely seen about the streets after 10pm. Nightlife — if so exciting a term can be used in Quito's case — heats up somewhat on weekends and holidays, while on weekdays you'll hardly find an open discotheque, not to speak of a genuine nightclub. Weekday-evening entertainment for those who wish it consists of movies, occasional concerts, or folklore shows. The *Sucre National Theater* on Calle Flores, between Guayaquil and Manabi, and *Casa de la Cultura* on Avenida 6 de Deciembre in El Ejido Park offer symphony concerts and ballet; admission to some of these is free.

E CUADOR

Folklore shows are presented several times weekly at clubs known as *peñas* as well as in the large hotels. A visit to at least one is recommended. Even those arriving from Bolivia and Peru will find that the music, rhythm and dance of Ecuador are different from those of its neighbors to the south, and are definitely worth a try. *Peña Pachamama*, Calle Washington 530 (closed Sun. and Mon.) is justly considered the best in town. *El Chucaro*, Reina Victoria 1335, is also recommended. *Nucancmi Canchi*, very close to "University City", attracts students. There's also *Peña Quito Libra* in the Old City. Though most *peñas* open as early as 9pm for drinks, performances hardly ever begin before 10pm, or even later on weekends.

Those who want to dance the night away will enjoy an evening in some of Quito's better discotheques. Heading the list is *La Licorna*, the Hotel Colon's prestigious disco club, where the elite of Quito's society — mostly sons and daughters of the city's well-to-do and dignitaries — move to the beat. Those of them who wish to save the carfare from North Quito downtown, choose *Discotheque Faces* in the north, just across from the municipal tennis and golf center. You'll find more conservative nightclubs in the *Hotel Humboldt* and *Le Club;* the former has a casino as well, while the latter, one of Quito's finest entertainment spots, is a combination restaurant and club which offers enjoyable shows each and every night. A number of hotels, in addition to the Humboldt, have casinos for the gamblers among us. One of the nicest is in the basement of the *Hotel Colón*. Here activity comes into life late at night (late in Quito terms, of course), when the cream of Quito's citizens and guests, dressed in their finest, try their luck — some at cards, others at roulette — at the gaming tables. The hall is lined with slot machines, which will happily swallow your coins to the accompaniment of whistles and shrieks. These should certainly be enough for the "poorer" visiting gamblers.

Sports

The men and women of Quito are known for their love of sports of every kind, many participate while others prefer watching the pros fight it out. Soccer is undoubtedly the most popular of all; the Olympic Atahualpa Stadium is packed every Saturday and Sunday, when the matches are held.

Quito has several tennis clubs, most rather high-priced. The large tennis and golf center on Avenida Brazil near the airport (Tel. 241-918) features tennis courts, a well-kept golf course and a swimming pool. Expensive. If you've got swimming in mind, head for *Hotel Colón*, or the *Intercontinental*.

Mountain climbing has become quite popular in recent

years; many Ecuadorians, along with many tourists, are great enthusiasts. Though the towering mountains around Quito guarantee ample opportunity for this sport, you would do well to remember the effort and the risks involved. Quito has a number of climbers' clubs, which will be glad to advise, organize outings and even to sell, buy, or rent professional climbing gear. Make inquiries at one of these before you set out.

Horse racing fans can visit the racetrack on Sundays, at the Hippodrome in La Carolina Park, and join the many spectators who follow their favorite thoroughbreds — on whom they have bet their hard-earned cash. Interesting.

Entertainment of a different kind — perhaps the most popular variety of all — is bullfighting. This unique Latin tradition, played down in its home-base Spain, is enjoying a renaissance in Quito. It arouses mixed emotions: some fervor and enthusiasm, some discomfort and revulsion. Quito's most important bullfights take place in early December, featuring some of the finest matadors from Spain and Mexico. Though the bullfights in the preceding months are less grand, almost all of them lead to the same outcome: the bull's demise before the eyes of a multitude who roar "oles" with no inhibitions. This warfare of man and beast is generally held on Sundays at **Plaza de Toros**, at the junction of Avenidas Amazonas and Cojanes. Tickets are rather expensive and are best procured in advance. Also, it is best to come early. A visit to the *corrida* (bullfight) is a unique experience. All told, it is a noble combination of rhythmic music, picturesque dress, a stylized struggle waged according to a rigid ritual and an uninhibited reaction of an audience including women and children. All these elements justify a visit to this special event, which will surely not leave you unmoved.

Festivals
Quito celebrates a variety of holidays between November and January, of which the greatest and most important marks the anniversary of its founding.

The merrymaking begins with a city-wide cleanup campaign (an enviable tradition in its own right) on a single day during November. On this day, called *Minga* after the ancient custom it preserves, everyone in Quito labors at cleaning, renovating, painting, washing and so on. Nothing — buildings, streets, parks, plazas — is overlooked. This marks the beginning of the carnival period, which compensates the populace for its trouble.

Quito's own celebration takes place during the first week of December (the city was founded on December 6) with a series of colorful events. Throughout the entire week there are bullfights

Mt. Cotopaxi

by day and balls, shows and the like by night. The feast reaches its peak with parades of marching bands and dance troupes, some local and others from the surrounding Indian villages. The dancers cavort down the packed streets with inexhaustible fervor, with spectators pulled along in their wake.

An all-night parade of celebrants, most of them costumed, takes place along Avenida Amazonas to the accompaniment of fireworks and tempestuous music.

The great party resumes the week of New Year's Day. Quito's citizens and entertainers take to the streets once again, as if to use up energy left over from the festivities of the previous three weeks. If you find yourself in Ecuador during that time of the year, a fascinating experience awaits you.

Banks and currency exchange

Changing foreign currency in Ecuador is unrestricted, involves no difficulty and is done at any bank branch or through official moneychangers (*cambio*). *Rodrigo Paz*'s moneychangers' network has a good reputation and branches all over town, but the exchange rates are not always the highest. The conversion procedures are simple and speedy, the hours convenient. The large American (*Citibank, Bank of America*), British and European banks have branches in town.

At the airport bank branch (open on weekends too) you can reconvert leftover sucres into dollars.

Postal service and telephones

We highly recommend sending all postal items to and from Ecuador by air mail only; even so, expect delays. The Central Post Office is at Av. Eloy Alfaro and 9 de Octubre. The *IETEL* offices (international calls) are on Av. Colón and 6 de Diciembre. International calls are rather expensive and involve a lengthy wait. Service at *IETEL*'s north Quito office (on Avenida Colón near Avenida Amazonas) is sometimes a little faster.

Shopping

Quito and its environs offer an inexhaustible selection of souvenirs, knickknacks, clothing, and so on. The combination of quality, beauty and reasonable prices makes Quito a bargain-hunters' paradise, as proven by the many visitors who've thrown economy to the winds in the face of such attractive buys. Always remember that any purchase, anywhere — marketplace, shop, plaza, or boulevard — should begin with stubborn bargaining, it's the local custom, accepted and in good spirit.

Most of the Indian crafts produced in the Quito area are brought into the city. If you have no way of going out and exploring the Indian villages and towns by yourself, you can buy their wares — at slightly higher prices, of course — in town. Beyond the monetary gain, the artists' villages (especially Otavalo, San Antonio de Ibarra and their neighbors) deserve a visit (see "North of Quito"), even though their goods, as said, may be purchased in town as well. In Quito you will find a wealth of wool products — sweaters, wall hangings, blankets — in addition to colorful ceramics, carved wood sculpture, silver jewelry, leather clothing and more. These can be purchased at any of the many stores along Avenida Amazonas and the adjacent streets, or in the less-elegant, lower-priced parts of town a short walk away. Some of the best shops are in Quito's new section. Of them, the best-known is *Folklore* at Avenida Colón 260, owned by Olga Fisch. She has opened branches in the *Hotel Colón* and the *Intercontinental* as well, where you will also find the well-known H. Stern jewelry chain, which does business in most Latin American capitals. In the same area you will also find the large *La Bodega artesanía* shop, at Calle Mera 641 (Tel. 232-844), opposite the *Libri Mundi* Bookstore. It has everything from wooden statuettes to furniture. The *OCEPA* government *artesanía* store is at Calle Carrión 13.

The areas closer to the Old City, especially around Calles Guayaquil and Venezuela, are noted for a large selection

— displayed in conspicuous disarray and distressing density, though at prices much lower than those in the places we have listed so far. Here — obviously — is where the locals shop. The Plaza Independencia area has a number of souvenir shops offering an exhaustive selection at convenient prices. The sidewalks of Avenida 24 de Mayo and in El Ejido Park are covered with seated Indians proudly offering their wares — fertile hunting grounds for genuine bargains.

Quito also has shops that sell various types of antiques, some of them genuine. Be careful to verify that what you have bought is authentic and — no less important — that the dealer is licensed. To be caught leaving Ecuador with an archaeological artifact for which you have no permit is an altogether unpleasant experience.

Foreign-language literature

One of South America's best bookstores is in Quito: *Libri Mundi* on Juan León Mera 851 (Tel. 234-791), a venerable institution in the town. Here you will find almost every book ever written about Ecuador, alongside an impressive selection of works on nature, science, economics and the like — in English, French, German and Spanish. *Libri Mundi* is near the *Hotel Colón*, where it holds a branch; we recommend a visit, if only to browse.

English-language newspapers are available in the large hotel shops and at kiosks along Avenida Amazonas.

Weather

Quito enjoys wonderful weather. Its proximity to the equator and its elevation give it a magnificent climate with enviable seasonal stability. Rains fall throughout most of the year and usually at the same hour every day. The driest months are from May until November, when much less rain falls. Quito's air is pure and pristine; the sun's rays burst through the thin mantle of clouds that frequently shades the city in a manner which can be troublesome for the sun-sensitive. Shield your head and face from radiation and use sunscreen. Contact lenses are liable to prove painful, because of the dryness and the high altitiude.

Days in Quito are warm; temperatures generally hover around 22°C (72°F). At night, however, the mercury plunges considerably. Warm clothing is necessary; a raincoat and umbrella will also prove most useful.

Important addresses and phone numbers

Police (Radio Patrol): Tel. 101.

Ministry of Tourism (*DITURIS*): Reina Victoria 514; Tel. 239-044.
Red Cross: Tel. 214-977.
Long Distance Calls: Tel. 116.
Ministry of Immigration (for extending visas): Av. Amazonas 2639.
Ecuatoriana Airlines: Colón and Diego de Almagro, Tel. 563-003.
Airport: Tel. 241-580.

Consulates
U.S.A.: Av. Patria 120, Tel. 562-890.
U.K.: González Suáres 111, Tel. 560-670/1.
France: Diego de Almagro, Edificio Kingmann, 2nd floor, Tel. 569-883.
Germany: Av. Patria, Edificio Eteco, 6th floor, Tel. 232-660.
Switzerland: Catalina Herrera 120, Edificio Xerox, Tel. 434-948.

Guayaquil and Southern Ecuador

Guayaquil is Ecuador's largest city, home to about 2 million people. It is Ecuador's major coastal city, and is also the country's industrial and commercial metropolis and the traditional home of most of its economic institutions. It is undoubtedly Ecuador's most "western" city, which tourists will notice immediately.

Guayaquil, founded as part of the Spanish campaign of conquest and settlement, established industrial, commercial and agricultural elites from its earliest days. The fertile areas that encompass it have made Guayaquil very important indeed, in determining patterns of national development in many spheres. The city is highly influential in determining the size and composition of the national foodbasket, the scope of the country's foreign trade and its economic strength.

With regard to tourism, Guayaquil is hardly one of the Seven Wonders of the World; if you are not passing through on the way to somewhere else, you probably would not miss much by skipping the city. Most people who come as far as Guayaquil do so on business; others take advantage of its convenient location en route from Peru to the mountains or as a point of departure for the Galápagos Islands. The city lies on the western side of Rio Guayas along the innermost reaches of the Gulf of Guayaquil, about 50 kilometers east of the Pacific coast. The city boasts the modern Bolívar Airport and a gigantic commercial harbor. The latter, known as **Puerto Nuevo** (New Port), provides exceptionally convenient and secure anchorage for enormous ships. The well developed port, which handles about 80% of Ecuador's import and export freight, is always bustling. At the same time, it is kept clean and almost never appears disorderly or chaotic.

Guayaquil was the arena for political conflict during the struggles for independence waged by the Latin American people against the Spanish monarchy. The most important encounter that took place here was in August 1822, when the Venezuelan general Simón Bolívar met his Argentine counterpart José de San Martín, to discuss the city's future. Bolívar, engrossed at the time in his dream of "Greater Colombia", sought to annex the city to the northern confederation, while San Martín, one of Peru's liberators, wished to attach it to that country. The conclusion of the secret meeting is shrouded in fog, but its results were to have long-term consequences: Guayaquil was included in "Greater Colombia", while an embittered San Martín went off to self imposed exile in France, where he remained till his dying day. His remains were brought to Buenos Aires and interred in the cathedral on Plaza de Mayo.

Transportation

Guayaquil has many and various transportation connections with most Ecuadorian cities, with Peru and the other Latin American countries, and with Europe and the United States. Many airplanes from Quito and elsewhere in Ecuador land every day in its modern, centrally located airport, along with others which stop over en route to and from neighboring countries. The daily flight from Quito to the Galápagos and back stops here as well (see "Galápagos").

Guayaquil is also easily accessible by bus. The trip from Quito takes about eight hours (about ten hours for the return — uphill — trip), passing through lovely mountain scenery. *Transandina* and *Empresa* provide convenient and reliable daily service. Local companies also run buses along this line, using more antiquated vehicles, though fares are adjusted accordingly. Transportation to Cuenca (five hours), Esmeraldas (seven), Riobamba (five) and elsewhere is also frequent.

The most enjoyable way to go from Quito to Guayaquil is by train (see "Quito — Transportation"). The railway station is in Duran, across the river; from there, take a ferry or taxi (the latter crossing the impressive bridge) into town.

A number of bus companies provide service between Guayaquil and the border city of Machala, with several departures every hour (see below: "Onward to Peru").

You can get around in Guayaquil itself by means of buses, minibuses and *colectivos* (fixed-route taxis) — all cheap and fast, but crowded and noisy. Regular taxis are in abundance; be sure to agree on a fare with the driver **before** you climb in. The international car-rental companies have branch offices at the airport and in town.

Where to stay and eat

Oro Verde: 9 de Octubre at the corner with García Moreno, Tel. 510-201. The best in town, luxury and high prices guaranteed.
Continental: 10 de Agosto, at the corner with Chile, Tel. 329-270, Fax 325454. Five star, with the usual facilities in this category, plus the old wing, with its classical charm and the superb restaurants.
Gran Hotel Guayaquil: Boyacá and 10 de Agosto, Tel. 329-690,

Fax 327251. Next to the Cathedral, at the very center of town.
Top level.

Palace: Chile 216, very recommended for business travellers.

Rizzo: Ballén 319, Tel. 325-210. Not as expensive as the others.
and very good service.

Plaza: Chile 414, Tel. 324-195. Moderate prices paid for moderate
service. It is off the Rizzo.

Imperial: Urdaneta 705, Tel. 308-586. Inexpensive, clean and
recommended.

Thrifty accomodation is available north of Avenida 9 de Octubre
along Calles Junín and Urdaneta, and south of Avenida 10 de
Agosto, on Sucre, Boyacá and nearby streets.

You'll find excellent restaurants in the luxury hotels, like the
Continental, the Oro Verde and the Grand Hotel Guayaquil. You
can also find many Chinese restaurants, mostly downtown.

On Avenida 9 de Octubre costumbrists will feel at home, no
matter where they come from, at the local *Pizza Hut*, the
Kentucky Fried Chicken or at *Burger King*. *La Govinda*, or
Parque Centenario, is a nice vegetarian restaurant. On food
and lodging, you may find the prices in Guayaquil somewhat
higher than in Quito.

Tourist services

Maps and printed material are available at the Central Tourist
Bureau on Aguirre 104, on the corner with the Malecón, Tel.
328-312; open until 5.30pm.

Though many tourist companies organize excursions in
Guayaquil and its surroundings, their main expertise is in cruises
to the Galápagos Islands (see below). Flights to Galápagos are
run by *TAME* airlines, at 9 de Octubre, edificio Gran Pasaje, Tel.
305-800.

Tourist sites

Though Guayaquil is not noted for fascinating sites, there are
a number of places worth seeing. The **Malecón**, a sort of
promenade, runs along the riverfront, bustling with people and
cars on one side and a procession of boats on the other. The
Government and Municipality buildings are along the Malecón
as are many public buildings. The entire area is crowded
during most hours of the day and the evening. At sunset, many
locals take their evening constitutional, ending at the **Clock
Tower** at the end of Avenida 10 de Agosto. This nineteenth-
century Oriental clock serves as a familiar landmark for locals
and visitors alike. Heading northward along the Malecón, we

come to Avenida 9 de Octubre, Guayaquil's main street, which runs perpendicular to the northernmost quay. Opposite the intersection of this boulevard and the Malecón is **La Rotonda**, a monument commemorating the fateful meeting of Bolívar and San Martín. One block north of here, at the intersection of the Malecón and Calle Icaza, *Banco del Pacífico* displays a collection of regional art. Recommended.

We now turn left — westward — up Avenida 9 de Octubre, passing the shops and restaurants that line this humming business street. Three blocks later we reach the Church of San Francisco. This church, one of the city's loveliest, is noteworthy for its interior decor, a well-preserved survivor from the colonial era. Beside the church, on Calle Chile, are a number of stalls which comprise a sort of small market. To visit another beautiful church, **La Merced**, cross the street opposite San Francisco, turn onto Calle Córdova and continue for a few meters.

Proceeding up Avenida 9 de Octubre, we arrive at **Parque Centenario**, Guayaquil's main square. The monument to the heroes of national independence dates from 1920. A **Museum of Pre-Columbian Art**, run by the Ministry of Culture, is at 1260 Avenida 9 de Octubre. Here you can feast your eyes on antique handicrafts, gold jewelry and more. Open Mon.-Fri., 9am-noon and 3-6.30pm; Sat. 9am-4pm. Recommended.

From here we'll head back, southward, toward the intersection of Avenida 10 de Agosto and Calle Chimborazo. Here we come upon a small park named for Simón Bolívar, and across the way, a relatively modern cathedral with white towers and broad dimensions, which may be visited during mass. We continue toward the river, passing the Municipal Library and reaching Calle Pedro Carbo.

Turning right, we arrive at the corner of Calle Sucre. Here we find the **Municipal Museum**, with its impressive display of gold implements and archaeological findings, alongside shrunken heads ... a reminder of the customs of the wild Indian tribes. Though the ground floor is occasionally used for exhibitions of modern art, most of it is set aside to display archaeological collections and colonial art objects. On the upper floor you'll find collections of handicrafts, folklore and the like. Open Wed.-Fri., 9am-4pm; Sat., 10am-3pm and Sun., 10am-1pm.

From here it's but a short walk to the Malecón, near the Clock Tower. Once we've come to know the city center, it is worthwhile to venture a bit farther. From La Rotonda you can keep going straight — northward along the Malecón — to **Las Peñas**, Guayaquil's Old Quarter. Though it is not a long walk, we do not recommend it, for it goes through a poor and dangerous

_E_CUADOR

GUAYAQUIL

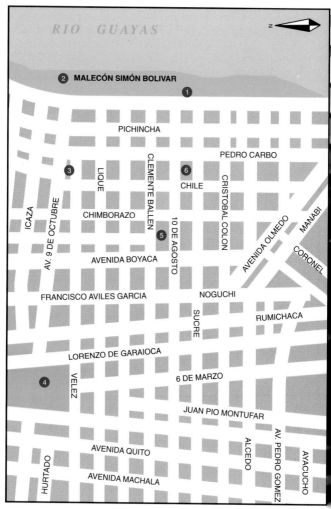

neighborhood. It is best to let a taxi take you there. In this rickety neighborhood, at the foot of Santa Ana Hill, you can roam the cobblestoned streets between squat houses, centuries old. Here you will find the **Santo Domingo Church**, Guayaquil's first, dating from the mid-sixteenth century. For a bird's-eye view of the area, climb a little way up the hill until you come to two ancient cannons, and contemplate the scene around you. The cannons were installed here centuries ago to defend Guayaquil against attackers from the sea and have remained ever since.

The prestigious suburb of Urdesa, with its many cinemas, fine restaurants, clubs, sports facilities and more, is northeast of the city center.

Night life

Guayaquil's status as Ecuador's most active city finds expression in entertainment, as well. Unlike Quito, Guayaquil does not excel in folklore activity though this too is available — but rather in more Western entertainment: discotheques, cinemas and nightclubs the like. The first two can be found in the large hotels, the city center and Urdesa. Most are open every night, though they are mainly active on weekends. The cinemas show first-rate films. A number of resort towns and recreation centers around Guayaquil offer a broader range of leisure-time pursuits.

Banks and moneychanging

Several foreign banks have branches in Guayaquil, which deal in matters of trade between Ecuador and their respective countries while handling all conventional monetary transactions. *Citibank, Banco Holandés* and *Bank of America* branches also handle the transfer of money to or from Ecuador. For changing currency it is best to turn to the moneychangers (*cambio*), most congregating along Avenidas 9 de Octubre and Pichincha. The airport *cambio* is open on weekends as well. For buying Peruvian *soles* it is best to wait until you reach Peru, though the exchange rate is sometimes better in Guayaquil. Check first.

Postal service and phones

The Central Post Office and the *IETEL* office for international phone calls are on Calle Carbo and Aguirre.

Resorts

Guayaquil is surrounded by several popular resorts where the locals spend their weekends and holidays. The most popular ones, **Playas** and **Salinas**, have frequent bus service to town.

Both of them have nice hotels, pleasant restaurants, sports and entertainment clubs and a casino.

The tourist office in Guayaquil will provide you with transportation details. If you are planning to visit during the holiday season, you would do well to make reservations in advance.

South of Guayaquil

The main highway south of Guayaquil skirts the Gulf, and connects Puerto Bolívar and **Machala**, Ecuador's fourth-largest city (pop. 170,000). Machala is the largest town near the Peruvian border. This rapidly developing city is the center of a large agricultural area — the main product grown here is bananas. Frequent bus connections link Machala with Ecuador's other cities and with Peru.

Cuenca

Cuenca (pop. app. 250,000; elev. 2600 m) is Ecuador's third-largest city and the center of the Ecuadorian handicrafts "industry", whose reputation has spread far and wide. This convivial town was founded in 1557, and its old homes and cobblestoned streets do not seem to have changed much since. Its climate is spring-like the year round, and its Indian population forthcoming and friendly.

The lovely *artesanía* market held on Thursdays (on Calles 9 de Octubre and San Francisco) offers a wide selection of the best local handicrafts. Try to arrange things so as to reach town on market day (there is a city market on Sunday as well, but it is much smaller and less impressive). For shopping, we can also recommend the *Productos Andinos* Cooperative, with its variety of wares at reasonable prices, or any of the shops throughout town, mainly along Avenida Gran Colombia.

Transportation

Many buses from Guayaquil, Quito, Ambato, Machala and elsewhere reach Cuenca. One train arrives every day from Sibambe, leaving it at 11am and departing back from Cuenca at 2pm. The trip from Sibambe is a little faster by bus, but less impressive and not as interesting. Take the bus only if you have missed the train. *SAM* and *TAME* have daily flights to and from Quito and Guayaquil.

Food and lodging

El Dorado: Gran Colombia and Luis Cordero, Tel. 831-390, Fax 831-663. The best in town. Expensive.

Crespo: Larga 7-93 and Luis Cordero, Tel. 827-857/825-837.
Less expensive then the former, recommended.
Milán: Córdova 989 at the corner with Aguirre, Tel. 835-351.
Basic, inexpensive, clean, recommended. Curfew during the
night.
In the central area of the town you'll find no problem to get a meal
that suits your taste and budget. Vegetarians will find a branch
of *La Govinda* behind the new Cathedral. Avoid fresh vegetables
and fruits!

What to see

The **Tourist Bureau** is at Hermano Miguel 686, at the corner
with Córdova and at B. Malo 725, Tel. 827-414.

Cuenca is renowned for its many churches, whose steeples
dominate the skyline. We recommend a visit to the El Carmen
Church on Calle Sucre, the cathedral in the central plaza and
the San Francisco and San Blas Churches.

No visitor to Cuenca should miss visiting the museums. The
Municipal Museum displays impressive Indian ornaments,
Incan and other pre-Columbian archaeological relics. The
Banco Central Museum houses a highly interesting,
unquestionably unique collection of antiquities, the Padre Crespi
collection. The priest, who died in 1982, amassed the collection
to support his contention that the first settlers in this part of the
world were Phoenicians, who had crossed the Atlantic Ocean in
their small boats and penetrated the continent along the Amazon
and its tributaries. The museum, in the Banco Central building on
Calle Gran Colombia, displays artifacts which, in Father Crespi's
view, attest to their owners' Mediterranean origin. Interesting.

Excursions in the vicinity

Las Lajas Park is located not far from town. The park is rather
hard to reach and has no facilities. Nevertheless, the area, more
than 4000 m above sea level, is lovely, with lakes, lagoons and
small streams. You could spend several enjoyable days hiking
here. Bring food and excellent camping gear.

Ingapirca, Ecuador's most important Inca ruin, is located two
hours out of Cuenca by train, bus, taxi or thumb. Though
deserted on weekdays, it is full of visitors on weekends when
transportation is easier to arrange. For lodging, you can pitch a
tent nearby or camp in a *refugio* (hut). The purpose Ingapirca
served is not certain, but it appears to have been used for sun
worship, as well as an administrative center. Today one can
see here ruins of fortifications, temples and courtyards, and get
a good impression of the Incan architecture.

After exploring Cuenca and its environs, we will return to the Guayaquil-Quito route and continue the climb from Simbote to Riobamba.

Loja

The town of Loja (app. 150,000 inhabitants), lies at over 2,000 m above sea level in a lovely scenery. This is South Ecuador's gateway to the eastern Amazon Basin. Its university has a good reputation and many young Ecuadorians come here for their studies. It has several nice churches, and a market takes place on Sat.-Mon.

Loja is connected by daily flights to Quito and Guayaquil (the airport is about 1/2 hour ride away). There are many buses to Quito (about 20 hours), Cuenca (6 hours) and Guayaquil (12 hours). If you are going south to Peru, there are buses to the border towns of Huaquillas (the common way) and Macará (less popular yet more scenic road).

The village of **Vilcabamba**, an hour away from Loja in a splendid valley, is a most popular place among young travelers, who come to spend here a few days after their long journey. Here one can enjoy lovely nature, excellent weather, relaxing atmosphere and good inexpensive hostels. The most recommended one is *Madre Tierre*, run by Jaime Mendoza, some distance out of the village. It offers beautiful setting, healthy food, excellent breakfasts and dinners; they also rent horses for day trips.

Onward to Peru — border-crossing procedures

Border crossing formalities between Peru and Ecuador are handled in the frontier town of Huaquillas, with all the standard immigration procedures carried out nearby. The checkpoint is open daily from 9am until 5pm with a two-hour afternoon *siesta*. Tourists entering Peru are sometimes required to present departure tickets from that country, and an MCO is not always enough. (If that is the case, buy an inexpensive bus ticket from any border town to some destination in a neighboring country). You must cross the border on foot. After completing departure procedures, you will have to submit to the bureaucracy of immigration regulations of the country you are entering. You can go to street moneychangers who congregate at the border area to change currency. It is worth remembering, however, that exchange rates here are lower than those prevailing in the nearby cities, so change only enough money for your immediate needs. On weekends and while the banks are closed, the rate of exchange is even poorer. Be sure to compare a number of moneychangers' rates — and check the amount handed to you.

*E*CUADOR

Direct bus service from Huaquillas brings you to Quito and to other large cities. From the Peruvian side, *colectivos* (fixed-route taxis) will take you to Tumbes, where you can get express service to Lima and other cities in northern Peru. Keep in mind that this area was one of the worst affected during the 1991 cholera epidemics. Avoid raw fruits and vegetables and drink only bottled water!

The Galápagos Islands

Though many places on earth are called "unique" or "exceptional", the Galápagos Islands, a thousand kilometers west of the Ecuadorian coast, are exclusive in their ability to actually back up the claim with statistics. Dozens of animals and hundreds of plant species flourish here, and a considerable number of the sea animals, about half the flora and almost all the reptiles exist nowhere else on earth

The Galápagos Islands — *Archipielago de Colón* in Spanish — were discovered in 1535, and ever since have aroused the wonder and admiration of zoologists and botanists the world over. The archipelago, named after the giant sea turtle (Sp. *Galápago*) consists of several dozen islands of various sizes. Noticeable differences in flora and fauna types can be discerned even between one island and the next.

Of the five thousand people in Galápagos, about half dwell on San Cristóbal Island (the administrative center) and many others live on the major island of Santa Cruz. Ships link the islands and also transport tourists from the island of Baltra, where the flights from the mainland touch down, to Santa Cruz where most island cruises begin.

The Galápagos Islands are home to hundreds of animal species. Among them: giant sea turtles, marine and terrestrial iguanas (huge lizards), sea lions, penguins and birds by the tens of thousands. The most famous animals are the large iguanas, which resemble prehistoric dinosaurs, and the huge turtles, which served for years as easy prey for pirates who feasted on their tasty meat. Since, historically, they have had little contact with man, the beasts lack an instinctive fear of people. For the visitor, this is perhaps the most astounding phenomenon of all. Not only do the animals not flee from one; they actually swim up to one and give one a friendly greeting.

The Government of Ecuador and the Darwin Foundation, with assistance from UNESCO, set up a research station on Santa Cruz in 1959. Most scientific research in Galápagos is concentrated here, along with a very interesting exhibit of the local flora and fauna. We highly recommend that you stop here **before** cruising among the islands. Thus you will acquire a basic familiarity with what you will see and increase your enjoyment of this strange world where time seems to have stood still since Creation.

The development of Galápagos

The Galápagos Islands were never part of any continent and are in fact the peaks of volcanoes that reach as high as 3000 m above sea level. Though actual eruptions are extremely rare, some of the volcanoes are still active; you can sometimes see smoke wafting from distant cones. The islands, commonly assumed to be three million years old, consist chiefly of volcanic basalt. Only limited areas are covered with top soil which supports the dense vegetation. The equator runs nearby; so does the Antarctic Humboldt current, which meets the warm El Niño current not far from here. Some regard this singular geographic combination as the key to the wondrous phenomenon of the Galápagos.

According to the accepted hypothesis, the animal and plant life on the Galápagos Islands developed over hundreds of thousands of years, during which various biological families were transported here by sea and wind, each finding its own niche in this odd environment. This theory underlay the conclusions of the British scholar Charles Darwin, who visited the Galápagos in 1835 as a crewman aboard the *Beagle* and came to know at first hand the archipelago's unique natural phenomena. Darwin's Galápagos observations laid the foundations for his famous work *The Origin of Species*, in which he presented his view of the evolutionary process. Its essence: animal and plant life undergoes a process of development influenced environmental changes in such a way as to make possible their survival in the new conditions.

The theory of evolution

Basing his theory on observation and research, Darwin concluded that all life originated from a single source. In search of support for his ideas, the British scholar turned to a variety of complementary theories, widely-held in his day, and integrated them into his own. Darwin's evolutionary hypothesis is based on the fact that animals and plants produce offspring in quantities far greater than those necessary for maintaining the species at its current population level, while those levels have remained

THE GALAPAGOS ISLAND

stable over extremely long periods of time. At the same time, each generation is somewhat different from its precursors. The first two arguments led Darwin to conclude that every generation's mortality rate is high; the third led him to infer that some individuals have better chances of survival than others. The survivors, claimed Darwin, are those who are better able to adapt to changes — and these will subsequently become dominant.

The theory of evolution made a big splash the moment it was published, and today it is widely recognized. New discoveries and scientific experiments tend to confirm the idea of change and the thesis that all creatures derive from a single primeval

Feeding an Iguana

Masked Boobies

source. Humans, land animals, sea animals and even birds have many common traits. Genetics, the biological frontier of our age, explains how the process of evolution actually takes place; its description of the mutation of genes tends to confirm Darwin's most important arguments.

Visiting the islands

Tourists with the Galápagos Islands on their itineraries may choose between two possibilities, both "organized". Because there is a quota of about 5000 visitors per month and because transportation among the islands is possible only by rented boat, we haven't many alternatives. The first option is a package tour which includes a flight to the islands and a cruise among them. The second possibility is to get there yourself and haggle with some local captain over renting his vessel. Though the first way is usually more expensive, it guarantees full utilization of your time, reliability and a comprehenisve pre-planned route. The second option, though liable to involve a lengthy wait until a boat becomes available — with the possibility of prolonged delay and waste of precious time — is sure to end up considerably cheaper than the "packaged" way.

A number of factors should be taken into account when you select a tour and determine the type of excursion best for you. First of all you must choose between a real ship and a bouncing boat. The former has a number of advantages, the most important being stability (especially since the sea around the Galápagos is rather stormy) and optimum use of time (since a ship can continue traveling throughout the night as well). The great drawback: you will be in a large group, with no possibility of a "one-on-one" contact with the animals. When you go ashore, you will march along in a tight little queue with an even tighter timetable. A small boat, by contrast, offers a significant advantage in this respect, for a group of eight to ten people is far more flexible about how it behaves on shore and how much time it spends on a given island. At the same time, the waves will rock your boat and you will waste precious daylight hours sailing between islands, since small boats are incapable of nighttime navigation. If you are young or young-at-heart — and if you do not suffer too grievously from seasickness — we would recommend a boat. The pleasant atmosphere, excellent food which the crew hauls out of the sea each day, plus the flexibility en route will definitely compensate you for the inconvenience.

When you rent a boat yourself, generally in Santa Cruz, it is essential to bargain with the boat owner over the rate and route, stipulating the precise route the boat will follow, the time to be spent on each island and the overall duration of your trip. Rates fluctuate depending on the type of vessel, speed, comfort and the like. Remember that the cheapest option is not necessarily the best, and be sure to ascertain that the crew has equipped itself sufficiently for the duration of your trip, otherwise you will waste valuable time restocking.

If you are on an organized excursion, the crew of your boat will meet you at the airport to take you to the vessel on which you will spend the coming week. Many travel companies organize Galápagos tours — some from Quito, others from Guayaquil — and their rates vary considerably. It is important to verify the quality, reliability and condition of the ship or boat and, of course, the duration of the cruise and its route. Among the reliable firms, we can mention *Metropolitan Tours* (Av. Amazonas 239, Tel. 560-550, Fax 564-655) in Quito, which offers many tours either by ship or by boat.

Though *TAME* Airlines flies to the Galápagos from Quito and Guayaquil every day, you have to buy tickets in advance, for the planes are always packed. If you are on your own, take a boat from the airport on Baltra to Santa Cruz, where you will start organizing your outing. Be prepared to wait a long time for a boat. Concluding an agreement with a boat owner is likely to take a week during the "hot" tourist season. Individual tourists will easily find potential partners on Santa Cruz with whom to team up to rent a boat

The ideal Galápagos excursion itinerary runs from seven to ten days and recommend the following islands:

Santa Cruz — the major island, with more than one thousand inhabitants. Here you will find the most important attraction: the Darwin Center for Galápagos Island Research, with its fascinating exhibit of various aspects of life and its development on the Islands, and the giant sea turtles cared for under special conditions to prevent their extinction. Open 9am-4pm weekdays. A must.

Lodging possibilities in the island's main village, Puerto Ayora, are limited and generally rather basic. Reservations are important between June and September and in December and January. Bear in mind, that eating, drinking and moving about freely are forbidden on the islands except in specified areas or by special

Seals

Albatrosses

permit. The restrictions are intended to guarantee a minimum of damage to the natural environment that the animals require.

On Santa Cruz you can hike to Tortuga Bay or Mount Crocker. Another recommended outing takes you to the turtle preserve, accessible by car from Santa Rosa (about 20 km from Puerto Ayora).

Española — one of the most beautiful islands, favorite playground of sea lions and frequented by tremendous flocks of birds, among them the albatross, masked boobies and blue-footed boobies.

Isabela — the largest island, populated by a great number of birds, as well as iguanas, penguins and more. If you are in shape and willing to make the effort, we recommend a climb to the top of volcanic Mt. Alcedo, with its splendid view.

Floriana — an island full of stunningly beautiful birds.

Plaza — covered with dense vegetation and populated by iguanas, birds and assorted marine creatures.

Santiago — a gorgeous island with thousands of iguanas, birds, sea lions and other marine species, who will gladly join you in a swim along Espumuilla beach. Games Bay is an exquisite bay with a basalt coastline where sea lions and birds bask in the many pools which have been formed in the rock surface. An exceptionally beautiful part of Santiago Island is that opposite the adjacent Bartolomé island (enchanting in itself). In this area the lava has solidified into strange and varied forms.

Daphne — on this island two types of boobies nest — the blue-footed and the masked booby.

Seymore — this is the nesting ground of the frigate. During the mating season one can observe the incredible breast of the male which inflates into a big red sack — protruding below its head — part of his attempt to court the female.

Other recommended islands — the more remote Tower and Fernandina Islands (a visit there requires an extra day or two). Tower Island is the only nesting place of the red-footed boobies.

Miscellaneous comments

For more information, consult the many books available on the Galápagos Islands. They are available in Quito, Guayaquil and on the Islands, as well.

Take along enough local currency. Prices are higher in the

Galápagos than on the mainland, since almost everything must be flown in. Moneychanging possibilities are limited. Those places — banks and other institutions — that are willing to change dollars will do so at a lower rate and a higher commission, and many places (like the taxes to be paid) accept only *Sucres*.

From Guayaquil to Quito —
up the Andes

One of the most beautiful and interesting routes that ascend the heights of the Andes, is that from Guayaquil to Quito. Though we have mentioned the railroad which plies this route, in our sections on Quito and Guayaquil, it is hard to refrain from taking it up again and recommending it.

A trip along this route is certainly unforgettable. Though two trains set out from Guayaquil up the mountain each day, only one, the *Autoferro*, reaches Quito. This train, with its comfortable, spacious cars (some designed especially for tourists) and relatively low fares, starts out a bit after 6am every morning and climbs towards the capital. This railroad, completed in 1908, reaches an elevation of 3609 m above sea level at Urbina (275 km from Guayaquil). The second train, *tren mixto*, hauls passengers and freight only as far as Riobamba; from there you will have to take a bus to Quito. It also departs each morning and takes about ten hours to reach Riobamba, after stopping in every village and hamlet along the way to take on and unload passengers and freight. It is a lively ride, full of peddlers — an experience in itself.

Remember that the trains do not run on Sundays and that it is advisable to buy tickets in advance at the office in Guayaquil (no need to go as far as the terminal, located across the river in Durán). Though the trains make a number of stops and the platforms en route are swarming with peddlers, we recommend packing food for the trip. First, you will not always have time to wait in line; secondly, the peddlers' "bargains" will not always favorably strike your palate.

Plenty of buses ply this route every day as well, using the Guayaquil-Quito highway. Most of the bus companies that serve this line are low-priced and reliable (see also "Quito — Transportation").

Some of Ecuador's most interesting towns lie along this route and we will visit them while traveling between the country's two largest cities.

Mt. Chimborazo

The route heads northeast from Guayaquil and we spend four hours crossing fertile, heavily farmed plains. The last stop before climbing the Andes is Bucay, a small provincial town 87 km from Guayaquil at the foot of the mountains (you can also reach Bucay from Guayaquil by bus, covering a route no less beautiful in half the time). Then the train begins its steep climb, the most captivating part of the trip and the reason for its fame. The first important stop is the town of Sibambe, 130 km from Guayaquil. The route to Cuenca branches off here. Past Sibambe the tracks make some astounding switchbacks up **Nariz del Diablo** (The Devil's Nose) — an utterly fascinating stretch — and continue toward the mountain cities.

Riobamba

Riobamba was founded by refugees from Cajabamba, a town about thirty kilometers away that was abandoned after being levelled by an earthquake in 1797. Riobamba, an attractive city 2750 m above sea level, is home to a population of some 150,000, who engage mostly in commerce, agriculture and the manufacture of decorative items. A delightful market held every

Baños

Saturday offers local *artesanía* and a view of the locals in their traditional attire.

The Guayaquil-Quito *Autoferro* train stops in Riobamba and continues on to Quito, while this is the end of the line for the *Tren Mixto* from Guayaquil. Many buses travel to Riobamba from Quito (three hours), Guayaquil and the other mountain and coastal plain cities.

Riobamba is full of restaurants. Among the city's many hotels, the best is the *Galpón* (far from downtown). We recommend the *Humboldt* (on Avenida Borja). You'll find very reasonable hostels along the streets near the train station.

The Tourist Bureau (at Tarqui 2248, corner of Primera Constituyente) will advise you concerning accommodation, transportation and outings in and around town. In Riobamba itself, we recommend a visit to the churches and the religious museum in the Concepcion Monastery. You should then head 10 km north to the village of **Guano**, renowned for the wonderful fabrics woven by the local residents.

From Riobamba we continue toward Quito, either by train or by bus, passing between soaring mountain peaks and broad plains. Our next stop: Ambato.

Ambato

Ambato (pop. app. 140,000), 150 km from Quito, is largely a new city built atop the ruins of its predecessor, devastated in the terrible earthquake of 1949. Today's reconstructed Ambato, with its handsome streets and buildings, is a quiet, rather sleepy town, which bursts into life in February when its **Fruit and Flowers Festival** attracts crowds of participants.

The city center is graced with a lovely plaza, where you will find the cathedral and a small museum displaying stuffed local birds and animals (closed weekends). Nearby are a number of *artesania* shops where you can acquire a selection of souvenirs.

Many buses from Quito, Guayaquil, Cuenca, Baños (see below), and other cities pull into Ambato.

Climbing Chimborazo

The most propitious time of year to climb this volcano (summit: 6310 m) is from June through August or December and January. The weather then is favorable, with almost no extreme changes. The most popular route up is via Pogyos (elev. 4000 m), an hour and a half from Ambato by bus. Rent mules to haul your gear the rest of the way. From Pogyos it is about a four-hour climb to Refugio Zurita, a hikers' shelter at 4950 m; spend the night there. The next day — **very early** — begin your final assault on the peak, a nine-to-ten-hour trek. The descent is far easier, usually taking about five hours. Be sure to wear comfortable hiking shoes and warm clothing; bring top-grade climbing and camping gear.

Warning: if you are not an experienced climber do not attempt this climb by yourself.

The city is the starting point for the ascent to volcanic Mount Chimborazo. If this is for you, make inquiries beforehand at the Tourist Bureau about climbing conditions, weather, transportation, necessary equipment, etc.

It should be noted that mountain climbing, a stormy adventure in its own right, requires experience, superb physical condition and appropriate equipment. Because of the high elevation you **must** be doubly cautious, spending several days in the area before setting out, to allow your body to acclimatize to the rarified atmosphere (see "Introduction — Altitude").

Baños

This resort town takes its name from the hot springs in the vicinity, which account for much of its popularity as well. The town lies 1800 m above sea level in the middle of a fertile valley. It attracts tourists in its own right and by being on the road to the eastern jungles, as well as serving as a crossroad of the hiking and mountain-climbing routes. Try not to come here on the weekends because this is when throngs of locals arrive. The hotels are fully booked and the warm water pools are packed with bathers.

Transportation

The city enjoys frequent bus service with Ambato, continuing to other destinations on the Quito-Guayaquil route. Buses leave for the eastern jungles several times a week, reaching the jungle towns Tena and Misahualli. The road is rough, but passes through gorgeous, tropical landscape (see "El Oriente"). Buses leave from the terminal located near the city center.

Where to stay

Baños has many hotels of various grades and price levels. You will find plenty of cheap hotels and pensions, but since Baños is a resort town, occupancy is high: you will have to move fast — even faster on weekends — to find a vacancy.

Sangay: Plazoleta Ayora 101, Tel. 740-490 (reservation in Quito by fax 432-622). The best in town, moderate price, sport facilities, good restaurant.

Café Cultura: Santa Clara at the corner of Montalvo. Low prices, very good value, also a restaurant, good vegeterian food.

Pensión Patty: Elog Alfaro 556. Near the marketplace, inexpensive.

Santa Clara: 12 de Noviembre and Montalvo. Very popular among young travelers. Quiet, nice garden, access to kitchen.

Residencial Las Delicias: Central plaza and Maldonado. Very basic, inexpensive.

What to see

Hot Springs are located in Baños itself and slightly out of town. The most distant of them, **Salado**, is about one kilometer west of Baños, with frequent bus service to bring you there. It is much less crowded and the experience of bathing in the pleasant water justifies the trip.

The **Agoyan Falls** are about 9 km out of town. Daily buses set out from Baños passing the Falls. Walk back to town along Río Pastaza.

The Zoological Gardens: At the eastern approaches to Baños there is quite an interesting zoo, and among the many jungle animals there, one may also see the gigantic Galápagos turtles.

Mountain hikes can be pursued along numerous routes around town. Some of the most beautiful ones are in the area between Baños and Puyo. A hike along the streams winding between the towns will expose you to pristine views, lush foliage and gentle falls. Hiking is not difficult and the pleasant climate permits hiking almost all year round. Bring along food and camping gear and spend a few days exploring the area.

You can continue from Puyo to the jungles of The Oriente.

Climbing Tungurahua

This active volcano looms 5016 m above sea level and it takes 2-3 days to climb. The volcanic activity of the mountain is restricted to emitting small amounts of sulphuric steam from the crater. The view from above is breathtaking; slopes covered in snow, and way below stretch green valleys. On the horizon more snow capped peaks can be seen, such as those of Chimborazo and Cotopaxi. About a 2 hour climb below the snow line is

Mt. Tungurahua

a mountain hut (*refugio*), where one can sleep and use the stove for a few pennies. It's about a 5-10 hour climb to reach here from Baños, but it is best to do most of the trip by car which leaves every morning from the *Santa Clara* and *Patty* hotels in Baños. These hotels also have climbing gear.

On the day of the climb one must get up very early and leave the *refugio* at dawn. The climb to the crater takes about 3 hours with an additional hour to the summit. It is worthwhile to make the descent from the *refugio* to Baños by foot and to enjoy the beautiful green pathway. The descent takes about 4 hours.

Latacunga and Laguna Quilotoa

Latacunga is a colonial town, about 50 km north of Ambato and 80 km south of Quito. To the west of Latacunga is the beautiful **Laguna Quilotoa** — a lake with green water, which fills a large volcanic crater. Take the bus from Latacunga to Quevedo (several buses a day), and get off at **Zumbahua**, a very small village 2 hours away (great views on the way). A colorful market takes place here on Saturday morning. From Zumbahua there is a dirt road to Quilotoa, and unless you are lucky to get a ride by a truck, you will have to walk a few hours (take water with you). The crater and the lake appear only as you get to the rim — a spectacular sight.

El Oriente

The journey to the *selva* (jungle) of Ecuador's east (*Oriente*) is one of the most exciting and interesting. Here nature has offered man a rare opportunity to observe a primeval, almost unexplored corner of the world. The enchanting scenery, dense vegetation, animal life, Indian tribes, fearsome rivers, little towns ... even the derricks which pump out the oil discovered here recently — all exude a unique essence. The wild jungle atmosphere accompanies the visitor's every step, and the feeling of Creation acquires a dimension of rare power.

Even though El Oriente accounts for about half Ecuador's territory, no more than 200,000 people live there. The predominant population is Indian, consisting essentially of three tribes: the tranquil Yumbos, the Jívaros (once known as head-shrinkers) and the wild Aucas. In addition, a community of Catholic missionaries has dwelled here for many years, engaging in linguistics and religious activity.

The climate here is hot and humid. Though temperatures usually do not exceed 32°C (89°F), humidity can reach 97%. Rain — lots of rain — falls almost every day. The greatest precipitation falls in the western section of the *Oriente*, along the eastern slopes of the Andes (5000 mm per year!). As one heads eastward toward the upper Amazon Basin, the amount drops to "only" 2000 mm. This is one of the world's rainiest areas, a fact which leaves its imprint both on the river-sliced topography and on the composition and amount of vegetation. The latter is dense and features hundreds of different species, with a considerable number belonging to the palm family.

The thick tropical growth, which imbues everything with a bold green hue, gives the observer a misleading sensation of inexhaustible fertility. In fact, it appears that the jungle soil is not rich at all; the very tangle of vegetation actually accounts for itself. This is the reason that most attempts to deforest the jungle and plant domesticated crops there have, at best, been modestly successful. Bananas, yucca and other typical Indian crops rapidly drain the soil of its nutrients. The growers have no choice but to abandon their holdings and migrate every few seasons.

THE ORIENTE

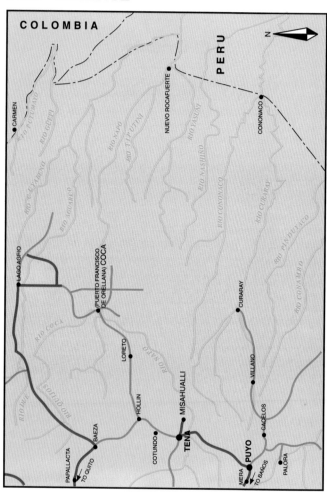

The first white man to visit here was Francisco de Orellana. Sent into the thicket in 1541 to hunt for gold, he succeeded in coming down Río Napo and reaching the Amazon intact after an exhausting and perilous campaign. He was the first to succeed in returning from the wild and unexplored region in one piece. Though he came back with no gold, he was greatly esteemed and respected. Orellana set out again for the jungle in 1546 — and never returned.

San Rafael Falls

Not much has changed since. Only in the twentieth century did the area begin to reflect signs of genuine change. The missionaries began to establish little settlement points, schools, hospitals and religious institutions. With the help of boats and light planes they began penetrating the depths of the *selva* intending to convert the natives. Their energetic activity first encoutered the Indians' intuitive opposition, for the indigenous people were culture-shocked by the foreign agent who had penetrated their territory. This sentiment later turned into an almost ideological hostility: the missionaries, the tribesmen claimed, were disrupting their ways of life and damaging their ability to preserve their tradition. The Indians demanded that the invading missionaries be ousted. The Ecuadorian Government, concurring, issued directives during the 1970's calling for downscaled religious activity in the *Oriente*. In so doing, the Government found it necessary to enter into confrontation with religious bodies of tremendous worldwide influence. The missionary institutions are funded directly by the Vatican (though not all the missionaries are Catholic). Their work is done on a voluntary basis, the priests receiving only their food and clothing needs. Almost all the priests own nothing and spend decades in the jungle without commitment to family, people, or country, save their religion and mission in life.

Only in recent decades has non-religious development also begun to take place in the *Oriente*. Growing numbers of whites have discovered the dormant potential of the jungle and have relocated there, establishing a number of villages and towns. The year 1967, when top-quality petroleum was discovered in commercial quantities, marked a dramatic turning point in *Oriente* history. A large-scale development boom followed.

American oil companies and the Ecuador Government have joined forces to exploit the fields, investing enormous sums to push through roads, build settlements and erect derricks. In 1972, a 500 km oil pipeline as far as Esmeraldas on the Pacific coast began conveying the local produce to the port where it is loaded on tankers for export all over the world.

The American companies, chiefly *Gulf* and *Texaco*, invested about a $1 billion in building a suitable oil production infrastructure. Their contribution was decisive in turning the *Oriente* into an area of utmost economic importance. The discovery of oil caused an upheaval in Ecuadorian economic thinking and its financial possibilities, and petroleum sales are still a decisive input in the country's income despite falling prices and demand.

Transportation

In *Oriente* you will surely notice a beefed-up military presence — a consequence of Ecuador's prolonged border disputes with Peru. If you wish to explore the area in depth, you will need to obtain special permits for the purpose. Daily flights serve the major towns, as do buses. Though dirt roads (some covered with asphalt) link some of the settlements and allow antiquated buses to bounce along them, riverboats appear to constitute the chief method of getting around. They reach most settlement points, including the most remote little hamlets.

TAME flies from Quito to Lago Agrio every day and to Puerto Orellana (better known as Coca) several times per week. Fares are low and flights are usually packed. Buses from Quito set out for Lago Agrio several times daily, making the difficult trip in about fourteen hours depending on weather and the quality of the vehicle.

The main highway heads eastward from Quito to the town of Baeza. There it forks — one leg south toward Tena, the other north to Lago Agrio. From Tena the road continues to Misahuallí and from Lago Agrio to Coca. The latter two — typical jungle towns — are points of departure for adventurous outings into the *selva* thicket.

Another route from Ambato to Tena passes through Baños and Puyoso. This, however, is much less convenient and entire stretches are washed out at times by flash floods.

The Ecuador Air Force operates non-scheduled flights to *Oriente* cities. You can sometimes get on board. *Texaco* flies several times per week to Coca and Lago Agrio and tourists occasionally get special boarding permits at the company offices.

How to get around

A tour to the *Oriente* is not the kind of experience you should pass up. Nevertheless, it is important to emphasize that the matter involves no few difficulties and obliges visitors to be willing and prepared to bear considerable hardships — primitive roads, harsh climate, mosquitos, irregular food and lodging conditions, two-legged "transportation" and so on.

Older tourists who wish to get a taste of the jungle with minimal effort, cruise aboard the *Flotel* the floating hotel on Rio Napo. *Flotel* excursions are organized by the *Metropolitan Tours* in Quito (Avenida Amazonas 239, POB 2542, Tel. 560-550, Fax 564-655). *Flotel* fares are rather steep ($300-$500 per person) for the three to five day trip. Fares include the flight to the *Oriente*, a comfortable room aboard ship, meals and outings. As *Flotel* sails down the broad river, passengers can avail themselves of small boats to explore side rivers and reach more remote villages. Those wishing to tour in this manner should be sure to make reservations and synchronize their itineraries with *Flotel*'s departure dates.

Young and daring travelers can set out on more lengthy voyages and wander deep into the thicket to extremely remote, interesting and unique primitive Indian villages. If you have this in mind, your first requirement will be a rudimentary command of Spanish. You will need to rent a boat and hire a crew for such an outing and this requires negotiating skills and ability to communicate continuously.

Another way to explore the jungle — in fact the most popular of all — is to reach Misahuallí, Tena, Coca or Lago Agrio on your own and hire a local guide to take you into the jungle. This is a convenient compromise between the previous alternatives. It is also interesting, relatively convenient, safe and unquestionably much cheaper than the others. Misahuallí, though somewhat commercialized, is known as a popular point of departure for such outings. See below.

Where to visit

The route covered below is a fascinating one incorporating most of what is worth seeing in the *Oriente* and delving into the remotest points of the *selva*. The means of transportation are varied, as is the amount of time required. It is a circular route beginning and ending in Quito. To carry it out in full you would need several weeks and lots of money. We present the matter this way so as to meet every visitor's needs, with no intention of having everyone go through it all. We mean to cover select sites in a logical, geographic sequence. We suggest that you read the entire route meticulously and then determine which of the sites you would like to see. A number of alternatives for integrating other routes are given for each of the places surveyed here. In this way, you can combine a visit to various sites according to your personal preferences and possibilities.

Start out in Quito. From here, take a bus or plane to **Lago Agrio**, Ecuador's oil capital. The overland route to this town starts out paved, though once you have crossed the mountains it deteriorates as it progresses eastward. Baeza, the missionaries' town on the eastern side of the mountains, is the last important point of settlement on this route. Once you have passed it, the road narrows and crumbles as it winds through enchantingly beautiful tropical scenery. We recommend that you make a brief stop at **San Rafael Falls** (150 m high).

Once you have reached Lago Agrio, the attractive lagoons in the vicinity (especially Quiarenos) also deserve a visit. In Lago Agrio you can rent a canoe for an excursion along the nearby rivers, relying on its owner to take you far enough for an impression of the bird and plant life. There are buses from this town to nearby hamlets which, however, are graceless places of no special interest.

Lago Agrio's tiny airport (far from town) is served by frequent flights from Quito. Open trucks equipped with seats await arrivals at the airport. These will take you either into town or straight to Coca past wooden houses with straw roofs, oil pipelines and other features of jungle life. If you're coming by plane, an enjoyable shock awaits you upon arrival — for the change in scene and climate is extreme and stunningly powerful.

In town you will find small, basic hotels along with bars, restaurants, shops and a small market. The bus company serving Quito and the surrounding area has its offices "downtown".

A main road out of Lago Agrio heads toward **Coca**, passing oil derricks, oilfield workers' camps, little concentrations of houses and more. A number of rivers cross our path; the bus mounts ferries to traverse them. Though bridges have actually been erected over some of the rivers, they are damaged at regular intervals by flash floods in which the rivers surge over their bank and wash away anything in their path.

Coca, situated at the confluence of Rios Coca and Napo, is the organizational center for the river communities. It is a faraway, rather desolate little place where the locals stick to their own affairs. There are several rather basic hotels and a number of convivial restaurants which serve good, plain fare. Coca, in the heart of the jungle, is a window opening onto a wonderful, unknown world. From here you can set out on the *Flotel* for a cruise on Rio Napo or rent a boat for a voyage far up its tributary streams. Boats also head upstream to Tena and Misahualli.

The most recommended outing takes us down Rio Napo for somewhere from two days to two weeks, depending on interest and budget. At the *Capitanía*, the riverside boat office, you can inquire into departure times or take off on your own by renting a canoe. Regular transportation down Rio Napo consists of boats which take passengers and missionaries to their villages, plus cargo and mail vessels which go as far as the town of Nuevo Rocafuerto. By regular transport you can reach the riverside settlements only. If you are interested in penetrating deeper into the jungle, you will require the services of a boat owner who's willing to take you. Negotiate persistently with these boat or canoe owners, and give them no more than an advance before you set out so they can purchase fuel and food. It is very important to bring along sufficient food, water-purification tablets, mosquito repellent, camping gear and lots of patience, for as the cruise goes on day after day, the distant coast and the scenery become monotonous and exhausting.

From Coca to Nuevo Rocafuerte

The cruise to Nuevo Rocafuerte takes about two days, though it isn't complicated. If you wish to head inland from this town (up Rios Tiputini and Yasuni) into the territory of the wild Aucas Indians, you will have to rent a canoe and equip yourself with a special army permit at the Defense Ministry in Quito. Before setting out, be sure to register at the army base across the river in Coca (cross the bridge and ask for Headquarters). Otherwise, military inspection stations downstream are liable to make you turn around and head back.

The first leg of the cruise down Rio Napo passes quickly and tranquilly. Along the banks of the broad river you'll notice isolated houses surrounded by gardens. They belong to placid Indians who engage in fishing and agriculture. About two hours out of Coca, you'll reach Primavera, a convivial little jungle hamlet where you can stop for rest and a light meal. A little later, you'll come upon the missionaries' village of **Pompeya** with its mission school and museum which you may visit. The latter houses an interesting display of ornaments, musical instruments, hunting tools and burial caskets belonging to the Indians who live along the banks of Rio Napo; nuns will instruct you about all these fascinating exhibits. Back on the water, you'll float past **Monkey Island**, so-called because of the numerous monkeys climbing its trees (they are seen chiefly in the early morning or late afternoon hours). A river channel off the Napo leads to **Limon Cocha**, a missionary town where you can meet a distinguished cross-section of the churchmen who have spent many years here in an attempt to bring the natives into the fold. Their activity arouses controversy, and their movements have been subject to restriction more than once. The mission's light plane is sometimes available for hire when remote places must be reached, though this is a costly undertaking. The village also has a number of canoes for rent, enabling you to tour the surrounding jungle with the help of a local guide. If you've arrived here on the freight ship, you can "hitchhike" back to Coca on one of the many boats which head there every week.

If you are continuing down Rio Napo you will reach **Panacocha**, a tiny village on the river's left bank where you can spend the night — in a sleeping bag. Panacocha has a sort of half-kiosk, half-restaurant which serves ample portions of local delicacies. The tastiest of these are the *plátanos* (fried plantains), whose flavor brings to mind fried potatoes.

From here, the watercourse becomes more monotonous. Apart from the military inspection point in Tiputini, where you will have to present army transit permits, no towns or villages are to be found — until **Nuevo Rocafuerte** (also known as Puerto Rocafuerte), a collection of several houses, a couple of tiny shops and only a few dozen inhabitants. Lodging though can be arranged in a local resident's home or at the boathouse.

Even if you have reached the town by "public transit", you have no choice but to rent a small boat if you intend to continue on. Make very sure that the boat owner knows his way around; bargain ... for even so the pleasure is unlikely to be cheap. At the same time, people who sail up Rios Tiputini and Yasuni into the heart of Aucas Indian territory can expect a trek of unequalled fascination, during which they will have the privilege of observing a multitude of animals and coming upon Indian tribes which live as their forebears did hundreds of years ago. This is undoubtedly an emotional and aesthetic experience.

From Nuevo Rocafuerte you can return to Lago Agrio by heading upstream on Rio Aguarico, traversing pulsatingly beautiful jungle areas, parts of which have been declared nature reserves. If you have come this far on your own resources, you can try to continue toward Lago Agrio on the mail boat which puts into Puerto Rocafuerte several times each month. This is certainly an interesting and enjoyable possibility. The only alternative return route is Rio Napo, by which we have come.

Up Río Yasuni

Ríos Tiputini and Yasuni — both narrower than Río Napo and both utterly desolate — wind into the depths of the *selva*. The motionless water in their tributaries is a comfortable environment for crocodiles, water tortoises, giant Anaconda snakes (up to ten meters in length, dangerous though not poisonous) and a host of other creatures. Monkeys clamber in the trees, while at ground level huge wild boars roam about, and birds soar above. It is a nature-lover's Paradise, a golden opportunity to explore one of the few places in the world which has not been ruined by the white man and the civilization which accompanies him.

The crowning point of our trip must certainly be a visit to the Aucas Indian villages. The tribe's name in Quechua means

The eastern jungles

"wild", and not without reason. The Aucas were the last to come into contact with the white man and submit to his sovereignty. Until a few decades ago they were wont to attack and murder visitors. During the 1960's, the tribesmen were in the habit of coming up to the bank of the Napo (considered the border of their hunting grounds) to shoot arrows and other weapons at the settlers who had attempted to settle there. During the 1970's, an expanded search for oil in the *Oriente* led to increased friction with the native Indians. Only after violent confrontations, some fatal, did a few missionaries find a way to bridge the gaps and make initial contact with the natives. As a result of this understanding, "exchange visits" between priests and the indigenous people commenced, with a few of the Indians reaching Puerto Rocafuerte in early 1982. The tribes at the western end of the vast territory, closer to the town of Tena, have maintained relations with the whites for many years and have long since abandoned their forefathers' ways. Accelerated exposure to Western civilization has brought in tow changed behavior patterns: most of the Indians have stopped going about naked and have begun using aluminium tools and fire. They even vary their diets now including rice, sugar, salt and candy in addition to the traditional monkeys, fish and yucca.

In the 1980's, it still was an "unspoilt" population. The tribesmen went about naked, hunting with the aid of long, well-maintained blowguns, fished with harpoons and plied the river in boats they had carved out of tree trunks. Today most of these Indians presently wear clothes and their customs have changed beyond recognition. Nonetheless, inasmuch as they were the last to be "discovered", a certain measure of that distant civilization, a rare ingredient of a vanishing world, is still preserved.

The Aucas and their culture

Little is known of the Aucas. They cast fear over the entire area by being known as a dangerous community from whom it was best to keep a healthy distance. Nonetheless, after the visitors overcome the fears instilled by their reputation, the Aucas prove to be forthcoming, pleased to host foreigners.

The language barrier is difficult and burdensome. The Aucas speak no Spanish, but rather their own unique tongue consisting of sharp guttural consonants and dissonances, which rarely exceed two syllables in length. The Aucas' violent image notwithstanding, their language is gentle. For example it has no command form.

The Aucas live in little thatched shelters and sleep in hammocks. The Aucas tribe and family structure has no "chief" in the accepted sense and decisions are reached freely among family heads. This is how settlement territories are determined and land distributed. The latter is worked according to the cycle of the yucca, the Aucas' staple crop. When the land loses its nutrients at the end of a lengthy nine to ten months' cycle, the tribe relocates five or six kilometers away and repeats the process. The calendar is determined by agricultural events: the monkeys' birthing season, for example, or by the growth cycles of the trees.

Their loyalty is to a single god, Uynuny, creator of all. The Aucas offer him no sacrifices of any kind; they have no symbols, gestures of honor, no prayers, no rituals.

Family celebrations are handled modestly, usually with quiet song, dance and *chicha* (a fermented yucca beverage). Burial of the dead is also handled in a special way: the body is left in the family's shelter while its occupants go somewhere else, never to return.

Especially interesting is the fact that despite their total isolation and unknown origins, their concepts of good and evil are very close to our own: no murder, no theft, no incest. Though Aucas youth are taught to be highly independent and tough, no ceremony or test of masculinity or femininity upon attainment of adulthood has been discovered.

In recent years, as the trend of Aucas integration into modern civilization gathers strength, the attitude towards them is changing as well. Things have reached such a state that these amiable, forthcoming Indians (today!) even wish to change their tribal name ... from Aucas — "wild" — to **Uarany** — "people".

From Coca to Misahuallí, Tena and Ambato

Regular boat traffic links Coca to **Tena**, capital of Napo Province, a quiet town populated mainly by Spanish-speaking Indians of the Yumbos tribe. The Yumbos have long been in touch with Western civilization and are subject to strong missionary influence. Tena offers a few hotels, small eateries and bars. There are daily buses to Puerto Napo, Puyo, Baños and Ambato, while less-frequent buses head for Quito via Baeza (the trip takes about ten hours).

From Puerto Napo, about ten kilometers from Tena, you can cross the river and go downstream another fifteen kilometers to **Misahuallí**. This town, at the confluence of Rios Napo and Misahuallí, is a popular departure point for jungle tours which are interesting though a far cry from those you can enjoy farther downstream.

Misahuallí is easy to reach from Quito by bus via Tena, from Ambato via Puyo or by boat from Coca (the latter a twelve-hour crawl upstream). Many boats to and from Coca make the journey every other day and some are designated for passengers.

If your visit to the *Oriente* has begun here, and if you intend to go on from Coca toward Puerto Rocafuerte, you will need a rented canoe to get there. It is worth your while to make inquiries about rentals as early as Misahuallí. This will save you time and considerable effort while it will not involve any significantly higher expenses.

The town of Misahuallí has a number of basic and intermediate-level hotels, along with little restaurants whose standard fare probably will not got over well with fussy eaters. A popular tourist spot, it has got a well-developed and flourishing tour industry with many guides eagerly waiting to be hired, each promising to take you into wholly unexplored sections of forest. Choose your guide carefully; check the route he has planned for you (it may include a lengthy hike) and bargain over the price. It is important to recall that Misahuallí and its immediate environs (i.e. anything within a one or two-day radius) are rather touristy and the local Indians have long since grown accustomed to Western faces which smile at them from behind Japanese lenses. Though this holds true for the animals as well, you cannot hope to encounter many of them during your outing around here.

If you are interested in more authentic experiences and are prepared to expend the necessary effort and time, you will need to go hundreds of kilometers downstream (see "Coca" above). This notwithstanding, Misahuallí unquestionably provides a relatively convenient and very interesting opportunity to explore the jungle from up close, getting to know its vegetation, life and ways. It would be a shame to pass it up.

Special instruction

Your number-one requirement when visiting the *Oriente* is willingness to tolerate tremendous lack of comfort, to cope with difficult sleeping, diet, hygiene and sanitation conditions, to put up with the humid climate... and more. Though it is undoubtedly an exciting experience, take into account the fact that it is recommended only for healthy, resourceful tourists with camping experience and an ability to improvise. Even these tourists would do well to conduct themselves with redoubled caution in light of the hazards to be expected here. You must obey safety rules and the authorities' instructions down to the last letter. First of all, obtain the appropriate military permits from the Defense Ministry in Quito and register at every inspection post. This way your movements will be traceable, something to be made use of should the need arise.

It is important to insist on a **reliable guide** with a river-worthy boat. Sudden storms, cloudbursts and floods are common occurrences and you would do well to minimize the unavoidable dangers by being equipped with the very best. Check and recheck before you decide, for the money you save is liable to prove a mistake which you cannot always correct.

Stock up on food, mosquito repellent, a first-aid kit, anti-malaria pills, water purification tablets, camping gear, a mosquito net and hammock. These will prove indispensible in this harsh, problematic environment; their absence may lead to unpleasant situations and needless suffering.

The *Oriente* is a wild, undeveloped area, and as a result malaria is rife; infectious and intestinal diseases doubly so. Again, be especially careful and prepare for the possibility of sickness. Since medical services here are rather basic, we recommend that you bring along medicines in sufficient quantity for an emergency. You **must** boil water before drinking it; if it is river water, add disinfectant.

The local population will warmly accept modest gifts. People you visit in their homes will greatly appreciate something simple such as chewing gum, picture postcards, simple metal crosses and the like. In certain places the value of hunting bullets for rifles is higher than that of money, and sometimes they will be welcomed in lieu of payment.

Moneychanging is no simple matter in the *Oriente*, for banks in this area are almost nonexistent and dollars go for low rates and high commission. Have enough local currency on hand before you get here, and remember that "enough" means a considerable sum. For one, prices here are higher than elsewhere in Ecuador (transportation expenses inflate the price of almost everything); for another, your expenses seem to multiply as you go along.

Warning: Be Careful! One cannot minimize the dangers of a trek through the jungle and every precaution must be taken. Apply wise, level-headed thought to every aspect of the decisions you make on your trip and use every strategy to lower risks. Even if most hazards are of nature and therefore unavoidable, many others are subject to our control.

From Quito to the northern coast

Another interesting area lies northwest of Quito and descends to the northern section of the Ecuadorian coast. The entire region is covered with dense jungles wholly different from those in the eastern sector. Here you will find a number of picturesque towns, Indian villages, concentrations of black Ecuadorians, white settlers' farms and more — which together form a unique and complex social matrix.

To reach this area, take the bus from Quito toward Santo Domingo de los Colorados (from where you can continue in various directions). The route will then take you to the coast and to the largest of its cities, Esmeraldas. A visit here will last several days, during which you can combine hikes, cruises and trips to remote settlements — remote in both the geographic and the cultural senses.

Santo Domingo de los Colorados

The provincial town of Santo Domingo de los Colorados (pop. 70,000) is a rather worn-out tourist attraction. In the middle of Ecuador's western jungle, the town is on the road to Quito, Esmeraldas, Manta and Quevedo. Its fame derives mainly from the Colorado Indians, whose villages are scattered in the surrounding forests and who frequent the town on Sundays — when they bring their wares for sale in the local market.

Transportation

It takes three or four hours to cover the 123 km from Quito to Santo Domingo; the difficult highway becomes even more so on rainy days.

Transportes Esmeraldas and *Transportes Occidental* operate buses that pass through Santo Domingo several times daily on the Quito-Esmeraldas route. The offices of both companies in Quito are next door to one another, in Calle Ambato. Other buses reach Santo Domingo from Guayaquil (six hours), Ambato, Manta and the other towns in the vicinity.

Where to stay

Santo Domingo has a rather large selection of cheap pensions, but only a few hotels worthy of the name. You will easily find pensions downtown, though on weekends you may well have to try a number of them before you find a vacancy. The *Hotel Zaracay*, on Av. Quito 16-39, Tel. 750-023, 2 km from downtown, is one of the best and most expensive hostelries, with a swimming pool and a good restaurant. The *Hotel Tinalandia*, with a golf course and swimming pool, is much more expensive, and is located in a quiet area about 16 km out of town.

What to see

Though the Indian market held every Sunday has brought fame to Santo Domingo, its charm has faded in recent years. The crowds of visitors and the commercialization of its traditonal "Indian-ness" have left their imprint on the entire event. Today, it is not much more than a tourist showcase. Much of the merchandise is made especially to serve as decoration and conversation pieces in European or American living rooms and the same holds true for the Indians' colorful attire, hairstyles and body paint.

The Colorado tribe is noteworthy for its unique style and mode of dress. The men used to smear a bright red paint — made from a local plant — over their bodies and short hair, in order to ward off evil spirits. The women too, painted themselves red and walked about their villages topless. Today's Colorados (some 2000 in number) are well-adjusted to the new reality, having been baptized and having adopted modern ways of life. Most engage in fishing and agriculture. Though they still dwell in straw huts open to the elements, little seems to have survived of their ancient traditions.

While in the Santo Domingo vicinity you should venture into the jungle for a close-up of the Indians' way of life. A number of tour companies organize guided excursions from Quito to Santo Domingo, with a visit to the jungle villages on the itinerary. It is best to reach the town independently and to use it as a base for short trips on your own.

The road south of Santo Domingo leads to Quevedo, a town whose population of about 100,000 includes quite a few of Chinese origin. The roads out of Quevedo (to Manta and Guayaquil on the coast and to Latacunga up the mountains) pass among fertile plantations, where you can see how the people of tropical highlands live.

If you wish to go on from here to Guayaquil, you may choose between the busy main road via Daule, or a quieter byway via the town of Babahoyo.

Many buses set out every day from Santo Domingo to the port town of **Manta** (pop. 140,000). Here coffee and bananas are loaded for shipment, a fishing industry thrives and the

San Lorenzo

commercial needs of the district are taken care of. Flights from Guayaquil and Quito land here several times a week.

Esmeraldas

The coastal city of Esmeraldas, Ecuador's fifth-largest (pop. app. 200,000), is the hub of most commercial and industrial activity along the northern coastal plain. Its port handles the local produce — tobacco, cocoa and timber. The oil pipeline from the *Oriente* terminates nearby, and the precious liquid it has conveyed is loaded onto tankers in Balao for export over all the world.

Esmeraldas' special ambience is a combination of geographic location, tropical environment and isolation. Restaurants and bars are packed — higher prices notwithstanding — and both locals and visitors seem to be in perpetual motion. Refinery and port workers, along with gold miners and villagers who visit the city, contribute to its unique atmosphere.

Transportation

Buses operated by *Transportes Esmeraldas* and *Transportes Occidental* make the trip from Quito to Esmeraldas in about eight hours, travelling via Santo Domingo. To reach Guayaquil, Ambato, or Manta, you must also go via Santo Domingo.

Esmeraldas is served by daily flights from Quito and Guayaquil, which land at the small airport across the river.

What to see

The **Tourist Bureau** is located in the City Hall, on Bolívar 541, and 9 de Octubre, and will be able to supply you with information and maps of sites in the vicinity. Wander through the city and observe how it lives. The main street is closed to vehicular traffic between 7:30 and 9:30pm, when the locals may stroll along it to their hearts' content. Most people in Esmeraldas are descendents of black slaves whom the Spanish brought here in the sixteenth and seventeenth centuries to work the banana plantations. They've preserved some of their traditions, mainly in the music and dance; African rhythms and the *marimba* dance are very common here, and you can enjoy them in dancing clubs and schools, especially on weekends and holidays.

Around Esmeraldas

Many Ecuadorians come to Esmeraldas for a pleasant seaside vacation. A thirty-minute trip south of town brings you to two popular resorts, **Atacames** and **Súa**, which offer little hotels and palm-spangled beaches. It is best to stay in these places which are cheaper and more pleasant than staying over in downtown Esmareldas. Here the beaches are suited to days of relaxing and tranquility.

Las Palmas, north of Esmeraldas, is also developing as a resort area; its pristine beach attracts many of enchanted visitors.

The northern coastal strip swarms with mosquitos. Be prepared by bringing a repellent and some netting to put over your bed.

The route to San Lorenzo

The trip to San Lorenzo involves bus and boat and takes eight hours or more. The bus part is difficult and exhausting, for the road is mostly unpaved and the vehicles are antiquated. You will go through the village of Río Verde and the town of Rocafuerte (where you can enjoy excellent seafood) until you reach Limones. From this town, located at the confluence of two rivers, you can take a side trip to the delightful Cayapa Indian villages of Borbon and Zapallo Grande. To proceed north to San Lorenzo, go by boat from La Tola for a cruise of several hours along a lovely seashore, rich in mangroves and bird life.

San Lorenzo

San Lorenzo, Ecuador's northernmost coastal town (situated next to the Colombian border) is especially famous for the local *marimba* bands which you can hear rehearsing practically every night.

It also offers a number of rudimentary hotels and an intolerable plague of mosquitoes (remember to bring netting and repellent).

From San Lorenzo you can either set out on short jungle trips to local villages or sail southward to the coastal towns. Between San Lorenzo and the city of Ibarra there is a decrepit railroad on which the *Autoferro* runs irregularly. The 200 km journey sometimes lasts many hours longer than planned as a result of technical delays and track problems.

North of Quito

The Pan American Highway north of Quito runs for 250 km to the Colombian border, crossing a serene mountain region of enchanting beauty and grandeur. Green mountain landscapes and volcanic peaks grace the road from either side and towns and villages come into view at every turn. Some of these villages are among Ecuador's most interesting, and they should be visited either on an outing from Quito or drop in en route northward to Colombia.

The route is well traveled by buses and minibuses, allowing you great flexibility and mobility. Though reserved seats are recommended, it is hard to imagine that you will run into trouble, for service is frequent, efficient and provided by a number of companies.

This pleasurable region of Ecuador is noted for its handicrafts and art. Each of the places we are about to visit has been graced with its own special character and is known for its particular wares.

Otavalo

The Indian market in Otavalo (pop. 20,000) is one of South America's most famous, a magnet which attracts hordes of tourist year after year. Otavalo, 110 km north of Quito, is laid out pleasantly with small, somewhat squat buildings, lining its handsome streets. The myriad shops in those structures offer an impressive selection of wool and textile clothing, the finest handiwork of the Indians who live in the surrounding villages. They have been long famous for the beauty of their wares, which suits the blazing color of their attire, their characteristic hairstyle and the manner of their speech and behavior. It is this successful combination which serves as the basis of the lovely market held in the central plaza every Saturday morning and afternoon. As early as 6am the main square is flooded from end to end, with an abundance of colors and pleasantries emanating from dozens of stands, offering enchanting wall carpets, ponchos, sweaters, dresses, shirts, leather handbags, sandals, ornaments — and so on.

Truth be told, the market's great popularity has slightly damaged its traditional character. At the same time, however, there is absolutely no doubt that this is **the place** to visit and shop. The

Otavaleños

Otavalo — at the market

prices are attractive — not before bargaining, of course — and the display is worthy of a king.

Because the market opens at the crack of dawn, it is better to reach Otavalo the day before, exploring the area and spending the night in one of the town's modest, clean, well-kept and inexpensive hotels. The best of them (not cheap) is the *Yamor*, which has a swimming pool. It is best to make reservations. Alternately, arrive early on Friday before the tourist rush begins. The bus-drive from Quito to Otavalo takes about 2 hours. It's easier bargaining in the afternoon, as most tourists are gone and the vendors want to get rid out of their stocks.

Around Otavalo

It is a good idea to spend a few days in Otavalo's charming and tranquil area of mountains, lakes and small villages, rather than just come for a visit to the Market.

You can explore the Otavalo vicinity — especially the area between the town and **Lake San Pablo** — on foot, enjoying two or three hours of pleasurable country hiking, wonderful scenery and crisp mountain air.

You can spend the night at one of the pleasant hotels at the lake — the most comfortable of which is the *Cusín*. It is a good alternative for lodging in Otavalo.

San Antonio de Ibarra

San Antonio de Ibarra, the "village of wood", is situated beside the main road between Otavalo and Ibarra. Many of its residents engage in woodcarving, their goods gracing marketplaces throughout the country. You will find a number of shops packed with statuettes around the central plaza. These, however, charge higher prices than those you will find farther away. Quite a few of these creations are true "kitsch", but many others are definitely estimable. Roam through the village and try to vist the workshops. Avoid visiting on Saturday afternoon, for then most of the shops are closed and your possibilities narrow down to a choice among those on the square.

Cotacachi

Northeast of Otavalo is the village of Cotacachi, which is known as the "village of leather". Here you can find a fine variaty of leather goods in attractive prices.

Laguna Cuicoch is a splendid crater lake a few kilometers beyond Cotacachi. You can either take a cab from Otavalo or Cotacachi, or walk a few hours to the lake. There is a very nice walk around the laguna, and you can also walk 6-8 hours from the lake back to Otavalo.

Ibarra

The largest town in the region (pop. 80,000), Ibarra is a tranquil, pleasant place whose light-colored buildings give it a clean, calm hue. Here you will find an *artensanía* market, hotels and restaurants. Many tourists prefer to stay the night here rather than in congested Otavalo. It is about ½ hour by bus to Otavalo, and 3 hours to Quito.

The **train to San Lorenzo** (see "From Quito to the northern coast") on the Pacific coast sets out from Ibarra irregularly. The route (*Autoferro*) is beautiful and interesting, passing mountains, valleys and lush vegetation. On the way the car stops in small villages and foods are sold by the locals. A road is under construction, so ask for updated information about this route before setting out from Quito.

Tulcán

This is Ecuador's northern border town, 250 km north of Quito (5 hours) and 3000 m above sea level. Its main and only attraction is... a visit to the **cemetery**, a gloriously well-maintained place with greenery pruned so painstakingly it is hard to describe. Trees and bushes have been shaped meticulously into images of animals, faces, buildings and the like.

Tulcán's 35,000 people host most of the travelers between Ecuador and Colombia and vice versa. Flights from Quito arrive here, as do buses and minibuses. You will also find a number of simple hotels and a few restaurants.

Onward to Colombia —
border crossing procedures

The international border runs four kilometers north of Tulcán. Ecuadorian immigration procedures must be completed as you leave town. From there, take a taxi or bus to the checkpoint itself, where the Colombian immigration procedures are implemented. There is a Colombian consulate in Tulcán which will issue visas to citizens of those states which require them.

Rumichaca, a natural bridge, serves as the border between the two countries. Here you will easily find transportation either to Tulcán or Ipiales, the Colombian border town.

The crossing station is open 6.30am-9pm, but closes for a one-hour *siesta* around noon. Dozens of buses and trucks cross the border every day, frequently causing lengthy delays. Crossing procedures are simple and speedy; on the whole, they involve no special difficulties.

Dispose of all your remaining local currency before leaving Ecuador; the same applies if you are arriving from Colombia. Except in Bogota, where there is black market, all currency changes into Colombian currency is done at the Banco de la Republica — a branch of which is found in most cities, including Ipiales. Remember, too, that on your arrival in Ecuador try to exchange the minimum of money until you reach Quito, because you get a higher dollar exchange rate there.

COLOMBIA

Gorgeous scenery, towering mountains, pristine beaches, dense jungles, fascinating archaeological sites, large cities, and little villages — all these and more await the tourist who has come to discover the hidden treasures of Colombia, South America's northernmost country. Just south of Central America, lying between the Pacific Ocean and the Caribbean Sea, is one of the continent's most exceptional countries and perhaps the most dangerous.

Colombia is a mass of contradictions. At one time, it was one of the most important countries in South America and its capital the site of crucial decisions. Simón Bolívar established it in the center of "Greater Colombia", his lofty dream of South American unity, which proved hollow even before his death. Today's Colombia lies on the fringe of the political map in South America. Perhaps due to the acute poverty and deprivation that plague the country, Colombia has become notorious as a world center for the production and export of cocaine and marijuana. Tourists are not warmly welcomed here and in no other South American country are they as prone to theft as in Colombia. While enjoying Colombia's splendid mountain and river landscapes, visiting its cities and villages, landing or departing at the airport, or reclining in the taxi that brings you into town, behave as if on a battlefield — alert, cautious, and ready to fend off any kind of attack.

Bandit gangs terrorize the country, and seem to have an affinity for vulnerable tourists. The local authorities often collaborate with the bandits, and, when they do not, are either unable or unwilling to help luckless tourists. Before deciding to visit Colombia, take this state of affairs into account.

Just the same, throngs of visitors have reached, seen and enjoyed Colombia, and left unscathed. The country offers a wide variety of possibilities for touring, rest, and recreation — whether in the extraordinary capital of Bogotá, on the Caribbean coast, in the Amazon jungles, or in the village of San Agustín in the south. Colombia is the gateway to the continent for those who arrive from Central America, and serves as a convenient departure point for the Caribbean or the United States.

COLOMBIA

History

Colombia was claimed for Spain in 1500 by Rodrigo de Bastidas, an early explorer who reached the area in pursuit of legendary treasures of gold. The first half of the 16th century was a period of exploration and conquest, which intensified in response to rumors that *El Dorado*, the legendary Inca city of gold, was sited on the plateau where Bogotá rests today.

The *conquistadores* encountered Indians of the *Chibcha* tribe, whose fondness for gold and treasure encouraged speculation concerning *El Dorado*. The Chibchas had a rich and well developed culture, with a strong central monarchy. Their major pursuit was agriculture, which they usually practiced in settled communities. Unlike the Incas and the Aztecs, they were not noted for monumental architecture, and their sphere of influence was restricted to the mountainous regions of Colombia.

The Chibchas yielded to Spanish domination without a fight, rapidly assimilating and giving rise to the major ethnic element in modern Colombia — the *mestizos*. The Indian character was gradually lost over the years, and today Spanish domination in language, religion, and way of life is more perceptible in Colombia than anywhere else in the Andes.

In Bogotá, the Spanish established a magnificent education system, including institutions of higher learning (the first university was founded in 1573) and highly-developed cultural and community life. During the 17th and 18th centuries cultural and colonial influences peaked and Bogotá was known as "the Athens of South America".

In Colombia, as in the other Latin American crown colonies, the ambitions of the Creoles, descendants of the Spanish settlers, began to grow. They were instrumental in the struggle for independence from Spain, and supported Bolívar's efforts to establish "Greater Colombia" as a sovereign state free of Spanish control. "Greater Colombia" declared its independence in 1810. (At the time, Spain was facing difficulties as a result of Napoleonic conquests in Europe). At first, called "Nueva Granada", it embraced Ecuador, Venezuela, and Panama, as well as modern Colombia.

Spain was not about to give up these territories without a struggle, and its troops spent the next decade trying to maintain Spanish dominion over the rebellious colonies. It was only in 1819, after Bolívar's famous victory in the battle of Boyacá, that Spain's colonialist dream finally ended and that the independence of the region was assured.

Bolívar's vision of unity faded swiftly. Ecuador and Venezuela left the Federation in 1832, and two opposing blocs, liberal and conservative, began squabling for power in Colombia, a struggle which persists to this day. This internal strife has come at the expense of national development and has severely damaged the country's economy and social order.

A two-year civil war broke out in Colombia in 1840, each side seeking total defeat of the other. Toward the turn of the century in 1899, a harsher and more grievous period of internal fighting erupted, which claimed more than 100,000 casualties in the ensuing four years.

One of the most bitter results of this war was Panama's withdrawal from the Federation. The Panamanians took advantage of the anarchy in Colombia, and, with the support of the United States, declared their independence. The act was of far-reaching consequence regarding subsequent U.S. relations with the states of South America. Colombia refused to recognize Panamanian independence and objected to the Panama Canal project. This brought the protracted dispute between Colombia and the United States which was resolved only after World War I. The United States agreed to generously compensate Colombia in return for Colombian agreement to waive its canal-based claims. This paved the way for the affluent 1920's and the emergence of a Colombian *nouveau riche*, which benefitted from American compensation together with soaring prices in the world coffee market.

The world-wide economic crisis provoked by the crash of 1929 put an end to the boom. Colombia once again sank into domestic difficulties and power struggles, with the Liberals finally coming out on top. The country's social and political contradictions radicalized both camps. Extremist factions emerged on both sides. Jorge Gaitán set up a leftist bloc in the Liberal Party, while on the right positions were influenced by European Fascism.

In the 1946 elections, the Conservatives defeated a factionalized Liberal party against the backdrop of an unprecedented recession. Domestic unrest grew and violent demonstrations rocked the country. Gaitán's assassination in April, 1948 unleashed the full fury of the embittered villagers, who streamed into Bogotá *en masse* and vented their rage on property and people, as the authorities stood by helplessly.

For 20 years Colombia was caught in a web of violence known as *La Violencia*, costing the country a quarter of a million casualties. The national economy was paralyzed, and polarization and hatred reached new extremes.

A military coup in 1953 brought General Pinilla Rojas to power, at the head of a repressive regime bent on quelling the violence. The imperatives of the times brought the Liberals and Conservatives together in an unprecedented accord: a united "national front" devoted ending Rojas' tyranny. The general was forced to resign in 1958.

The United States government met Colombia's ongoing crisis with grants and long-term loans that helped stabilize the economy and restore tranquillity. In 1966 Llaras Restrepo was elected President and his tenure is considered one of the most successful. Rising coffee prices helped Restrepo stabilize the country's economy and political scene — but not for long.

Leftist guerrilla movements began operating in Colombia in the early 1970's, countered by a new right-wing party led by the former-dictator Rojas. Domestic ferment continues today, though the Government is making a tremendous effort to stabilize the country and restore order. By endeavoring to narrow economic and social inequities and by diverting resources to programs for the poor and disadvantaged, the Colombian government is attempting to reduce the frustration and rage that underlie crime and violence, but without success.

A volcanic eruption of Nevado del Ruiz in 1985 buried entire villages, claiming 25,000 lives. In 1991-1992 Colombia suffered a long drought. Much of the country's electricity mains is based on water power, and since rivers became dry hydroelectric stations could not supply electricity. Many cities, even Bogota, had no electricity for long periods. All this exposes the lack of infrastructure and add to the feeling of social unrest. The government initiated a strong campaign against the barons of drugs after the assassination of presidential candidate Luis Galán on 1989.

President Gaviria, elected in march 1990, has to face not only the dangers of the cartels, but also of the extreme right, as hundreds of members of his own party were killed, and of the extreme left, as remains of leftist guerrillas refused to join the talks with government (some are even related to the drug trafficking, in order to finance their activities). In many areas of Colombia, the main reason for death among adults is not cancer or heart diseases, but murder.

Geography and climate

Colombia is the fourth-largest country in South America and covers 1,140,000 km^2. The country has a varied topography and climate. Colombian landscapes range from beaches to plains and mountains, and the climatic zones range from tropical in the jungles and along the coast, to temperate in the mountains and valleys. In addition, the differences in population and their culture is especially prominent.

The Andes jut into Colombia, splitting into three ranges (*cordilleras*) — eastern, central and western. In between and almost parallel to them flow the Magdalena and Cauca Rivers, which originate in the south of the country and converge before emptying into the Caribbean Sea. The rivers serve as convenient transportation routes from the seacoast to the interior.

The central *cordillera* is the highest of the Colombian Andes, with peaks soaring to over 5,500 m. The central and western ranges are composed chiefly of granite, while the eastern range (*Cordillera Oriental*), which continues into Venezuela, consists of volcanic rock and limestone. Colombia is known for volcanic activity, and some of its many volcanoes remain active. The river valleys are filled with volcanic ash — the remains of eruptions in former geological epochs.

Lower mountain ranges run along the coast. The most important of these is the Sierra Nevada de Santa Marta. Its loftiest summit, at 5775 m, is the highest point in Colombia.

The mountain plateaus break down into several types: volcanic plateaus in the southwest at the foot of the central *cordillera*; and basins covered with ancient sediment in the central and northern highlands. Bogotá is located in such a basin.

The jungles (*selva*) and **the plains** (*llanos*) run along Colombia's east and southeast, where the climate is hot and muggy. The *llanos* stretch across the upper watersheds of the Orinoco and the Amazon. These regions, which account for more than half the country's territory, are nearly uninhabited: fewer than two per cent of Colombia's people live there, in harsh climatic conditions and cultural isolation.

A humid equatorial climate dominates the lowlands, where temperatures remain the same throughout the year. Precipitation rates are among the world's highest, with about 3000 mm of rain per year along the Pacific coast and in the Amazon basin. The Venezuelan border area in eastern Colombia enjoys a relatively dry savannah climate, with an average of 600 mm annual rainfall.

The climate in the mountain areas changes gradually, in keeping with elevation, from tropical in the low-lying zones to chilly and temperate above 3000 m. The high humidity causes clouds to form on the *cordillera* slopes, which are usually shrouded in fog.

Colombia lies on the migration route of more than 1500 species of birds, who nest or pass through on their way to and from North and South America.

Population

About half of Colombia's 34 million people, and the dominant social and political group, are *mestizos* of mixed Spanish-Indian descent. About 25% of the population is mulatto, 20% is European ancestry, 4% black and only 1% are Indian, descendants of the *Chibcha* tribe who refused to intermarry with the Spanish colonists.

About 80% of Colombia's population lives in the mountainous central region, the heart of economic and political activity. Another 15% dwell along the Caribbean coast. The Amazon and Orinoco plains, which account for 60% of Colombia's land area, are home to only 2% of its people.

The Spanish colonial tradition is most jealously preserved in Colombia. Spanish is the national language, though 180 different Indian dialects are spoken in various areas. Catholicism is the state faith, and the Church enjoys a special social status and broad influence in the country's education system.

Though Colombia boasts 35 functioning universities and compulsory, free elementary education, about 10% of its citizens are illiterate.

Economy

The Colombian economy can draw on many natural resources some of which only began to attract attention in recent years. The 1960's marked the turning point in Colombia's economy. Until then, 90% of the country's income derived from the export of one crop, coffee. Industry has since been developed extensively, mineral deposits have been exploited and other economic activity has been increased. Although Colombia's superb coffee still accounts some 20% of its export income, and other 20% come from oil and petrochemicals, the country also exports gold, emeralds, uranium, and various metals — in addition to consumer goods, chiefly textiles and paper.

Colombian oil, coal, and natural gas reserves are being exploited at an ever-accelerating pace. The country is nearly self-sufficient in oil and natural gas and many industries have relocated so as to use gas as an energy source. Colombian coal mines produce more than 60% of all the coal in South America, and vast amounts of equipment have been purchased in recent years to lay the infrastructure for further expansion of the mining industry.

About 30% of Colombia's labor force is agrarian, and the country is agriculturally self-sufficient. Apart from coffee, Colombia exports cocoa beans and bananas. According to unofficial estimates, however, all these together fail to equal even half of Colombia's income from the export of drugs.

Colombia needs a tremendous energy system to power its industrial development and technological progress, and huge sums have been invested in the project. A high priority for the government is the exploitation of the country's hydroelectric potential. Construction (industrial and residential) and road building have also enjoyed massive government aid, and local authorities take advantage of such projects to solve severe social problems and reduce unemployment.

Colombia's external debt did not begin to trouble the world banking system until 1984, when the country sought to exploit the financial situations of Brazil, Argentina, and other Latin American states by assembling a debtors' cartel which would negotiate interest and repayment terms with the creditors. Colombia's own foreign debt amounts to some $21 billion, and still the country's economy is well equiped to handle it; in 1989 some drugs barons offered to pay the external debt if they were given *carte blanche* in the country, a generous offer, which the government refused. The inflation rates never reached the astronomic figures of other South American countries, and the government labors aggressively to keep it that way.

General information

How to get there
By air: From Europe, *Air France, British Caledonian, Lufthansa*, and *Iberia* all fly from their respective capitals. *Viasa* and *Avianca* (the latter from Madrid, Frankfurt or Paris) also reach Colombia from Europe. *Avianca*, Colombia's national airline, offers low-cost flights from Madrid, Frankfurt, and Paris to Colombia, with connections to other destinations through its local agents. This may be the least expensive way to fly. *Avianca, Eastern, Aero-Peru,* and *Varig* fly from the United States (the latter from the West Coast). The lowest airfares are available via Panama or the Miami-San Andrés lines. San Andrés is a Caribbean island that belongs to Colombia, and from it one can fly to the mainland at little cost.

Colombia has four international airports, — Bogotá, Barranquilla, Cali, and Medellín. Each is served by several airlines. All South and Central American countries have air service to and from Bogotá.

Coffee plantations

By land: Colombia is linked by highway with Venezuela and Ecuador. Cross into Ecuador at a point south of Pasto. Venezuela has two border crossings: the little town of Maicao on the Guajira Peninsula in the north, and the town of Cúcuta in the mountain region. Maicao and Cúcuta are unpleasant as border towns. From Brazil it is possible to take the river as far as Leticia and continue by air (see "Leticia"). Regular bus service links Bogotá and the Andean countries.

Documents

A passport and tourist card are usually enough for Colombian immigration officers, though they sometimes ask for a departure ticket or proof that you can afford one. Visits to Colombia are restricted to 90 days and a visa is required to extend the stay. A transit visa, together with a passport and a ticket for the next leg of the trip, is good for 15 days. Tourist cards are issued on the plane or at border checkpoints.

A $15 departure tax is levied when leaving Colombia by air, except for stopover visits less than 24 hours long. Tickets purchased in Colombia are subject to an 15% excise tax, as are tickets bought elsewhere for journeys originating in Colombia.

COLOMBIA

When to come: national holidays

The climate in Colombia is the same through most of the year,
with variations according to elevation. The rainiest months are

April-May and October-November; the dry season runs from December through February.

The coastal zones, the plains, and the eastern jungles are hot and muggy the year round, while nights in the mountains may be rather chilly. The weather changes rapidly in southern Colombia: days that start out like spring and end up wintry are not uncommon.

Much of Colombia goes on vacation from early December through mid-January, and many businesses are closed. Peak seasons along the Caribbean coast are December-April and June-August.

Colombia's national holidays are January 1, May 1, July 20 (Independence Day), August 7 (Battle of Boyacá Day), October 12 (Columbus Day), November 1 (All Saints' Day), and December 25.

Accommodation

A National Tourism Company ranks Colombian hotels on a star system according to quality, sets each hotel's maximum rates, and handles complaints of overcharging. A 5% tax — but no service charge — is added to hotel bills. As for tipping, 10% is certainly sufficient.

The big-city hotels and seaside resorts are up-to-date and modern. Hotels in small cities, towns, and villages are much humbler, though most are clean and tidy. *Pensión*, modest guest houses, can be found in the villages and on the outskirts of most cities. Colombia's few **campgrounds** are located in parks. Most come without service facilities, showers, and the like, and one dare not leave anything unattended there.

Note: Some inexpensive hotels, especially in outlying areas, have an electric device over the water tap with which one heats water for a shower. **Be very careful** in operating it; one false move can lead to disaster.

Food and drink

Hotel restaurants in Colombia's major cities serve high quality international fare. Restaurants in every city specialize in local foods. Menus vary from one region to the next, reflecting the country's wide variety of cuisine. Popular-class restaurants are not noted for their hygiene. Prices are rather low; even in better restaurants one can eat for no more than the cost of a moderate meal in Europe or the United States.

The national drink of course, is coffee, black strong and

COLOMBIA

nvigorating, served with lots of sugar in a little cup. When ordering it, ask for *tinto*, because *cafe* means instant coffee. Colombia, like several of its Caribbean neighbors, produces several types of rum, (the most popular is *Aguardiente*), which are served both straight and mixed. *Canelazo*, a popular cocktail, consists of rum with lemon, sugar, water, and cinnamon. The local wines are rather poor, so treat yourself instead to Chilean or Argentinian wines, which certainly lend support to the dictum: "Who loves not wine, women, and song, remains a fool his whole life long". Carbonated soft drinks are called *gaseosa*. Stick to bottled water, especially outside the large cities. In jungle zones, water must be purified with chlorine tablets.

As for the national cuisine, all the varieties are delicious. Soups, *empanadas, arepas* (cornflour rolls), and fruit can be purchased at very low prices on every streetcorner, but keep in mind that they must be carefully washed (with bottled water) before you eat them.. Restaurant menus are based on beef, chicken, and seafood. Common dishes include chicken with rice (the popular *arroz con pollo*, tasty enough for any connoisseur); *ajiaco*, a chicken-and-potato ragout; and *sancocho de gallina*, a thick vegetable chicken soup. Seafood in great variety is most easily available along the coast and in Bogotá. Recommended are *arroz con chipichipi* — rice with crabs — and *criolla*, smoked fish with salad. Popular beef dishes are *bistec a caballo*, steak topped with a fried egg, with a side dish of bananas; *muchacho relleno*, beef with rice and vegetables; *puchero santaferneo*, a delectable stew with several kinds of meat and vegetables; and *chicharrones con frijoles*, deep-fried pork served with red beans. Most restaurants serve fixed-price menu, called *comida* which includes soup and main dish, inexpensive and satisfying.

Currency

The currency of Colombia is the **peso**, divided into a hundred *centavos*. Its symbol is "$". Coins go up to 50 pesos, while the largest banknote is 10,000 pesos.

Cashing traveler's checks is complicated and requires documented proof of identity. Many moneychangers and banks do not cash traveler's checks, but the national bank, *Banco de la Republíca*, does honor them. It is hard to convert currencies other than the U.S. dollar. Hotels cash traveler's checks only for their guests and even then at a low rate. When traveling outside the large cities, take enough local currency to meet requirements, since it is difficult to cash checks in outlying towns, and the rates offered in those locales, especially in the jungle and coastal areas, are lower. An official receipt affirming that you have converted foreign currency in Colombia entitles one to buy dollars back before leaving the country, though only after completing an exhausting bureaucratic runaround. Credit cards, especially *Diners Club* and *Visa*, are very common.

Business hours

Stores open before 9am, close for *siesta* 12:30-2:30pm, and reopen until 6:30pm (7pm in city centers). Companies and offices are open for business 8am-noon and 2:30-5pm. Banks in Bogotá are open Mon.-Thurs. 9am-3pm, Fri. till 3:30pm, and half day on Sat. (though not all). Banks in other cities open at 8am but close for *siesta*. Government offices in Bogotá are open 8am-3pm.

Domestic transportation

Air service: The fastest and most convenient way to cover Colombia's tremendous distances is, of course, by air. *Avianca SAM*, and more than a dozen other airlines provide regular service on a scale rarely equalled in South America, to almost all Colombia's cities and towns.

Though *Avianca* charges more than the other airlines, it provides the most reliable, convenient and frequent service to any destination. *Avianca* offers a 25% discount on many of its routes and takes stand-by passengers on flights between major cities. It also offers a "Get-to-know-Colombia" (*Conozca a Colombia*) ticket, good for unlimited air travel anywhere in the country except to Leticia and San Andrés Island for thirty days. The ticket must be purchased outside of Colombia, and no place can be visited twice.

Satena, the army airline, provides inexpensive air service to Leticia. *SAM* and other small companies have low cost flights to San Andrés.

Bear in mind that every flight in Colombia is subject to an airport tax.

Buses: The quality of bus service in Colombia varies from place to place. In and between the large cities, the vehicles are modern and comfortable. Off the main routes, however, the service deteriorates severely. Most roads are not paved, and the buses are old and prone to breakdowns. Stops are far apart, and terminal employees and just about everyone else have access to the unlocked luggage compartment. The best thing by far is to take one's gear on the bus. Even if most drivers object insist on it. Be firm!

For long-distance trips, bus travel usually costs nearly as much as airfare. Both possibilities are worth investigation. Buses are frequently stopped for police inspection; passengers must open their bags and, at times, submit to body searches.

Train: Though the large cities are linked by rail, passenger trains run only between Bogotá and Santa Marta. Most of the trains are antiquated and slow, though some relatively modern carriages have been introduced in recent years. Buy tickets in advance, and keep an eagle eye and a tight grip on your gear.

Car: Driving is no more complicated in Colombia than elsewhere in South America, though road service is hard to obtain, and highway conditions invite breakdowns. Try to stay off the road at night, and always carry essential spare parts.

The international car rental companies have branches throughout Colombia and provide well maintained, late model vehicles. An ordinary or international driver's license suffices for the local police, as long as a Spanish translation is attached.

Taxi: Most taxis in Colombia are equipped with meters; be sure they are turned on. If there is no meter, always negotiate the fare in advance! When you get out of a cab at your destination, or if the taxi breaks down, always have your bags in hand. Cab drivers have been known to ask passengers to help fix something, push the car, or get out at the journey's end... and to take off with the luggage.

Hitchhiking: Thumbing it is no problem along major highways, which are used mostly by trucks. Hitchhike from police inspection points, and refrain from getting into cars occupied by several men. Make sure your would-be benefactor is not driving an unmarked taxi; if he is, he may charge for the trip at the end. Do not hitchhike at night. Young women must not travel alone.

Photography

In comparison to other South American countries, Colombia is relatively advanced in the sphere of photography. In most parts of the country there is no difficult in finding film at reasonable prices. It is more difficult to get film for slides. In Bogotá there are many places which develop films very adequately.

Measurements, electricity, and time

The metric system is used. Electricity is usually 110V though in some places it is 220V, therefore it is advisable to enquire before using electrical instruments. Colombian time is GMT −5.

Personal security

Colombia has acquired a reputation in recent years for harassing and harrying tourists. Thousands of innocent visitors have paid for their trips the hard way — getting robbed on the one hand and undergoing humiliating police inspections on the other. It is hard to describe every hardship a visitor may encounter here. It suffices to mention several episodes where passengers on Colombian buses treated tourists to food laced with sleeping drugs and robbed them the moment they dozed off. Other visitors have been mugged under threat of *machetes* (long jungle knives) while enjoying a quiet stroll in the San Augustín archaeological park. It is important to stress the severity of the problem.

Colombian thugs have no qualms about how they obtain their loot. Be vigilant at all times! Trust no one; deal correctly but suspiciously with even the most respectable looking people. Sad as that attitude is, the alternative could be much worse. Never agree to carry parcels for strangers, and never let people on the bus place their baggage near your seat! When the police get on board for an inspection, your neighbors might claim it is yours.

Look out for your gear everywhere and at all times. Be sure to keep bags, packs, and suitcases locked, and **never** leave them unattended. Get off at every bus stop, and make sure that no fellow passengers or bus company employees have taken your belongings "by mistake".

Never wear jewelry, cameras, watches, and the like. They serve only to attract thieves. Keep your money and documents in inner pockets.

The local police, too, are a nuisance. Routine highway inspections are known to develop into destructive forays through tourists' luggage. Airport customs inspections and drug searches in hotel rooms are much the same story. All too often, police plant drugs in a tourist's personal belongings and then threaten the frightened foreigner with arrest unless he forks out over hundreds of dollars in bribes.

When being searched, never let the policemen touch your belongings; instead, remove and display the contents yourself. It is important to behave politely and patiently, never picking a fight. If complications develop, notify your country's embassy **immediately** and ask for help.

In case of theft, the police are likely to make trouble when you apply for a form to show the insurance company in order to prove your loss. Victimized tourists often need to bribe the police to be so kind as to fill out the forms properly.

A suggested itinerary for your visit to Colombia

Visitors to Colombia coming to or from south will most likely follow a south-to-north route, with detours east and west. One can then visit southern Colombia — San Agustín, Cali and the surrounding area (perhaps even the jungles), Bogotá and north to the Carribean coast (Cartagena). From there one can continue on to Panama, Venezuela or to the Islands of San Andrés.

This long route is recommended as it covers most of Colombia and offers a wide range of special sites — from the captivating south, to the industrial heartland, to the pleasant Caribbean coast.

Those arriving in Bogotá and making excursions from there to other parts of Colombia, would be best advised to take a circular route — to the south (San Agustín), to the jungles (Leticia) and to the north (Carribean coast).

Trips to the area of *Cordillera Oriental* (towards Venezuela) and the Pacific coast are not essential.

An interesting route from Bogotá to Venezuela is via Tunja and Cúcuta.

Bogotá

An interesting story of conquest preceded the establishment of Bogotá in 1538. Upon hearing of legendary treasures of gold owned by the *Chibcha* or *Mochica* cultures that populated the lovely plain where the Colombian capital now stands, no few Spanish adventurers got the urge to set out in search of the mysterious place. *El Dorado*, "the Golden City", was every Spaniard's dream from the day America was discovered, and quite a few fortune hunters penetrated the unexplored recesses of the continent in search of it. Together with various localities in Peru, Venezuela, and elsewhere, the Bogotá plateau was considered one possible location of the hidden treasure. Gonzalo Jiménez de Quesada reached the area from Santa Marta on the Atlantic coast in 1538, beating his competitors by only a few days after a grueling and bloody march. He came from Santa Marta along the shores of the Atlantic ocean and he founded Santa Fe de Bogotá, on the lovely mountain ringed plain, 2640 m above sea level.

Bogotá developed and expanded quickly. The Spaniards looted every speck of gold they found among the *Mochica* Indians, and herded the natives into a restricted areas. Some Indians opposed the Spaniards; they were ultimately annihilated or driven east into the jungle. Most, however, submitted to the new regime and assimilated into the Spanish community, laying the foundations of the *mestizo* society that still exists.

Today Bogotá and its suburbs are home to a population of almost 4.5 million, engaging in business and industry. Northern Bogotá boasts exclusive residential neighborhoods and elegant office buildings along wide boulevards. In the south, by contrast, are *barrios* where hundreds of thousands live in shameful poverty, a miserable mix of want and deprivation, rage, frustration, and daily insecurity. Western Bogotá is the industrial zone. In the city center, near Plaza Bolívar, Colonial and modern architecture converge in a rare harmony, as 17th century edifices coexist side by side with modern high-rises.

Bogotá is an interesting, effervescent, rather tempestuous city. It is a topsy-turvy metropolis, where a facade of serene grandeur overlays social unrest and unspeakable poverty — a breeding ground for crime and violence. Its temperate climate (average temperature 14°C or 57°F) and special geographic location

COLOMBIA

BOGOTA

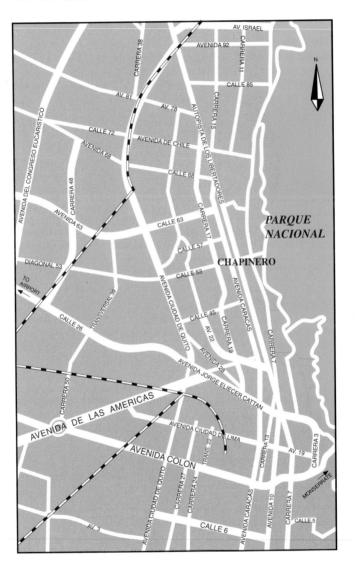

lends it a pleasant, charming ambience, and a grandeur and grace which few cities enjoy.

How to get there

By air: Bogotá's El Dorado Airport, about 10 km from the center of Bogotá, provides tourist police service, car rental companies, services for hotel reservations, elegant duty-free shops, and currency exchange (the rates are better in town).

Taxis ply the route from the airport to town. A fixed sum is added to the meter reading, depending on the time of day and day of the week. Verify this information before getting into the cab. Buses and *colectivos* (shared taxis) are much cheaper and are recommended. When they set out for the airport (from Calle 19), they are marked *Aeropuerto*.

By land: Buses from everywhere in Colombia and from Ecuador, Peru, and Venezuela arrive at the big and modern bus terminal situated between the airport and the city center, on Av. Boyacá. Buses set out for Medellín, Cartagena, Cali, Popayán, and San Agustín many times each day. Passenger trains run between Bogotá Santa Marta, only once a week in the dry season.

Where to stay

Bogotá boasts not only some of South America's most modern and luxurious hotels, but also hundreds of less expensive ones. Most hotels are clean and tidy. The Ministry of Tourism ranks them and fixes their maximum rates (to which one must add a 5% tax and a 15% VAT). Don't leave valuables in your room; lock the door when you are inside. Here, more than in many other countries, it is important to leave money and jewelry in the hotel safe.

Tequendama: Carrera 10, No. 27-51, Tel. 826-8111, Fax. 282-2860. A very expensive and excellent hotel, it also runs an apart-hotel in downtown Bogotá.
Orquídea Royal: Carrera 7, No. 32-16, Tel. 287-0788. Still refered as the Hilton by local people, towering over Bogotá with hundreds of rooms, swimming pool, lobby, etc. Very expensive.
Dann: Calle 19, No. 5-72, Tel. 284-0100, Fax. 282-3108. Very good, it is only one of the Danns in town, varying in price; all of them are well located and have a good service.
Continental: Av. Jiménez No. 4-16, Tel. 242-5901. Near the business and shopping districts, somewhat less expensive than the former ones.
San Diego: Carrera 13 No. 24-82, Tel. 284-2100. Nice, about the same price as the Continental, centrally located.

COLOMBIA

Bogotá Internacional: Carrera 7A and Calle 21. Medium priced, good location, good value.
Residencia La Escalinata: Calle 15 at the corner with Carrera 10. Basic, but good value; inexpensive.
Rey: Carrera 5 and Calle 20. Despite its name ("king") — very simple and basic, yet safe and central.

What to eat, when and where

Bogotá's business district and northern areas have hundreds of eating establishments. Bogotá offers a tremendous selection of restaurants for every taste and pocket. Every streetcorner has a creole restaurant (indigenous food), or something of French, Italian, Chinese, and more. Recent years have witnessed a proliferation of pizzerias, ice-cream shops (*heladerías*), and little pubs with inexpensive meals in an informal atmosphere. These places where young people and students congregate, are near the University area.

With the wealth of possibilities, only the best known restaurants can be mentioned here, together with some which deserve special mention for their special decor, location and the like. This is not meant as a slur to the others; visitors are sure to quickly find the restaurants most amenable to their tastes.

Elegant hotel restaurants present a combined menu of indigenous and continental dishes. The *Orquídea* and the *Tequendama* have opulent rooftop restaurants with splendid views of the city. Another restaurant at the *Tequendama* serves a relatively inexpensive, top quality buffet lunch. *El Chalet Suizo* at 21-51 Carrera 7 is a good Swiss restaurant.

The prime attraction, of course, is typical Colombian food and the restaurants that specialize in it. Few visitors, after all, cross oceans and continents in order to eat American style pizza or steak. Try the national delicacies mentioned in the introduction at *Casa Vieja*, Av. Jiménez 3-73. This is one of Bogotá's classic restaurants and, though it is a bit old, it treats its customers to delicious food at reasonable prices, with folk music in the background. Other possibilities are *Casa Vieja de San Diego* (across from *Hotel Tequendama*), and *Zaguán de las Aguas* at Calle 19, 5-61.

A more expensive and festive place to eat is *Los Sauces*, which offers a full evening of Colombian folklore and delicacies: excellent service, superb cuisine, and a folk music performance — certainly one of Bogotá's most pleasurable Creole restaurants; it is worth visiting for lunch or dinner. Vegeterians can find branches of *El Vegetariano* at Calle 22, 8-89 (upstairs, hard to spot it); calle 18, 5-74; and Carrera 8, 21-39 (open only for lunch). *El Integral Natural* is a health-store with a small restaurant which serves inexpensive meals, at Carrera 11, 95-10.

Transportation

In Bogotá, taxis are recommended. Bus service is fast and frequent, but one is at the mercy of thieves. If you choose public transportation anyway, the best choice is a *buseta*, a minibus which charges twice the regular bus fare and does not take on standing passengers, or a *colectivo*, a fixed-route taxi for six to eight passengers.

The green and beige taxis at special stands beside the major hotels are meant exclusively for tourists. They charge more than regular taxis, but the drivers speak basic English and are relatively reliable. Taxi fares are determined by meter; drivers are allowed to add a surcharge for night, holiday, and Sunday trips. Should you find a taxi without a meter, be sure to negotiate the price before you set out.

For car rental, try *Hertz* at Carrera 10, 26-35, Tel. 334-7961 (at the *Tequendama Hotel*) or *Avis* at Carrera 10, 27-79; or their desks at the airport.

Renting a car for in-town driving is not recommended. Never leave valuables in the car, and park only in supervised parking lots, called parqueaderos. When driving out of town keep small change for the quite frequent tolls.

Tourist services

The Government Tourist Bureau (*Corporación Nacional de Turismo — CNT*) is at Calle 28 No. 13a-15, Tel. 281-4341, ground floor of the building with the *Banco Cafetero* name at its top. There is a Municipal Tourist Bureau at Carrera 35, No. 26-18. The National Parks Authority (*INDERENA*) has offices at Carrera 10, No. 20-30, 8th floor, Tel. 283-2598. It is best to arrange in advance your visit permits to Parks here. The Auto-Club, at Avenida Caracas (14) No. 46-64, has road maps. For hiking maps go to the Instituto Geográfico Codazzi, Carrera 30 at the corner with calle 45. The offices of the *DAS*, the immigration service, are at Carrera 28, No. 17A-00.

Foreign airlines have modern offices downtown. Local companies are *Avianca* at Carrera 7, No. 16-36 (Tel. 266-9700); *SAM*, Carrera 10, No. 27-91 (Tel. 266-9600), and *Satena*, Avenida 19, No. 13A-18 (Tel. 283-5557).

Guía de Bogotá, a tourist publication that covers events and places to visit in town, is distributed free at the hotels. More

COLOMBIA

DOWNTOWN BOGOTA

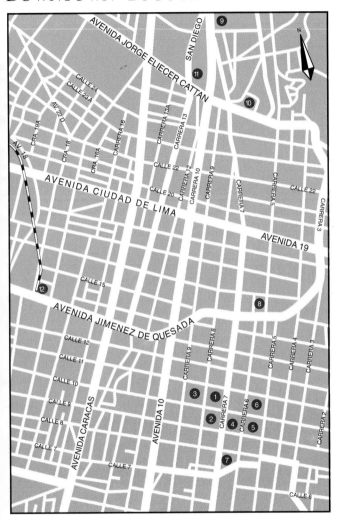

159

detailed maps and a weekly, up to date brochure are available at almost any newsstand.

Tourist sites

For the tourist, most places of interest in Bogotá are near the city center or in the colonial district to its south. To the east, the city is flanked by a green mountain range. The south is a slum district, as is the western district, which also has industrial zones. Since these areas are not only uninteresting but also dangerous, we concentrate rather on the more pleasant sides of Bogotá, a city that becomes more modern as one heads north.

First, a brief outline of the street numbering system. Here, as in all other cities of Colombia, streets have numbers, not names. East-west arteries are called *calles* (streets), while north-south thoroughfares are *carreras* (avenues). The roads are numbered in ascending order from south to north, and from east to west. Buildings have two numbers, the first being the number of the nearest street, and the second indicating the number of the building on that street. Thus, for example, Calle 13, No. 24-45 is the equivalent of 13th St., No. 45, between Carreras 24 and 25.

The tour starts with a visit to the observation point atop the **Monserrate**, the mountain bordering the eastern part of town. Use the cablecar, which runs daily, 9am-6pm. Try to avoid Sundays if possible, since you will have to wait in line for the cablecar for a long time. Do not attempt the ascent or descent on foot as the place swarms with tourists — and, therefore, with muggers who do not hesitate to waylay pedestrians at knife or gun point. The foot of the mountain, near the cablecar station, is also dangerous. The summit itself is safe, due to a heavy police presence. On top are a small church, souvenir shops, a cafe and a restaurant. At 3153 m above sea level, the mountain peak provides an excellent bird's eye panorama of the entire city. The transition from old to new, highlighted by the modern skyscrapers downtown, is easily discerned from this vantage point.

Down at the bottom, near the cablecar station, is **La Quinta de Bolívar** (Bolívar's House), built in 1793 by a Spanish merchant who presented it to the liberator, Simón Bolívar, in 1820. Bolívar lived here until leaving Bogotá shortly before his death. The estate has been preserved in its original condition, including the furniture and *objets d'art*. The gardens, too, have been well maintained, with a wealth of flowers and trees. Some of Bolívar's personal possessions and arms, as well as numerous documents preserved from that era, are kept in the back of the house. (Calle 20, No. 3-23, Tel. 284-6819, open Tues.-Sun. 9am-5pm).

The next stop is the colonial district, with **Plaza Bolívar** in its center. (Since traffic is always heavy here, it is best to arrive by public transportation or on foot.) A statue of Simón Bolívar stands in the middle of the square, which is surrounded by public buildings. To the south is the **Capitolio** (the National Congress); facing it is **Palacio de la Justicia**, Colombia's renowned Supreme Court of Justice. It was here in October 1985, that a band of guerrillas seized a large group of hostages, including the President of the Supreme Court. The government, true to its iron fist policy in dealings with guerrillas, refused to negotiate. Instead, they sent in the armed forces with tanks and mortars. The guerrillas and their hostages (about 150 people) were massacred.

To the west of the square is the **City Hall.** The house in the northeast corner is the spot where Colombia's independence was declared on July 20, 1810. Today the edifice houses the **Museo 20 de Julio** (July 20 Museum) with a collection of documents and paintings relating to that historic event. Calle 11, No. 6-94, Tel. 334-4150, open Tues.-Sat., 10am-6pm and Sun., until 4pm. On the southeast corner is the **Church of San Ignacio**, the most impressive of Bogotá's colonial churches. Its sophisticated, progressive architecture contrasts with the simple design of the other churches. The interior houses a rich collection of paintings and sculptures by Bogotá's principal 17th century artists. One block farther on is the **Palacio de San Carlos**, the president's residence which once was Bolívar's house. Across the street is the fine **Teatro Colón** (see below "Entertainment and culture").

Plaza Bolívar is in the **Candelaria** Quarter, formerly known as **Barrio de los Príncipes** (the Princes' District) because the Spanish nobility made its home here. A stroll through its narrow streets between the colonial houses, provides a picture of how Santa Fe de Bogotá developed socially, culturally, and architecturally under the Spanish between 1550 and 1810. The **Archaeological Museum** off Plaza Bolívar (Carrera 6, 7-43, open Tues.-Sat. 9am-noon and 1:15-5pm, Sun., 10am-1pm), was once the home of the renowned Marquis San Jorge. The building gives one a glimpse of the life style of its former occupants. It is a beautiful example of colonial architecture with its large windows, balconies and spacious patios. Today it exhibits a fine collection of ceramics found in the ruins of various pre-Columbian civilizations.

Another recommended stop in this vicinity is the **Arts and**

Crafts Museum, on the corner of Carrera 8 and Calle 9, with its splendid collection of handicrafts from all parts of the country. Open Tues.-Sat., 8:35am-5:30pm (the main galery opens at 9:30am). In the premises, once an Agustinian monastery, there is also a restaurant serving dishes from the different areas of Colombia.

Slightly north of Candelaria, at Calle 16, 5-41, is Colombia's most important museum, the best known institution of its type in the country, an establishment renowned throughout the Americas, and a "must" for any visitor — the **Museo del Oro** (Gold Museum).

The museum contains one of the world's largest collections of gold objects — approximately 25,000 items! Most of these are relics of pre-Columbian civilizations, which attributed divine properties to gold. The artifacts on display, salvaged by the *conquistadores*, represent but a tiny fraction of the original treasure. The museum was founded by the Central Bank in 1939 in order to avert the mislaying of such treasures as could still be found. Most were purchased from antiquity looters, and only a small percentage from archaeologists.

The gold itself, as well as most of the processing techniques, reached the pre-Columbians from Central America. Since pure gold is difficult to shape, most artists worked in a gold and copper alloy with a gold content of no more than 80%.

Of the museum's three floors, the first houses temporary exhibitions of gold items, the second exhibits a representative sample of pre-Columbian gold relics of various civilizations, and the third is a large safe with long corridors, in which most of the museum's collection is kept. Here, too, the items are classified by different cultures. Note the great delicacy of the workmanship. Some of the exhibits are placed behind a magnifying lens, to enable the viewer to appreciate the finer details. Open Tues.-Sat. 9am-4pm, Sun. 9am-noon.

Bogotá's business hub is between Calles 19 and 34 and Carreras 7 and 13. This area has the best selection of top hotels and stores, and the largest number of travel agencies and embassies in town.

On the corner of Calle 28 and Carrera 7, in a building that once served as the city jail, is one of Colombia's most important museums: **Museo Nacional** (The National Museum). It houses a wide variety of exhibits of Columbian and pre-Columbian ethnography and history. Open Tues.-Sat. 9:30am-5:30pm, Sun., 11am-5pm. On Thursdays entrance is free. A guided visit in English can be arranged a few days in advance. Tel. 342-5925.

Aficionados of the avant-garde will certainly want to visit the permanent and seasonal exhibitions of contemporary art at the **Museum of Modern Art**, Calle 24, No. 6-55, open Tues.-Sat., 10am-7pm and Sun., noon-6pm.

Northern Bogotá

Northern Bogotá, though hardly "touristy", is worth visiting if only to sense the vast disparities among the various sections of town. This is an area of modern neighborhoods, luxury homes, and shaded avenues. Bogotá's wealthy citizens, diplomats, and foreign dignitaries live here. However, in spite of — or rather because of — the high standard of living, the residents of northern Bogotá live in constant fear of robbers and burglars. One who has visited the slums of Bogotá should not find it hard to understand why.

Zipaquirá

This town (pop. app. 40,000), a short ride from Bogotá, is the capital of cattle country. Of special interest to us, however, is the magnificent **Salt Cathedral**. The region has vast salt deposits, which were discovered and first exploited by early Indians. Over time, a large salt mine was built into a rocky hill in the area, and the church was hewn out of the center of this hill.

One approaches the church by walking 120 m through the mine tunnel. Its nave can accommodate up to 8000 worshippers, and the central altar is made of a block of salt weighing 18 tons!

Bus service to Zipaquirá (from Avenida Caracas in Bogotá) is very frequent. The trip takes over an hour. Travel agents also organize guided tours. The Cathedral opens Tues.-Sun., 10am-4pm.

General information

Entertainment and Culture

Bogotá is not famous for its exciting night life; the locals seem to prefer staying home rather than braving the city's outlaws. Movie fans will find plenty of good, modern cinemas. The local cinematheque, for one, is at Carrera 17, 22-79.

The major nightclub and discotheque district is the north side of the town. The most popular nightclub, however, is actually in the city center at *Hotel Tequendama*.

On Friday and Saturday you can enjoy the Colombian Symphonic Orchestra at the **Teatro Colón**, Calle 10, No. 5-32, facing the

Palacio de San Carlos. This century-old hall can be appreciated on guided visits, Mon.-Fri., 10am-5pm.

Shopping
Bogotá's several shopping centers are best for leather goods, gold items, and handicrafts. Colombia has been blessed with large deposits of emeralds, which are therefore relatively inexpensive. Beware of street peddlars who may approach you furtively and offer you stones for sale; most are fake.

Many shops with large stocks of high quality merchandise are situated on Avenida 15. The area between Calles 50 and 65, known as **Chapinero**, abounds in cut rate leather and textile stores. The lobbies of the *Orquídea Royal* and *Tequendama* have shops with souvenirs, gold items, and superb leather goods — prices are sky-high!

Stores belonging to the *Artesanías de Colombia* chain, situated around town, sell handicrafts (*artesanía*). The main outlet is at Carrera 10, 26-50. On the corner of Calle 127 and Carrera 15 is *Unicentro*, a modern shopping center and one of South America's largest. Apart from stores, *Unicentro* has movie theaters, restaurants, and nightclubs.

Banks and currency exchanges
Colombia's national bank, *Banco de la Republíca*, has branches around town, where one can exchange dollars (cash or travelers' checks) for local currency without any problem. Here, one can also perform all standard business banking transactions — international currency transfers, obtaining letters of credit, etc.

Postal and telephone service
Try to send letters and parcels by air mail only. Parcel postage is not costly at all. Poste restante service is available at the post office in Edificio Avianca, Carrera 7, 16-36, open Tues.-Sat. 8.30am-12pm and 3.30-5pm.

The local phone company, *Telecom*, has its central office at Calle 23, 13-49 and a branch office in the commercial center of *Hotel Tequendama*. International collect calls cannot be made from the *Telecom* offices, though private phones permit this.

Climate
At 2600 m above sea level, Bogotá can be a little chilly, with an average temperature of 14°C (57°F). Because of its proximity to the equator, there is little seasonal variation in the weather, and the plentiful rainfall is distributed throughout the year.

Beware: thieves!

Pickpocketing and mugging are rife in Bogotá. Keep constant watch on your possessions. Never put a purse or wallet in a back pocket, and never wear jewelry. Steer clear of any group, since it is liable to be a set up. Aggravated armed robbery is a routine occurrence, and the bandits are not reluctant to use their weapons.

Tourists are best advised to confine their movements to city center and northern Bogotá. Be careful around the foot of the Monserrate. To ascend or descend the mountain on foot is to tempt fate! The area around the lower terminus of the cablecar, too, teems with muggers.

The Bogotá police sometimes work hand in hand with the bandits by turning a blind eye to their forays. Just the same, report any case of robbery or theft to the tourist police, at Carrera 7, 27-50. Tel. 283-4930 or 284-5047.

Important addresses

Red Cross: Tel. 231-9008.
Tourist Police: Carrera 7, No. 27-50, Tel. 283-4930 or 284-5047.
National Tourist Bureau (*Corporación Nacional de Turismo — CNT*): Calle 28, No. 13a-15, Tel. 281-4341.
Municipal Tourist Bureau: Carrera 35, No. 26-18.
National Parks Authority (*INDERENA*): Carrera 10, No. 20-30, 8th floor, Tel. 283-2598.
Automóvil Club de Colombia: Avenida Caracas (14) No. 46-64.
DAS (immigration service): Carrera 28, No. 17A-00.

Consulates

United Kingdom: Calle 98, No. 9-03, Tel. 218-5111.
United States: Calle 38, No. 8-61, Tel. 285-1300.
France: Carrera 7, No. 38-99, Tel. 285-4311.
Germany: Carrera 4, No. 72-36, Tel. 212-0511.
Italy: Calle 70, No. 10-25, Tel. 235-4300.

From Bogotá to Cúcuta

Transportation
A number of direct buses travel the Bogotá-Cúcuta (650 km) route daily, along with several flights per week. The buses are comfortable, and the journey takes about 24 hours. Regular bus service links the towns en route. A direct road connects Bucaramanga with Santa Marta on the Caribbean coast.

Tunja
Tunja, the capital of Boyacá province and one of Colombia's oldest towns (fouhded in 1539 by Gonzalo Suárez Rendón), is about a two hour ride from Bogotá. It is home to more than 100,000 inhabitants. Its old quarter still preservcs its grand Spanish colonial character, but the new areas are rather undistinguished. At 2800 m above sea level, Tunja is fairly cold.

The most important surviving colonial buildings are the **Church of Santo Domingo** (const. 1594), **Santa Clara Monastery**, today a hospital, and **La Casa del Fundador** (Founder's House). The latter, built in 1540, was the residence of the town's founder and houses some of the most interesting relics left by the Spanish conquerors.

Food and lodging
Hostería San Carlos: Carrera 11, 20-12, Tel. 42-3716. A bit expensive, but good value, nice building, very good.
Hotel San Francisco: Carrera 9, 18-90, Tel. 42-6645. On the central Plaza, moderately priced and recommended; it also serves good meals.
Residencias Lord: Calle 19, 10-64, Tel. 42-3556. Inexpensive, friendly and recommended.

For satisfying, reasonably priced meals, some places in the old part of town can be found, among them the *Bodegón de los Frailes* off plaza Bolívar, behind the church of San Ignacio.

The Boyacá Bridge
About 16 km south of Tunja is the site of the famous Battle of Boyacá, the decisive campaign in Colombia's War of Independence. Tunja fell to Bolívar on August 6, 1819. The following morning, he led his troops with reinforcements to the

Tunja — the old quarter

marshy banks of Rio Boyacá, where they challenged British battalions which had come to the aid of the Spanish army. Through audacity and good strategy, Bolívar's army overcame the Spanish forces despite their superior numbers, inflicted numerous casualties, and got away almost unscathed. The handful of Spanish who managed to escape reported to the Spanish governor in Bogotá, who fled the town and left his royal treasures behind. This, in effect, marked the end of Spanish rule and paved the way for Colombia's independence.

The Boyacá Bridge on the Bogotá-Tunja highway is graced with a large statue of Bolívar, a monument to that glorious triumph. Its anniversary, August 7, is a national holiday.

Villa de Leiva

The small town, founded in 1572, was well preserved architecturally over the years, and it was declared national monument, not allowing the progress to be seen.

This town was home to some of Colombia's most famous patriots, such as Antonio Nariño, who translated Thomas Jefferson's *The Rights of Man* into Spanish in 1794. Nariño's house is a museum today, open Tues.-Sun. 9am-12:30pm and 2-6pm.

Stroll through the town's pleasant plazas and peaceful streets, and visit the house where the first joint committee of the States of "Greater Colombia" met in 1812. The **Luis Alberto Acuña Museum**, on the central plaza, is named after the famous Colombian painter and houses a collection of his works. The stores along the plaza stock the usual selection of handicrafts, and a market is held here on Saturdays.

Just out of town is the **Monastery of Santo Ecce Homo**, a stone and clay edifice built by the Dominicans in 1620. To reach it, there is a bus daily at 9:30am from Villa de Leiva to Santa Sofía, and about 2 km walk to the Monastery.

When planning your visit in town, bear in mind that most museums and places of interest here are closed on Mondays, and that it is very crowded with visitors on weekends.

Food and lodging
Accommodation to most hotels in Villa de Leiva can be arranged in Bogotá thorugh *Servicios Hoteleros Boyacá*, Carrera 15, 77-90, Tel. 218-0321.

Hostería del Molino La Mesopotamia: Calle 117, 6-33. The street of this good and pleasant hotel is also known as "calle del Silencio"; the building of a mill built in 1568 with beautiful and well tended gardens, highly recommended. Medium price.
Hospedería del Convento de San Francisco: On Plaza San Francisco. It also has a pool and is recommended for its high quality service.
Estancia El Olivo: On Calle 12 and Carrera 7. For low budget accommodation.

There are several good restaurants on the central plaza. One of the best in town is *Los Balcones*, just off the plaza.

Beyond Tunja
The road to Cúcuta forks at Tunja into two alternate routes, both of which pass through spectacular mountain scenery: a smooth paved road via Bucaramanga, and an especially scenic, but largely unpaved and difficult eastern route through Capitanejo and Málaga. The latter road passes through little towns and villages, where one can enjoy a convivial and relaxing visit and spend the night. The two routes converge at Pamplona, forming a single paved road that leads directly to Cúcuta.

From the town of **Capitanejo**, about half way to Pamplona, a right (east) turn leads to the Sierra Nevada del Cocuy, a beautiful mountain range over 5000 m high. The main villages are El Cocuy and Guaican, both with basic accoommodation facilities. Guaican is a better starting point for trekking.

Back on the main road, 40 km beyond Capitanejo, is the town of **Málaga**, another pleasant place to spend the night. Its surriounding is picturesque with many colourful small villages.

From Tunja to Bucaramanga

The road to Bucaramanga (290 km) offers many picturesque sceneries, green mountains and small colonial towns. The bus ride takes 9 hours. A good place for a break is **Socorro**, a nice town with small houses and a large church; also there is a daily market. The town has two comfortable hotels, the relatively expensive *Tamacara*, and the basic and cheap *Venezia*.

The town is proud of its two native heroines, who led the locals to violent struggles. The first led a peasant revolt in the 18th century; and the other, whose statue is in the town's square, led the local struggle for independence.

20 km beyond Socorro is the town of **San Gil** in a lovely valley. **Barichara** is a splendid colonial village off the main road, some 20 km west of San Gil. This charming place preserves the colonial atmosphere, and it was designated as a national monument.

Bucaramanga

Bucaramanga, the capital of Santander province, was founded in 1622. Until the second half of the 19th century, Bucaramanga was simply a small town, but has since, developed at a fantastic pace, and now has a population of more than half a million. Its burgeoning growth is due largely to the success of its coffee plantations, which export their produce worldwide. Reminders of the past are easily discerned in the modern city, with its spacious parks and squares. Parque Santander graces the heart of the modern section, while Plaza García Romero marks the center of the colonial district. Near this plaza is **Casa de Bolívar** (Bolívar's House), where he stayed for two months in 1813. The mansion is an archaeological museum today, with a collection of pre-Columbian pottery. Opposite Bolívar's House is **Casa de Cultura** (House of Culture).

Transportation

Bucaramanga lies about 10 hours' travel from Bogotá, on the junction of three main highways — northeast to Venezuela, north to Santa Marta and the Caribbean Sea, and south to Bogotá. *Berlinas del Fonce* (offices at Carrera 18, 31-06) provides good bus service to and from Bogotá. The trip to Cúcuta takes about 6 hours. Because the buses to Cúcuta are often full (the routes

*Villa de Leiva — **Monastery of Santo Ecce Homo***

begin in Bogotá), it may be best to travel by *colectivo*, which, though slightly more expensive than the bus, is faster and more comfortable. The trip to Santa Marta takes about 10 hours, or even more in the rainy season. *Copetran* provides bus service on this route.

Food and lodging
Chicamocha: Calle 34, 31-24, Tel. 34-3000 (reservations in Bogotá, Tel. 249-9420). The best in town, fairly expensive. Hard to get rooms, because of the many conventions held in town.
Bucarica: Calle 35 at the corner with Carrera 19, Tel. 42-3111. On the main plaza, moderate prices, swimming pool and a good restaurant. Recommended.
El Pilar: Calle 34, 24-09, Tel. 45-3147. Low prices, clean and good service.
Residencias Amparo: Calle 31, 20-29, Tel. 42-2255. Low prices, good and clean.
Hostal Doral: Calle 32, 21-65. Inexpensive.

For restaurants, Bucaramanga has a fair range of places all over the town. A local dish are the *hormigas* (large fried black ants!). Vegetarians can find good meals at *Govinda* in Carrera 20, next to calle 35.

Pamplona
Pamplona, 120 km northeast of Bucaramanga on the main road

Barichara

to Cúcuta, is where the two alternate roads north from Tunja converge.

Although a junction, not much have been changed since its foundation in the mid 16th century. The town of 50,000 inhabitants preserved many colonial houses and churches, and it has several pleasant hotels, most of which are inexpensive.

From Pampluna it is another 3 hours bus ride to Cúcuta.

Cúcuta

This town, with a population of about half a million, is the capital of Santander del Norte province. Founded in 1734 and leveled by an earthquake in 1875, Cúcuta was rebuilt as a modern city with wide avenues and parks. The climate is hot with an average daily temperature of 28°C (82°F). Coffee and tobacco are grown extensively. Due to Cúcuta's proximity to the Venezuelan border, however, many of the locals deal in smuggling. Its location also affected its role in the War of Independence. After capturing Cúcuta in 1813, Bolívar set out from here for Caracas at the head of his forces. A modest statue marks the spot where Bolívar billeted his troops before the campaign.

The small town of **El Rosario de Cúcuta**, some 14 km from Cúcuta en route to the border, is the place where representatives of the Confederation of "Greater Colombia" first convened. They ratified the unification of Colombia, Venezuela, Ecuador and Panama, elected Bolívar president, and selected Santander (who was born nearby) as his deputy.

Shopping
Cúcuta is recommended for inexpensive leather goods, such as boots and wallets.

Transportation
The bus ride from Cúcuta to Bogotá takes about 20 hours, or more in the rainy season. *Berlinas del Fonce* and *Bolivariano* buses leave Bogotá almost every hour. *Berlinas* also provides frequent bus service to Bucaramanga, on the way to the Caribbean coast. The bus station is on Avenida 7, and this is not a place to stay alone!.

Avianca provides air service to Bogotá daily from Cúcuta's airport, located just out of town.

Currency exchange
Cúcuta offers a good exchange rate for both Colombian *pesos* and *bolívares* (Venezuelan currency). Street moneychangers, who wander around the main square, usually outbid *Banco de la República* (Calle 11 at Av. 5). Convert all leftover *pesos* in Cúcuta, since this is hard to do in Venezuela. Travelers' checks can be cashed at the bank.

Food and lodging
Tonchalá: Calle 10 and Av. O. Has a fine restaurant, a swimming pool, air conditioned rooms and high prices.
Casa Blanca: Avenida 6, 14-55. Good, low priced, with swimming pool.
Residencias Leo: Av. 6 and Av. O. Recommended for low budget travelers.

For restaurants, the *Bahia* (near the main plaza) is good, pleasant, and affordable. *Chez Estevan*, with its continental cuisine, is recommended.

On to Venezuela
From Cúcuta, take a taxi or a bus to **San Antonio**, the Venezuelan border town. Because the border itself has no immigration offices, passports must be stamped for exit at the *DAS* office in Cúcuta at Avenida 1, 28-55. Open daily 8am-noon and 2-8pm. Closed Sun. To enter Venezuela, one must also obtain a tourist pass at the Venezuelan Consulate in Cúcuta, on Calle 8. Open Mon.-Fri. 8am-1pm. It is always best to obtain entry visas,

where required, in one's country of origin. Failing this, visit the Venezuelan Embassy in Bogotá.

Upon entering Venezuela, passports are stamped at the immigration office in San Antonio. *Expreso Occidente* buses leave San Antonio twice daily for Caracas — a 14 hour journey.

The Caribbean Coast

Colombia's northern coast, on the Caribbean Sea, offers history sun and lots of fun. Here the Spanish colonists founded their first cities on Colombian soil, as bridgeheads for the numerous explorers sent from the Old World to the South American interior The coastal towns were also used as ports for the huge cargos o gold that left for Spain. As such, they attracted hordes of pirates and the numerous fortresses erected to guard the approaches to the cities stand as silent witnesses to the cruel battles tha raged along this beautiful coast.

The Santa Marta mountains, with their snow capped peaks loom in the distance and extend as far as the tropical, sur drenched beaches. The climate, consistently hot, seems to have produced people of similar nature. The *costeños* (coasta people) are descendants of intermarriage between Europeans Indians, and Blacks. On the whole they are warm and outgoing people.

Note: All previous warnings about pickpockets and thieves are even more relevant here. The coastal area is even more prone to violence than the interior. Guard your possessions, and try not to tour alone.

Bearing this in mind, we now explore the coastal area — from Cartagena east to Venezuela, including San Andrés Island.

Cartagena

History
The first Spaniards to reach the many inlets of the Northern Colombia shore found a local population of *Calamari* Indians, a nation of warrior tribes with enormous quantities of gold and a fairly sophisticated culture.

Rodrigo de Bastidas of Spain discovered Cartagena Bay in 1501 and large numbers of Spaniards followed. The great influx o conquerors and explorers who reached Cartagena on their way inland made it necessary to establish a port. Thus, in 1533 Pedro de Heredia founded the city of Cartagena at a well choser location — an indented, flat coastline, with two precipitous hills that provided a good view of the maritime approaches to the city.

The exploration parties, heading inland, soon encountered the indigenous Indian population with their spectacular treasures of gold. Entire Indian villages were devastated, the gold was plundered, and melted down into ingots which were then shipped back to Spain. Ships returning from Spain were loaded with goods for sale. Cartagena became a rich town, and one of the most important ports of the Spanish Empire. This, however, proved to be a mixed blessing. Its wealth attracted many enemies, including the legendary Sir Francis Drake who attacked the city in 1586. Only a ransom of ten million gold coins dissuaded him from razing the city to the ground. Consequently, the Spaniards built a system of fortresses along Cartagena Bay, blocking all approaches to the city, which was itself surrounded by a wall. The construction work spanned the late 16th century and the first half of the 17th. As for the cost of this endeavor, the story goes that the King of Spain, gazing from his palace window in Madrid and musing on the enormity of his expenses, was surprised not to see the outcome of his investment on the horizon...

The long arm of the Spanish Inquisition reached this area as well, and set up its regional courts in Cartagena, in a beautiful palace built for this purpose. Until the city declared its independence, putting the Inquisition to an end, almost a thousand people fell prey to its *autos-da-fe*.

A large French force under Baron de Pointis attacked Cartagena in 1697. De Pointis mounted a siege and attacked the fortress of Bocachica, which blocked the approaches to the Bay. Once Bocachica fell, after a hard and bloody battle, the other fortresses fell more easily until the entire city was conquered. After methodically plundering the city and destroying most of its defenses, de Pointis was forced to retreat due to epidemics which were decimating his forces.

England's decision early in the 18th century to deploy troops in the Caribbean area caused a rupture in Anglo-Hispanic relations. When the Spaniards launched a provocative attack on an English ship in the area, the English reacted harshly. In March 1741, 186 English warships — the largest naval force ever employed in the region — appeared off Cartagena. The commander of this armada, Admiral Vernon, spent an entire week deploying his forces around the city, and only then ordered an attack on Bocachica. The fortress fell, and the English ships entered the Bay. After bombarding the city for a week, the English attacked the mighty fortress of San-Felipe de Barajas. After a short and fierce battle, the tables were turned: the English were routed with heavy casualties, and were forced to hoist anchor and flee.

Cartagena flourished during the second half of the 18th century. The defenses were repaired and renovated, and the great markets (*ferias*) in the area attracted thousands of merchants from the interior. Trade in black slaves, too, was a booming business. The victims were the forebears of the large black population that resides in the Caribbean to this day.

Cartagena played a decisive role in Colombia's struggle for independence. On November 11, 1811, the city declared itself free of Spanish rule. It spent several years thereafter fighting off relentless attacks by opponents of independence and Spanish royalists. In 1815, for example, a Spanish expeditionary force under Pablo Morillo managed to subdue the rebellious city and control it. A third of the population was killed in this cruel battle, for which Cartagena came to be known as *La Ciudad Heróica* (the Heroic City). Only in 1821, after Simón Bolívar's final victory, was Cartagena completely liberated from the Spanish yoke.

Today, Cartagena is a large, modern city of 600,000, the capital of Bolívar province, and an important port. Various monuments — palaces, colonial houses, fortresses — testify to its glorious past. The town also boasts bustling tourist facilities, shopping centers, and beaches alive with color and action.

When to visit
During December and January, the peak of Colombia's tourist season, Cartagena swarms with tourists. It is essential to make advance hotel reservations. Hotel prices are 25% higher at this time.

Cartagena's 4-day Independence Day festivities begin on November 11th. The locals turn out in their best clothes, don masks, and dance in the streets to the sound of folk music.

How to get there
Cartagena's Crespo International Airport has regular flights from all of Colombia's major cities and San Andrés Island in the Caribbean. One of the most economical ways to fly to Colombia from Central America is to fly first to San Andrés and then to Cartagena on a domestic flight. Another low-cost way is by boat from Panama.

Expreso Brasilia buses run between Cartagena and Medellín (17 hours) and Bogotá. Comfortable and regular bus service links Cartagena with other towns on the Caribbean coast. There is also a direct bus to Maicao on the Venezuelan border.

Food and lodging
Cartagena Hilton: El Laguito, Tel. 65-0066, overlooking the sea at the edge of El Laguito in the Bocagrande beach area, about 10 minutes from town. Very good.

Capilla del Mar: Calle 8 and Carrera 1, Tel. 65-1140. Also at the Bocagrande area and also first class, it has a good French restaurant.

Flamingo: Bocagrande beach, Tel. 65-0301. Intermediate class hotel with good service.

Hostal Santo Domingo: Calle Santo Domingo 33-46. In town, simple and fairly economic; a good deal.

The in-town hotels are more modest than the ones along the Bocagrande beach. Several low budget hotels are available on Calle Media Luna (the area of the Crescent). Two of these are the *El Refugio*, on No. 10-35, and *Media Luna*, at the corner with Calle Centenario. But beware: not all are safe; do not leave valuables in the rooms. You can reach Bocagrande by bus from Plaza Independencia.

To give Old Cartagena a new profile, its alleyways have been renovated and quite a few good restaurants have opened along them. One of these is *Nautilus*, located at the city wall across from the statue of La India Catalina. *Nautilus* is noted for its excellent seafood and good service. For good low budget restaurants, try the Plaza Independencia area.

Tourist services

The official **Tourist Office** is at Casa de Marques de Valdehoyos House on Calle de la Factoría. There is another information office at Crespo Airport. The **tourist police** station and a *Telecom* office are at La Maluna, in the city center.

Car rental: *Hertz* at Av. San Martín 6-84, tel. 65-2852 in Bocagrande; *Avis* at Carrera 6, 6-94.

Tourist sites

The Old City is partitioned by a wall into inner and outer sectors. Both comprise houses no taller than one or two stories, done in Spanish colonial style. The narrow, winding streets were built this way on purpose, to provide shade from the searing sun.

The inner section consists of two neighborhoods: the **Centro**, once home to the city's nobility, governors, and Inquisitors; and **San Diego,** which housed the middle classes, merchants, priests and the military. The outer section is known as **Getsemani**. The best way to know the town is to take a leisurely walk along the narrow lanes and to imbibe the atmosphere. In this manner one cannot help but encounter places of interest.

The tour starts at **Plaza de los Coches**, where the inner and outer sections meet. It was once the site of the huge slave market, and has a clock tower dating from the mid-19th century.

CARTAGENA

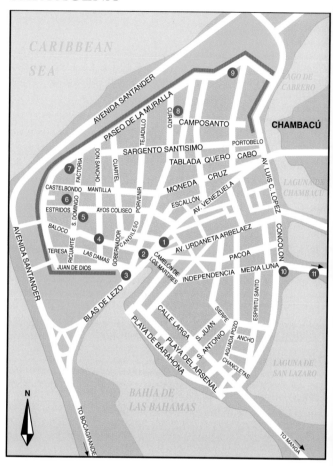

Index

Cross into the inner section via **Plaza de la Aduana** (Customs Square) with its stone statue of Christopher Columbus. Here *El Centro* begins , with its narrow lanes and elegant 2-storey houses. Near Plaza de la Aduana is another plaza, graced with a monastery and church built by Jesuits in 1603. It is named after **San Pedro Claver**, a Spanish monk, who dedicated himself to the cause of the black slaves brought from Africa. He was canonized more than two hundred years after his death, and his body is preserved in a glass coffin inside the church.

Turning north towards **Plaza Bolívar** (a statue of Bolívar stands in its center) is the **Palace of the Inquisition** — a splendid example of colonial architecture, which served as the Inquisition's Court of Justice. The first floor of the palace has a display of torture machinery used on heretics. The second floor houses two small museums: a **Museum of Anthropology** with archaeological exhibits from local pre-Columbian civilizations, and a **Colonial Museum** with an exhibit of documents, weapons and other items in daily use. Open Tues.-Sat. 10am-5pm, and Sun. 9am-1pm. Also on Plaza Bolívar is a branch of *Banco de la República*'s **Museo del Oro** (Gold Museum) — smaller than the main branch in Bogotá, but worth visiting nonetheless.

The **Church and Monastery of Santo Domingo**, on the street of the same name, was built in the late 1500's and is Cartagena's oldest church. At Calle de la Factoría 36-57, is **Casa de Marqués de Valdehoyos**. This magnificent colonial residence, used today as a tourist bureau, was built in the early 1600's by Don Fernando de Hoyos, a slave trade tycoon.

Further north is the **San Diego** quarter. There, on the grounds of San Diego Park, is the **Church and Monastery of Santa Clara**, originally built in the early 17th century. The monastery was subsequently converted into a hospital. Not far from here is **Plaza de las Bóvedas**. From this spot, one may assess the grand dimensions of the city walls — 12 m high, 16 m wide! The niches, once prison cells, now serve as souvenir shops.

We cross into **Getsemani**, the outer section of Old Cartagena, built of low houses and streets so narrow that a person standing in the middle can sometimes touch the walls on either side. At the end of Calle Media Luna is a huge sculpture of a pair of shoes. It is a monument to a native son, poet Luis Carlos López, who once described the city as being as inspiring as an old pair of shoes.

Nearby is the most important of Cartagena's fortresses — **San Felipe de Barajas**, completed in 1657. Though it fell to Baron de Pointis of France, it bravely withstood the onslaught of Admiral Vernon of England (see "History" above). The defenders' homes and offices, as well as a system of secret subterranean passageways, lie under the walls and fortifications. A sound-and-light show on the glorious history of the fortress and the city is staged here on Saturdays at 9pm.

Another link in the port's defenses is **San Sebastián de Pastelillo**.

An earlier fort (16th century) built here to ward off pirate attacks was completely destroyed in one of those assaults. The current fort, built in its place, is equipped with a dock used by the *Club de Pesca* (Fishing Club) and an excellent seafood restaurant.

Around Cartagena

About 20 minutes east of Cartagena is the fishing village of **La Boguilla**. Its weekend evening dance parties, powered by the lively rhythm of local music, are recommended. The mangrove swamps around the village are excellent bird-watching territory.

Lovely indigenous handicrafts are available at the village of **San Jacinto**, 1 ½ hour's ride from Cartagena.

The Rosario Islands

The lovely Rosario Islands, outside Cartagena Bay, are reached by a pleasurable but expensive 10-hour round-trip ride from Cartagena (departures every morning). The trip offers a good view of the fortifications that formerly guarded the city's approaches. Once ashore, note the palms, the dazzling white sands, and the color of the water — which changes from the lightest turquoise to dark blue as it gets deeper. You may wish to spend the night in one of the islands' picturesque houses, and enjoy the area's typical seafood.

Mompós

Santa Cruz de Mompós, one of the best preserved colonial towns in Colombia, stands on the banks of Río Magdalena some 200 km south of Cartagena. It was founded in 1530 on the commercial waterway; but in the 18th century the river's course was changed, and Mampós became isolated, as it no more served as an important river port. Today the 20,000 inhabitants grow cattle and tobacco, and enjoy a special charm and tranquility.

There are regular flights from Cartagena and Barranquilla to Mompós. Otherwise, you need to take a bus either from Cartagena or from Barranquilla (both about 4 hours) to the town of Magangué, and from there by boat (2 hours) to Mompós. The town offers several inexpensive hotels, the best of which (also most expensive) is the *Hostal Doña Manuela*, a colonial house from the 18th century.

Barranquilla

On the west bank of Rio Magdalena, several km from the river's mouth, is Barranquilla. The city began as a small rural settlement populated first by livestock breeders and later by fishermen. Over time, however, it has become a large industrial center and Colombia's largest and most important port. Of its population of approximately 1,250,000, most are employed in the sophisticated industries typical of a modern, progressive city.

Barranquilla is no tourist attraction, but as a major sea and air port it is the place most tourists reach first when approaching Colombia from the north.

Once a year the city shakes off the humdrum of its daily existence for **Carnaval Joselito**, a 4-day festival held in January. Everyone in town — together with throngs from the entire Caribbean coastal area and even inland — pours into the street in fancy dress to watch the parades, and to dance and sing to the local music. Hence a nickname that has stuck to Barranquilla — *La Ciudad Loca* ("Crazy City").

How to get there
Cortizzos International Airport is a modern, spacious facility about 10 km out of town; local buses, airport buses and taxis serve the airport. Air service to and from Cortizzos is available from all Colombia's main cities, as well as from Mexico City and Caracas.

Ships from all over the world dock at Barranquilla's huge port. Tourists wishing to head north by sea have a variety of options (to sail for Panama, however, it is best to embark from Cartagena). If you brought a car on board, be prepared to spend up to two days clearing through red tape.

Regular bus service links Barranquilla with Santa-Marta (about a 2-hour journey) and Cartagena (about 3 hours). It's about 16 hours to Medellín, and approximately 20 to Bogotá. Direct buses also set out for Maicao, on the Venezuelan border.

Food and lodging
El Prado: Transversal 7, 101-07, Tel. 218-1798, Fax. 256-9773. The best in town, though a bit far from downtown, it is also the place for locals to be seen, to be "in"; fairly expensive.
Cadebia: Calle 75, 41D-79, Tel. 45-6144. Swimming pool, sauna, casino and moderate prices.
Caribana: Carrera 41, 40-02, Tel. 41-4277. Modest, good service.
Majestic: Carrera 53, 54-41, Tel. 32-0152. Far from center, but recommended.
Zhivago: On Plaza Bolívar. For those on a low budget, very basic.

Keep in mind that hotel rates skyrocket at carnival time, and rooms are hard to get.

In Barranquilla you will find decent meals downtown, around

Plaza Bolívar, and at the Altos del Prado more expensive ones. Apart from the Local dishes you can find some Oriental, Chinese and Italian restauarants.

Tourist services
The **Tourist Office** has a main desk at Calle 72, 57-43. *CNT* has a branch at Carrera 54, 75-45.

Various countries have consulates in Barranquilla, including the United States (Calle 77, 68-15, the mall opposite the zoo garden) and the British (Carrera 44, 45-57).

Tourist sites
Barranquilla is not exactly a major tourist attraction, but there are some things worth seeing. The main street, **Paseo Bolívar**, is a pedestrian mall, and the city's shopping district is along Calle 72. Plaza San Nicolás is graced with a beautiful church which is guarded by a statue of Columbus. An attractive, colorful market is held daily along a channel of the Río Magdalena known as the Caño de las Campañas. **Parque 11 de Noviembre** and the port area are pleasant to visit. The port was originally intended to serve river barges plying the Magdalena. Over time, the need arose for a large sea port and the harbor was deepened and widened. Today it serves enormous ocean-going vessels.

Barranquilla's residential quarters are in the hilly area north of downtown. One of them, **Alto del Prado**, still retains the town's original architecture.

During the annual 4-day carnival, each neighborhood organizes its own parades and celebrations, so there is no shortage of amusement. Nightclubs provide a variety of evening entertainment and dances, and it is advisable to inquire as to the current year's favorite.

On to Santa Marta
The coastal road heads east from Barranquilla, crosses a bridge over the Río Magdalena, and continues through marshland rich in marine vegetation, birds, and wildlife. The route passes through the town of **Ciénaga** (pop. 80,000) and its backdrop of cotton, banana and cocoa farms. Another 100 km brings us to Santa Marta.

Santa Marta
Santa Marta, Colombia's first city, was established in 1525 by Rodrigo de Bastidas. It was the territory of the *Tairona* Indians, a tribe famous for its gold handicrafts. In the 16th and 17th centuries, the city became a center of the pearl industry and

Santa Marta

repeatedly suffered attacks by pirates, notwithstanding the two fortresses on the island off shore. Simón Bolívar spent his last days here.

Today, Santa Marta (pop. 300,000) is the capital of Magdalena province. Its scenery includes the deep harbor, the snowy peaks of the Sierra Nevada de Santa Marta in the distance, and beautiful "sandscapes" on the road from the airport to El Rodadero Beach. These make Santa Marta a popular resort for lovers of sea and sun.

How to get there
Simón Bolívar Airport, some 20 km from the city, has flights to and from all of Colombia's major cities.

An express passenger train with only one class (the *Tairona*) makes the 24 hour trip from Bogotá to Santa Marta once a week during the dry season only. The rest of the year there is a train twice a week between Santa Marta to La Dorada, and from there you can follow by bus to the capital.

The bus terminal is at Calle 24 on Carrera 8. Service to Barranquilla, Cartagena and Riohacha is frequent. The road south to Bucaramanga is long and difficult; from Bucaramanga, however, there is frequent bus service to Bogotá. Buses also leave Santa Marta for the Venezuelan border and Maracaibo.

Food and lodging
There are two hotel districts: Rodero Beach, for the luxury, and in town.

Irotama: Kilometer 14 on the road Santa Marta-Barranquilla, Tel. 23-7140, Fax 23-2961, reservations can be made in Bogotá, Tel. 217-4311. Good service, a beautiful private beach and one of the highest fares in the country.
Yuldama: Carrera 1, 12-19, Tel. 23-2479. Moderate prices, good location in town.
Miramar: Carrera 1, 18-23, Tel. 23-7238. Well situated, near the beach and the train station, clean, safe and inexpensive, recommended.

Santa Marta has plenty of good restaurants, most specializing in seafood. Like the hotels, the restaurants at Rodadero are more expensive than those in town.

The **Tourist Office** is at Carrera 2, No. 16-44.

Tourist sites
Avenida Bastidas is the long thoroughfare along the shore, with well-tended gardens alongside the beaches. **Punta de Betín,** the bluff that closes off Santa Marta Bay, affords an excellent view of the city.

The **Customs House** (*Casa de la Aduana*) in Parque Bolívar presently houses a branch of Banco de la República's **Gold Museum**. Its rich collection of archaeological findings includes gold handcrafts discovered in the Parque Tairona and Sierra Nevada area. Open Tues.-Sun. during tourist season and Mon.-Fri. the rest of the year.

About 15 km from downtown is **El Rodadero Beach**, tourist country. The best hotels, restaurants, and shops are situated here, as is the best of local nightlife. The nearby **Aquarium** has interesting specimens of the underwater life of the Caribbean coast.

Another museum worth visiting is the **Hacienda de San Pedro Alejandrino**, a colonial estate about 5 km southeast of the city. Here Simón Bolívar spent his last weary, destitute days, before he died at the age of 47. Though he was buried in Santa Marta, his remains were later reinterred in the Pantheon in Caracas, Venezuela. The estate is surrounded by beautiful, well kept gardens, and the house still contains some of Bolívar's personal effects. Open Tues.-Sat., 1:30-8pm; buses to the hacienda leave from Carrera 1 quite often for a ten minutes ride.

Parque Tairona

About 35 km northeast of Santa Marta, along the slopes of the Sierra Nevada de Santa Marta, is Parque Tairona, named for the Indians who predated the Spaniards in Colombia. The scenery is gorgeous — golden beaches, abundant tropical flora, five enchanting lagoons and indented coastlines. There is also an archaeological site in the area: a former Tairona village called *Pueblito*.

There are several ways to visit the park, including an organized tour that lasts a few hours, or a trip by taxi. Hikers with plenty of time can take a bus to the park entrance, walk the 5 km or so to the park's major beach — Cañaveral — and spend the night at its parking area. The beaches and the lovely lagoons are just right for a leisurely stroll or a lazy afternoon in a hammock.

Note: The thieves find this area attractive, too. Do not walk around alone, and try to sleep only in official campgrounds.

Sierra Nevada de Santa Marta

This great mountain range plunges into the Caribbean from a height of 5775 m, over a distance of only 50 km as the crow flies! The lower slopes, covered with tropical flora, are the habitat of natural wildlife and the home of Indians who retain and live by their cultural heritage. Higher up, the slopes become rocky and icy, and the peaks are snow capped.

Taking the mountains of Santa Marta on foot is an arduous and complicated venture. One way to do so is to travel to Valledupar via Riohacha, where jeeps continue to the Indian village of Pueblo Bello.

Ciudad Perdida

One of Colombia's most interesting and important archaeological sites is the "Lost City" (Ciudad Perdida), which was discovered in the depth of the mountain forest only in the 1970's.

The site, covering some 2 km^2, stands on the northern slopes of Sierra Nevada. It was the center of the Tairona civilization since the 8th-9th century, and most of the remains are large terraces which enabled the construction of the stone houses despite the steep slopes, and interconnecting steps and paths.

In order to reach this isolated site the only transportation is helicopter. Adventurous travellers can hike — a trip that takes one week. Ask for details at Santa Marta's Tourist Office.

Riohacha

The capital of the Guajira district, Riohacha (pop. app. 90,000), is 160 km east of Santa Marta. Founded in 1545 by Nicolas Federmann at the mouth of the Río César, the city first flourished because of its pearl industry — which motivated Sir Francis Drake to attack the city in 1596.

Today's main industry in Riohacha is smuggling. Thus it is no surprise that the locals are not too friendly to strangers.

Riohacha is the place of origin of the legendary Macondo, about whom the celebrated Colombian author, Gabriel García Márquez, wrote in his famous book *One Hundred Years of Solitude.*

The **Indian market** held every day in Riohacha is well worth visiting. The main highway out of Riohacha leads straight to Venezuela. Before leaving, however, it is worth visiting the **Guajira Peninsula**. This is an arid zone, sparsely populated by *Guajiro* Indians who fish and raise sheep for a living. To get there, find a place in the car that sets out twice a day for Manaure from the Riohacha Indian market. The trip lasts about 3 hours. Occasionally someone with a car continues on to Cabo de la Vela, with its marvelous, untouched beaches, and lagoons with flocks of flamingos. From Manaure, one can reach Maicao via Uribia.

On to Venezuela

The Colombian border town of **Maicao** is the capital of the smuggling industry between Colombia and Venezuela, and much of the trade involves drugs. It's obviously a dangerous place. **Do not linger here!** Proceed straight to the nearest large town in Venezuela, Maracaibo.

If you need an entry permit, try to obtain one in your country of origin, or failing that, in Bogotá. The Venezuelan Consulate in Riohacha (9-85 Calle 3) is slow.

There are flights to Maicao from Barranquilla, and buses to Maicao from all cities along the Caribbean coast.

Darién Gap

Colombia and Panama are linked by a marshy, sparsely populated, and completely undeveloped strip of land. Nearly half of eastern Panama consists of such territory, and is known as the Darién Gap. The region has no land transport, and the few Indian villages are reached only by air, boat, or foot. The area has therefore become something of a challenge for an

The Cuna Indians — Darién Gap

ever growing number of adventurers. The trek takes from one week to two, and it costs more than the airfare from Colombia to Panama. The amount the Indians charge for their various services, increases in relation to the number of travelers who need them, with a corresponding decrease in the friendliness.

Special guidelines
The trip is easiest to take during the dry season, between mid-December and mid-April; the paths are not marshy then, and the mosquitos are scarcer. Nevertheless, bring mosquito-repellent ointment, a mosquito net, chlorine tablets for water, and malaria pills. Pack enough food for at least 5 days (although one can usually find some along the way).

Do not overpack. Bear in mind that everything has to be carried and borne, along with the heat, humidity, and mosquitos. Unnecessary equipment can be mailed to the next station en route. Send everything by air mail only, and use the postal services only between major towns. Remember, too, that a return flight ticket must be presented to the Panamanian immigration authorities in order to get an entry permit for the country.

There are several options and routes to cross the Darién Gap — along the Pacific Ocean, along the Caribbean coast and then in land by canoe and walk. The one we chose to describe below is a third one — the most interesting, although the longest and most complicated.

The route

The route begins at the port town of **Turbo**, on the coast of Urabá Bay. Daily buses reach Turbo from Medellín (about 15 hours away) and Cartagena. Turbo has several hotels; banks are closed on Mondays and Tuesdays, and travelers' checks cannot be cashed. Be sure, too, to stop at the *DAS* office for an exit stamp from Colombia, since this is the last Colombian immigration office on the route.

Further progress is made by cargo boat, canoe and on foot. The route traverses remote areas and interesting Indian villages. The Indians in several of them greet visitors warmly and may even offer you hospitality for a few days. The *Choco* Indians, who live along the last stretch of the route, are noted for their hearty hospitality. On the first part of the tour, you will get to know the *Cuna* Indians, survivors of a superbly constituted pre-Columbian empire which dominated all of Panama.

Entry stamps to Panama are obtained in the village of Boca de Cupe. The route ends in the town of **Yaviza**, from where a daily bus leaves for Panama City.

For further details, see *Backpacking in Mexico and Central America*, by Hilary Bradt and Rob Rachowiecki.

San Andrés Island

This enchanting Caribbean island has a lot to offer: white beaches, palms, clear water, sun all year round, places to dive, and reggae music. The island, 3 km wide and 14 km long, was discovered in 1527 by Spanish navigators on the eve of the Festival of San Andrés, whence its name. Since 1827, the island, like its neighbor Providencia, has belonged to Colombia. Most of the local population, some 50,000, are black.

San Andrés Island is a duty-free zone, so it is usually packed with Colombians combining a vacation with a shopping spree on imported goods.

How to get there

By sea: Cruise ships make the 3-day cruise from Cartagena twice a month; ships from Colón, Panama, make the trip in 48 hours.

By air: *Avianca, Sam, Sahsa,* and *Satena* airlines fly to and from San Andrés and all major Colombian cities. There are international flights to San Andrés from Miami, Guatemala, Costa Rica and Panama.

Fleets of taxis wait at the airport to take travelers into town. The fare is fixed, and the rates are on display at the airport tourist office. Make sure you are not being overcharged. The airport is a walking distance from town.

Food and lodging

Cacique Toné: Av. Colombia, Tel. 24-251, excellent establishment, air conditioned rooms, a fine restaurant and a beautiful view of the Caribbean.

Abacoa: Av. Colombia, Tel. 24-133, with a sea-front.

Bahia Sardinas: Av. Colombia 4-24, Tel. 23-793. High standards, slightly less expensive than the formers.

Capri: Av. Costa Rica 1A-105, Tel. 24-315. The same standard and prices as *Bahia Sardinas.*

Las Antillas: Av. 20 de Julio 1A-81. Medium prices.

Residencia Restrepo: Near the airport on Av. 8. For truly tight budgets, noisy, but clean and safe.

The characteristic cuisine here, of course, is seafood. An excellent local dish is crab soup (*sopa de congrejo*).

Local women set up stands along Av. La Playa in the evenings; the selection of local home-made dishes they offer is well worth trying.

Tourist services

The main **Tourist Office** is on Av. Colombia 5-117, with a branch at the airport.

Currency exchange: Obtain local currency at *Banco de la República.* Open Mon.-Fri. 8am-1pm.

Car Rental: Rental cars are available for 2 hours or more at the *Abacoa Hotel* (on Av. Colombia), Tel. 25-6950. A pleasant alternative is a bicycle, which can be rented at the seashore.

White sand and clear water of the Caribbean islands

Tourist sites

As the capital of a duty-free zone, the town of San Andrés has become a noisy and drab shopping center packed with Colombians on their shopping sprees. Av. La Playa, parallel to the beach, is lined with hotels, restaurants and bars. Concerts of local reggae music have become popular. The beaches, too, are crowded — and not particularly clean.

From a vantage point on the beach, a tiny island crowned with palm trees comes into view. Known as **Johnny Key**, it can be reached by a motorboat which sets out from the beach opposite the *Abacoa Hotel*. Johnny Key is an enchanting spot: white, pristine sand, clear, clean water, and leafy palms which provide shade from the burning sun. In the center of this tiny island is an outdoor bar. The ambience is young and friendly, and the bar turns into an instant discotheque as the music moves the vacationers.

Motorboats setting out from the same place on the San Andrés beach drop anchor at **Aquarium**, another tiny island. This is a diver's spot, where the marvels of underwater life come into view. Other lovely beaches are yours at San Luis and nearby

Bahía Sonora. At *Hoyo Soplador*, the pounding of waves against the face of a cliff has created subterranean tunnels. The end of the tunnel has openings where the water bursts out. When the wind is blowing in the right direction, the place looks like a geyser field.

Shopping

Coral ornaments are the most typical of local handicrafts. Shops stock a variety of imported goods: photo and electronic equipment, decorative items and fabrics. Though the prices are low in South American terms, they are lower still, naturally, in Western countries.

Providencia

This little, hilly island (17 km^2; pop. 4000) lies about 70 km north of San Andrés and is linked to it by daily flights and irregular boat trips. Again, the beaches are breath-taking, the water clean and clear, and there are a variety of marine sports to enjoy. Providencia is much less "touristy" than San Andrés. The locals make use of the fertile soil for cultivating crops, especially fruit. The island offers a few campgrounds and several simple hotels, among them the *Cabañas El Paraíso* (Tel. 48-036), the *Cabañas Antiqua Mar* (Tel. and Fax 48-181) and the *Royal Queen* (Tel. 48-138).

The Cordillera Central

The Cordillera Central range is flanked by the Rio Cauca on the west and Rio Magdalena on the east. This is Colombia's most developed region, both highly industrialized, containing two of Colombia's largest cities, and a fertile agricultural zone.

Before the arrival of the Spanish conquerors, the area was inhabited by Indians who practiced subsistence agriculture and mined silver and gold.

The Spanish arrived in 1539, and two years later they founded the city of Antioquia. At the beginning of the 17th century, a wave of Spanish immigrants founded the city of Medellín. Strongly opposed to slavery, they refused to use black or Indian labor. Their lands were therefore divided into small farms, which each family worked individually. Besides farming, the immigrants mined gold for export.

Later, during the second half of the 19th century, the settlers started growing coffee. By the beginning of the 20th century coffee production had begun to play an important role in the economy of the Antioquia and Caldas provinces. Today these regions supply about half of Colombia's total coffee production. The success of the coffee industry led to rapid economic development and the establishment of other industries, particularly textiles.

Medellín

Medellín, the capital of Antioquia province, is Colombia's second largest city, with a population of approximately two million. The city lies in a valley, 1540 m above sea level, and is surrounded by lofty mountain peaks. The weather is springlike year round, but there is a certain industrial haze in the air.

Medellín was founded in 1616 by European immigrants. The old colonial structures have almost entirely disappeared, replaced by modern buildings. Only a few churches remain from days gone by. The city has become an important industrial center: about 80% of the Colombian textile industry is concentrated here, and this accounts for only half of the total local industrial production! The climate lends itself to horticulture, and Medellín is one of the world's orchid-growing centers. There are four large universities, and other institutes of higher education as well. Medellín's citizens are justifiably proud of their town, nevertheless you should keep in mind that this is the epicenter of drugs-related violence in the country.

How to get there

Medellín's international airport operates only by day, since the mountainous terrain makes it dangerous to land or take off by night. Numerous daily flights link the city to Bogotá — a 45-minute flight. There are also scheduled flights to all of Colombia's other main cities. The *Copa* company flies to Panama several times a week, as does *Sam*.

The train runs from Medellín to Barrancabermeja. Those wishing to reach the Caribbean coast can pick up the Bogotá-Santa Marta train at Puerto Berrío. If you reach Medellín by rail late at night, you might decide to spend the night in nearby Barbosa, at one of the two modest hotels in the central plaza; trains are available only during the dry season.

The *Flota Magdalena* company operates an efficient bus service between Bogotá and Medellín. There are several buses a day; the trip takes about 12 hours. There is a very frequent bus service to Cali (a 12-hour ride) and likewise to Manizales (a 7-hour ride).

The *Brasilia* and *Pullman Ocha* companies run buses to Cartagena. The second company is slightly more expensive, but its buses are also faster and more comfortable. The trip to Cartagena takes 14 hours.

Note: All the bus company offices are located in the Caribe quarter — a very dangerous area. Avoid lingering there, especially if you have luggage with you. Take a taxi to the bus station of the company you will be traveling with.

Food and lodging

Intercontinental Medellín: Calle 16, 28-51 (Variante Las Palmas), Tel. 266-0680. Excellent service, high prices; far from downtown.
Amarú: Carrera 50A 53-45, Tel. 231-1155. Also top-prices and service, well located.
Veracruz: Carrera 50, 54-18, Tel. 231-5511. Slightly less expensive, with swimming pool.
Horizonte: Carrera 47, 49-24. Central, medium prices, good restaurants.
Doris: Carrera 45, 46-23. Inexpensive, clean.

Medellín also has its share of good restaurants. We will mention just a few: *La Posada de la Montaña* offers exquisite local fare, in a beautiful colonial-style building, surrounded by gardens with a fountain. The place is expensive, and rather far from downtown. Meat lovers should definitely try *La Res*. An excellent, if somewhat expensive, French restaurant is *La Bella Epoca*.

Tourist services
The main **Tourist Office** is at Calle 54, 46-66; there is a branch office at the airport.

Currency exchange: Money can be changed at the *Banco de la República*, whose main branch is at Calle 50, 21-51 .

Car rental: *Hertz* has an office at Carrera 43A, 23-50 and another office at the airport.

Telephone: The *Telecom* office is at Calle 49, 49-73.

Tourist sites
Although Medellín is a busy industrial town, its spacious avenues, green parks, quiet residential neighborhoods, and cleanliness belie its industrial nature. The buildings are modern, especially downtown; ancient monuments are virtually nonexistent. Only a few old churches have escaped the relentless march of progress. The oldest is the **Church of San José**, built in 1646, at the corner of Calle 49 and Carrera 46. The **Catedral Metropolitana,** at the corner of Carrera 48 and Calle 56, is one of the world's largest brick buildings. The cathedral's impressive steps lead down to **Parque Bolívar**, with its statue of the Liberator. A market — known as the **Mercado San Alejo** — is held here on the first Saturday of each month when craftsmen sell their wares.

Medellín has been the home of many of Colombia's famous artists, as can be seen by the numerous statues and fountains that adorn the city. The most famous of the city's sculptures — Rodrigo Betancur's *La Fuente de la Vida* (Fountain of Life) — stands opposite the Centro Residencial Sudamericana Building.

Medellín has a fair selection of museums. The **Museum of Anthropology**, located on the new campus of Antioquia University, has a collection of pre-Columbian pottery. Open Mon.-Fri., 10am-12 noon and 2pm-6pm. Closed on Sat. and Sun. The **Museo de Zea**, at the corner of Calle 52 and Carrera 53, has an important collection of the works of contemporary Colombian artists. Open Tues.-Sat., 9am-1pm and 3pm-6pm. **El Castillo**, in the El Poblado quarter, was formerly the residence of one of the town's wealthy notables. Today its imposing rooms house art objects from all over the world. Chamber music concerts are sometimes held here. Open Mon.-Sat., 1pm-5pm. Closed Sun. The **Museum of Modern Art** is at 51-64 Carrera 64B. Stamp collectors will be interested in the **Museo Filatélico**, in

In Honda

the Banco de la República Building. It has a large collection of Colombian stamps, as well as from other countries.

The beautifully tended **Joaquín Antonio Uribe Botanical Gardens**, near the new campus of Antioquia University, are well worth a visit. The gardens, which are open daily between 9am-5.30pm, have a rich collection of flora. South of the city, the **Santa Fe Zoo** has a collection of South American animals and birds.

Shopping
Most of Medellín's business and commercial life is concentrated downtown. Several roads have been closed to traffic and converted into shopping malls, with shops and boutiques selling various goods of very high quality and price. The town also has several modern shopping centers; the largest is the Almacentro.

Locally produced textile and leather goods are especially inexpensive. Silver products are less costly here than in the rest of Colombia.

The Medellín vicinity
Santa Fe de Antioquia, north-east of Medellín, was founded in 1541 by Spanish gold miners. Until 1826, when Medellín assumed this coveted position, it was the capital of the

Antioquia province. The city's colonial character and unflurried atmosphere survive together with its cobbled streets. Of special interest are the Catedral Basílica and the Church of Santa Barbara. The City Hall building (*Palacio Municipal*) was the seat of the colonial government during Spanish rule. The road to Santa Fe crosses the Rio Cauca over a wide bridge that is 350 m long.

The trip from Medellín to Santa Fe takes about 2½ hours. The town has two hotels.

There are several places worth visiting east of Medellín. The area is pastoral and picturesque, dotted with villages and hamlets that still preserve their ancient lifestyle. The road from Medellín to El Retiro passes by the **Hacienda Fizebad**, an old estate whose interior has been preserved exactly as it was two hundred years ago. Its beautiful gardens feature a marvelous display of orchids.

The town of **Rionegro**, named after the river on whose banks it lies, was founded in 1663. Rionegro was the birthplace of José María Córdoba, one of Bolívar's generals, and a hero of the War of Independence. The town has a monument to his memory, and the local bank preserves the triumphal crown bestowed on him after the Battle of Ayacucho.

The surrounding villages are famous for their ceramic and leather products. Most of the work is done by hand — sophisticated technology is almost unknown here. Two villages of special interest are **La Ceja** and **Carmen de Viboral**. The inhabitants of both villages are used to tourists, so don't expect to find any bargains. The road to La Ceja passes near the **Tequendamita Falls**. We recommend a stop at the *Parador Tequendamita* restaurant, near the falls. The little town of **Marinilla** should be visited for its cathedral, its Town Hall, its museum, and the Church of Jesus Nazareno. A little further on is **El Peñol**, famous for the nearby bluff — 200 m high!

Manizales

This town, the capital of Caldas province, was founded in 1848. The area is known as the "Coffee Zone" (*La Region Cafetera*), since about 30% of Colombia's coffee crop is grown here. Manizales was twice the victim of huge fires. Today its multistorey buildings are constructed of modern, fireproof materials. Textile and leather industries provide employment for Manizales' half a million inhabitants.

The city lies 2153 m above sea level, and has a very humid climate. The average temperature is 17°C (63°F). Rainfall is plentiful. The most pleasant season begins in mid-December and continues until March. January is the month of the traditional coffee carnival, with its parades, folk dancing, and bullfights.

How to get there

The local airline *Aces* provides good service from Manizales' small airport to Bogotá, Medellín, and other major cities. An alternative is to fly *Avianca* to Pereira in the Cauca valley, and then travel the remaining 50 km along an excellent road that passes by breathtaking scenery. Good bus service links the town to Bogotá (a 9-hour trip), Cali, Medellín and Pereira. Local roads are good, and the scenery spectacular.

Tourist sites

The most famous building in the city is the modern **Teatro de los Fundadores**, which supposedly has the largest stage in all of Latin America. There is also a large Gothic style unfinished cathedral. The **Museum of Gold,** located in the *Banco de la República*, has a display of locally discovered gold artifacts. The **Museum of Anthropology** has an interesting collection of pre-Columbian finds, discovered near Mt. El Ruiz (Nevado El Ruiz). The museum offers a fantastic view of the mountain.

The El Ruiz volcano erupted in November 1985, causing heavy casualties. The immediate effect of the explosion caused the snow to melt on the volcano's peak, resulting in floods which carried away entire villages with their inhabitants. The town of Armero was particularly hard-hit. About 25,000 people lost their lives in the disaster. Massive international assistance helped save and rehabilitate thousands of victims.

Honda

Half way from Manizales to Bogota is the colonial town of Honda. Only 40,000 people live in this town today, but thanks to its important location on the west banks of rio Magdalena, it was in times one of the most important Colombian towns. Many old colonial houses have survived in Honda, and its streets are narrow and pleasant. It is considered a good place for fishing, and many locals make their living on the river.

If you are traveling by bus from Manizales to Bogota (or vice versa), Honda is a good break in the long ride. There are frequent buses to Bogota (4 hours) and Manizales (4-5 hours).

Southwest Colombia

Southwest Colombia is an enchanting area, one that combines the natural beauty of fertile mountain ranges with varied and interesting man-made attractions. The Andes divide here into three sections, and the scenery keeps changing as you travel east: from the temperate plains of the Pacific coast, across high, verdant mountains with snow capped peaks and volcanos, to the hot and humid tropical jungle in the east.

The terrain makes many areas isolated and difficult to reach. This inaccessibility is exploited by guerrilla fighters, as well as coca growers and cocaine smugglers. Consequently, the army is deployed in greater numbers here — especially in the towns and along roads — than anywhere else in Colombia. Roadblocks and thorough searches are extremely common. Be patient during such searches, and obey the soldiers' instructions.

This chapter surveys various places along the Cauca Valley, occasionally branching off the north-south axis to outlying areas. Most travelers, in fact, use this axis as their baseline. The area is full of beautiful landscapes and places of interest.

Cali

Belalcázar, one of Francisco Pizarro's officers, founded Cali in 1537, in the Cauca Valley. During its first years, Cali experienced numerous Indian attacks, prompting the eventual removal of the entire town to its present location. It was only at the beginning of this century that Cali changed from a small provincial town into an important and modern one — the agricultural, industrial, and cultural center of the Cauca Valley. This revolution, once begun, continued at an amazing pace. Today Cali is Colombia's third largest city, with some 1,700,000 inhabitants.

The city enjoys a pleasant climate: eternal summer, with rainfall year round. The inhabitants are very friendly; the beauty of Cali women (*Caleñas*) is legendary. This combination of human and climatic factors makes Cali a pleasant place to visit, although it lacks places of particular interest.

Note that violence is rampant in the poorer neighborhoods, therefore avoid outlying areas, and stick to the center of town.

The Tourist Office, Calle 12N, 3N-28, provides information on dangerous areas.

SOUTHWEST COLOMBIA

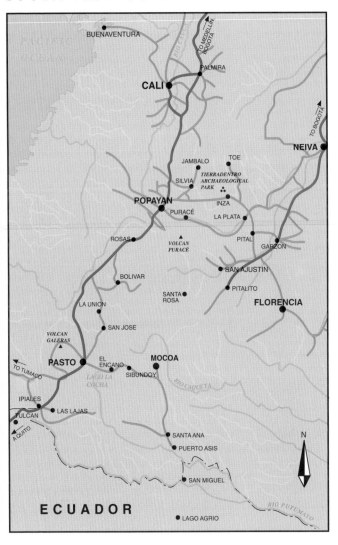

Transportation

There are a number of flights each day from Bogotá and other large Colombian cities to the international airport of Palmaseco, near Cali. The *Avianca* office in Cali is situated at Carrera 7, 13-52. The *Satena* airline office is on the same street, at 8-20.

Cali's modern and spacious bus terminal is situated near the center of town. Frequent bus service links the city with Bogotá (a 10-hour trip). The *Expreso Bolivariano* is recommended. It also runs buses to the south — to Popayán (3 hours) and Pasto (10 hours). Other companies run buses on these routes daily. The *Empresa Arauca* runs buses to Medellín. All these roads are good, paved roads, and the buses are fairly modern and comfortable.

Food and lodging

Intercontinental: Carrera 1 (Av. Colombia) 2-72, Tel. 82-3225, Fax 82-2567. Close to the center, super-first-class, good restaurant.

Don Jaime: Av. 6N, 15N-25, Tel. 67-2828. Quite expensive, but recommended; excellent location — in the heart of Cali's shopping and entertainment district.

Apartahotel El Peñon: Calle 1, 2-16, Tel. 83-4444. A very good deal.

La Merced: Calle 7, 1-65. Medium price, good service.

Miami: Carrera 7, 13-57. Good basic hotel, good location.

The famous Avenida 6 has a number of restaurants, most of them both good and expensive, although it is possible to find some cheaper ones. For a good meal with a beautiful view, try *La Torre de Cali* on Calle 18N. The restaurant, which features international cuisine, is located on the 41st floor of the tower. Expensive.

Night life

Unlike other Colombian towns, which are generally closed as soon as the working day is over, Cali has a flourishing night life. In Avenida Sexta (Sixth Avenue) there is activity all night long. There are two modern comfortable cinemas, an abundance of restaurants, coffee shops and bars. In the streets near this avenue you will find exclusive restaurants and nightclubs. The nightclubs in Cali are called *Griles*. The Juanchito quarter is another center for night life. Here there are many discotheques, which are packed over the weekends, playing popular *Salsa* music as well as Western music.

Tourist sites

The **Plaza de Caicedo**, a green square with numerous palm

trees, lies in the heart of the business district. On its western side stands the *Banco de la República*, the first modern building erected in Cali.

Two blocks away is the Río Cali, bordered by the tree-lined Avenida Colombia. Beware of thieves in the area! On that street, at No. 5 West-105, is the **Museum of Modern Art**, which has seasonal exhibits. The municipal cinematheque is next to it.

Also worth visiting is the **Archaeological Museum**, whose modest collection of ceramics offers a chronological survey of pre-Columbian civilizations. The museum is situated on Carrera 5, between Calles 8 and 9. Open Tues.-Sat., 9am-12:30pm and 2-6pm. Closed Sundays and Mondays. Nearby is the Museum of Religious Art, **La Merced**.

Not far from Plaza de Caycedo, near the river, stands the ornate Gothic church, **La Hermita.** Looking east from this church, you will see a 43-story skyscraper, the **Torre de Cali** (Cali Tower). There is an observation deck on the top of this building, which is the tallest building in town.

The town's modern shopping and entertainment district runs along the **Avenida Sexta**, on the other side of the Rio Cali. The avenue has numerous boutiques and luxury shops, cafes, restaurants, and two movie houses. Mingle with the pedestrians during evening hours, or sit in one of the many cafes and feast your eyes on the town's beautiful women.

Buenaventura

This town lies some 130 km west of Cali. It is Colombia's most important Pacific port, with a hot and humid climate. It has no particular attractions, apart from a number of attractive beaches. (Be on the look out for thieves!). This is a duty-free zone.

Popayán

This town predates the arrival of the Spanish conquerors, and owes its name to a local Indian ruler. The Spanish town was founded by Belalcázar in 1537. Over the years the town grew and prospered, largely due to its role as a link between the northern and southern parts of the "New World". It also became a center for the gold, silver, and other metals that were mined in the area. Although an important cultural center today, Popayán preserves its pleasant and modest character.

In March 1983, a considerable portion of the town was destroyed by an earthquake. The town's 250,000 residents embarked on a campaign to restore and renovate many of the ancient buildings that had been damaged. Thanks to widespread international assistance, new attractive residential neighborhoods were built

Cali — La Hermita

around the town to accommodate the many citizens left homeless by the earthquake.

Each year, the city holds celebrations during Holy Week (*Semana Santa*) before Easter. This festival, a 400 year old tradition, includes the festival of religious music, which fills Popayán's churches with enthusiastic audiences.

Transportation
A new and spacious bus terminal has been erected within walking distance of downtown. Buses leave for Cali every 20 minutes; the trip takes about 2 hours. There is also regular bus service to Pasto, about 8 hours' ride away. The small airport,

near the bus terminal, serves scheduled flights from Bogotá, Cali and Pasto.

There is a daily bus to San Agustín from the bus terminal. This trip, which passes Parque Puracé and the village of La Plata, takes about 11 hours. Jeeps for La Plata leave from the avenue near the terminal. These take a difficult, tortuous route, but the journey takes only 5 hours. Both routes cross the *Cordillera Central*, so take warm clothes.

Tourist services
The municipal **Tourist Office** at Carrera 6, 3-69, provides good service and up-to-date information.

There is a *Telecom* office at the corner of Calle 4 and Carrera 4. Putting through an international call involves a lengthy wait.

Food and lodging
Hotel Monasterio: Calle 4, 10-50, Tel. 22-191. Formerly a Franciscan monastery — whence the name; a good hotel with a swimming pool, fairly expensive.
Hostal Camino Real: Calle 5, 5-59, Tel. 21-546. Good with a fine restaurant, recommended, medium-priced
Residencias El Viajero: Calle 8, 4-45, Tel. 23-069. Low price, clean rooms and a friendly atmosphere, recommended.

Good meals can be found along the central parts of the main streets, and also across the bridge on Carrera 6.

Tourist sites
Although Popayán is a bustling center for the Cauca Valley, one would never know it from its slow, peaceful atmosphere. The locals are friendly, and the narrow downtown streets are not jammed with traffic. The pleasant weather throughout the year, with an average temperature of 18°C (64°F), contributes significantly to this ambience.

Downtown, around the central plaza, you can still see the ravages caused by the 1983 earthquake. Not all the damage has been repaired, and some of the ancient buildings are still surrounded by scaffolding. The modern *Banco de la República* stands out from most other buildings in the area, which were built in the colonial style. At the beginning of Calle 6, near the central bank, is Río Molino, spanned by a bridge that dates back to 1868. The bridge, known as *Puente del Humilladero*, is built on eleven stone arches, and is about 250 m long.

Silvia
For centuries, the Cordillera Central was the home of various

Indian tribes. The only tribe to preserve its traditions is the *Guambianos*. They are dispersed among several villages in the mountains northeast of Popayán.

The friendly *Guambianos* are peaceful farmers who live in a communal society based on cooperation in work and production. They preserve their language and dress: the men wear long blue skirts, and the women wrap themselves in a sari-like dress of the same material. The women wear an impressive amount of jewelry around their necks, like the Indians of northern Ecuador. Both sexes wear identical hats and have similar hairstyles, except that the women's hair is slightly longer.

On Tuesdays, the *Guambianos* gather in their main village, Silvia, situated in the valley, between the green mountains. They travel in vans laden to bursting point, in order to sell their produce — mainly potatoes of various kinds. Their handicrafts are quite similar to those of the Otavalos of Ecuador. At their colorful market you can see the *Guambianos* in their traditional costume. Eavesdrop on their conversation and catch snatches of their ancient Guambiano tongue. The market opens at dawn, and closes at 1pm.

Behind the vegetable and handicrafts market is the smaller livestock market. This market is run by the men, whereas at the other market women are in charge. You can see them discussing at length the value of a cow or pig.

Those with strong stomachs should not miss tasting the excellent *empanadas*. After enjoying the market, its smells and colours, take a short walk in the town and its outskirts.

The village outskirts make a pleasant contrast to the sights, sounds, and smells of the market. The road to the village of Guambia meanders through captivating scenery. After a short distance you will come across villagers working in the fields.

Try to reach Silvia as early as possible on market day. You may spend the night at one of its modest hotels. Those who stay the night in Popayán can take the 6am bus to Piendamó (it takes about half an hour). Plenty of jeeps travel the lovely and verdant road to Silvia, which is only another half an hour away. A direct bus from Popayán to Silvia leaves every Tuesday (market day) at 11am from the bus terminal.

To proceed to Tierradentro, take the bus which leaves Silvia for Totoró at noon on market days. Catch the Popayán-La Plata bus at Totoró (see "Tierradentro — Transportation").

Parque Puracé

The road from Popayán to Tierradentro and Neiva passes

through *Parque Puracé*. This park stretches over the highest section of the Cordillera Central. The view is breathtaking: rivers, cliffs, large waterfalls, snow capped volcanos, and hot sulfur springs.

The 7am Popayán-La Plata bus passes through the park. Detailed information on recommended sites are available in Pilimbala, although it's better to obtain this information at the tourist office in Popayán.

To brave the snow capped peaks of the **Purace Volcano**, take the 4am Popayán-La Plata bus and get off at Pilimbala. Note the stone pools of sulfur water from the sulfur springs (closed Tuesdays). The path to the summit of the 4700 m high volcano begins here.

Another recommended spot is the **San Juan Springs**. Here 112 hot sulfur springs combine with melted snow to form a multicolor mixture of volcanic rock and moss. A restaurant is located nearby and one can spend the night in the park ranger's hut for a small fee.

Tierradentro

Near the village of **San Andrés de Pisimbalá** is an important and interesting archaeological park, **Tierradentro**, which means "territory within territory". This strip of land was so named by the Spanish conquerors, who met with stubborn resistance on the part of the local Indians. The name reflects the fact that the Spanish infiltration was slow and painful — for conquerors and conquered alike.

The area is a valley high within the *Cordillera Central*. The mountains are steep and green, criss-crossed by many rivers. This fertile agricultural zone is currently inhabited by whites, mestizos and Indians — members of the *Páez* tribe. They are descendants of the Indians who lived here before the Spaniards arrived. The 25,000 *Páez* make their living from agriculture, in particular corn and vegetable crops. They have retained their ancient language and original social structure, headed by a ruling council, which is elected annually. This council is responsible for the functioning of an organized hierarchical body that governs cooperative labor. On Wednesday mornings, many *Páez* congregate in San Andrés to participate in the colorful market.

The archaeological findings discovered here testify to the existence of a number of civilizations, each with its own economic and cultural development, although very little is known about them. Clay and gold handicrafts were fairly advanced, but most remains had been plundered by the beginning of the

Spanish conquest. The few relics that remain are exhibited in the small local museum, and in the Gold Museum in Bogotá.

The most interesting of the local relics are the subterranean burial shrines, hewn out of soft rock by means of a hard flint. Spiral stairs lead down into the burial caves, whose roofs are supported by pillars. The dead were cremated; the burial chambers have niches where the urns containing the ashes of the dead were placed. The walls, roof, and pillars are decorated with various shapes, the most common motif being the rhombus, colored red and black against a white background. About one hundred burial caves of various sizes have been discovered in the area. Their depth varies from 3 to 9 m below ground level. Researchers do not know who built these caves, but there is no doubt that they were members of a developed and wealthy civilization, since considerable planning and manpower must have been required for such work.

Transportation
A number of buses leave Popayán daily on their way to La Plata, via Inza. The trip takes about 6 hours. Get off at the San Andrés junction. Then walk about 2 km to the park administrative offices, and another half hour to the village itself. After visiting San Andrés, get back on the Popayán bus and continue to La Plata. From La Plata there are buses to San Agustín and Neiva.

Food and lodging
Simple and inexpensive pensions can be found along the road leading from the park's administrative offices to the village of San Andrés. Of these, the best is *El Bosque*, a clean, good pension, with friendly owners. There are no really good hotels or restaurants in the area. Some of the houses near the administrative office serve as restaurants.

The archaeological park
The park at Tierradentro has several sites worth visiting, most within a short walk from the adminsitrative offices. The small museum, housed in the administrative office itself, exhibits some locally discovered pottery. Most of the archaeological treasures were plundered long before the arrival of archaeologists. Furthermore, many local finds are displayed in museums in Bogotá.

The most important area of the park is known as **Segovia**. Fifteen burial caves of various sizes were discovered here. The decorations on some of them survive. The area is about a 15 minute walk from the museum. At **El Duende** (a 10 minute walk from Segovia) four more burial caves were discovered. On the way to El Duende you will pass the houses of the Páez Indians.

The next place to visit is **El Aguacate**, about an hour and a half's walk from the museum. Here the whole of Tierradentro spreads out around you. The place also has a number of ornate burial caves.

El Tablón, near the museum, has eight statues with features similar to those of the San Agustín statues. This indicates that there was some connection between these different cultures.

For those wishing to tour the park and its environs on horseback, horses can be rented at San Andrés.

San Agustín
One of the more famous sites in Colombia is the village of San Agustín, with its archaeological treasures. Here you can see remnants of an ancient culture which has long since vanished; the art and sculpture are of rare quality. In order to appreciate these puzzling relics and the people who produced them, we have included a short introduction, which briefly describes the story of the Agustín culture.

The San Agustín Civilization
For more than two hundred years scholars have been trying to shed some light on one of the most interesting Andean civilizations, the San Agustín, so-called because of the proximity of its remains to the town of that name. This civilization, which flourished for 1500 years, still remains largely a mystery.

A Spanish priest visiting the area in 1758 was the first to report the existence of ancient relics in the area. The site began to attract researchers, but only in 1913 was the first comprehensive scientific study undertaken, by the German archaeologist Theodor Preuss. Further investigations have since been carried out by various official expeditions, and excavations continued intensively until the 1970's. About 500 statues were unearthed, as well as many graves and some gold and pottery. The most ancient statue discovered dates back to the 6th century BC.

From their various findings, the researchers concluded that the San Agustín civilization reached its peak between the 2nd and 8th centuries AD, a period they termed its "classical period". Nevertheless, the place was clearly inhabited centuries before this period, and settlement continued to exist until approximately the 10th century.

The origins of the San Agustín people are not clear, but they apparently came here from the jungles of southern Colombia. This deduction is based on the fact that Indian tribes living there still celebrate spiritual rites using masks (made out of tree bark), which are identical to the faces of the San Agustín statues.

The San Agustín economy was based mainly on agriculture. They cultivated corn, peanuts, and yucca, and gathered wild fruits and vegetables. They were also hunters, and to a lesser extent, fishermen (since the strong current of the rivers prevented large scale fishing). Stoneworking was fairly developed, as one can see from their many stone tools, the most significant of which were those used for quarrying. The San Agustíns were familiar with metalworking processes even before the Christian era. Their widespread use of gold-copper alloys testifies to the influence of central American cultures. This is also evident in the various motifs prominent in the sculptures. Little is known about the structure of Agustín houses, since significant remains of buildings have not been found. Nevertheless, various traces indicate that their houses were round, with bamboo walls and straw roofs.

The family was the basic social unit of the Agustíns. The various family groups were connected by economic and religious ties. From the end of the 5th century AD, the growing power and influence of the tribal leaders on the social stucture becomes apparent. The dead were buried in chambers covered by a large stone slab. Sometimes a statue would be erected at the entrance to the chamber, its size varied according with the importance of the deceased. It was customary to place the deceased's personal effects next to him, including jewelry, and clay, metal, and stone implements that he used in his lifetime. Religious rites were held near water sources, and many of the Agustín divinities were water or rain gods.

No one really knows why the San Agustín culture vanished. One theory suggests that the area was attacked by other Indian tribes — possibly the Tierradentro Indians. Just as little is known of the life of this civilization as of the reasons for its disappearance hundreds of years before the arrival of the Spanish conquerors. The Agustíns left behind only graves, daily work tools, and a wealth of statues. All the rest has disappeared.

Agustín sculpture
The quantity and quality of the sculptures discovered, testify to the high social status of the Agustín sculptor. It is clear that the

sculptor was allowed to devote most of his time and energy to his craft.

Stylistically, the statues can be divided into various levels of sophistication. While some are rough and simple, others are so intricate and detailed that it becomes possible to discern individual features. The Central American influence can be seen in the various motifs, such as large facial features. In most cases, only the front is carved, while the back of the statue is smooth stone. Very few sculptures depart from this rule.

Religious significance was attached to the figures. The eagle, for example, was a symbol of power and light, and the serpent symbolized the god of rain. Feline figures, such as the jaguar, symbolized the dark underworld. Monkey figures were used in fertility rites. Frogs, lizards, and salamanders were used in water ceremonies. Some of the statues consist of two overlaid human figures. The lower figure represents man's ego, and the top figure his spirit.

By studying the statues, something of the Agustín culture and life can be learned: the male figures generally hold tools or skulls in their hands, while the female statues hold their children. The heads are out of proportion to the rest of the body. Paint residues have been discovered on some of the statues. Most of the statues served as gravemarkers.

The quality of Agustín sculpture indicates an advanced and developed civilization, to which researchers attribute considerable influence over other Andean cultures.

The San Agustín village
The village lies in southern Huila province, an area of rolling green hills. Río Magdalena, Colombia's largest river, has its source in this area, and flows through a deep canyon near the village. San Agustín has some 18,000 inhabitants. The weather is very pleasant all year round, with an average temperature of 18°C (64°F). From November to February, the weather is particularly temperate, but this is also the height of the tourist season. Since San Agustín is one of Colombia's most important tourist attractions, many local residents depend on the tourist industry for a livelihood. There is a fairly large number of restaurants and hotels, and people are generally friendly. Nevertheless, the many tourists attract thieves and pickpockets to the area: guard your possessions well!

Transportation
The Pitalito airport, about half an hour's journey from San

San Agustín — the archaeological park

Agustín, is served by *Satena* and *Aires* flights. Beware of thieves in Pitalito. This is one of the most dangerous places in a dangerous country!

The town of Neiva is about 5 hours away. *Aeropesca* and *Satena* airlines fly there.

The daily bus from Bogotá to San Agustín passes through Neiva. The trip, on a fairly good road, takes 11 hours.

From Popayán there are two ways to reach San Agustín. The bus leaves Popayán bus terminal every morning and travels via La Plata; the trip takes about 11 hours. One may also travel by jeep-taxi, direct to San Agustín. This route is difficult and tiring, but takes only about 5 hours. There are no fixed departure times for the jeeps — they simply leave when they are full. The jeep fare is only slightly higher than the bus fare. Both routes are beautiful and cross the Cordillera Central. High up it gets extremely cold.

Food and lodging
Yalconia: Tel. 37-3001. Located out of town, just 2 km from the

The Forest of Statues

archaeological park, the best and more expensive in the area, perfectly adequate, with swimming pool.

Motel Osoguaico: Slightly farther from town and closer to the park, low priced and very good.

Residencias Luis Tello: Calle 4A, 15-33. Very friendly and pleasant, basic.

Camping is possible in San Agustín, but for obvious security reasons, it is inadvisable!

As for restaurants, do not expect an outstanding gastronomical experience here. The local diet is based on vegetables, eggs, meat, and, of course, rice. The better restaurants are situated in the two good hotels mentioned above, the *Yalconia* and the *Osoguaico*. The *Brahma*, offering low cost vegetarian fare, is located on Calle 15, 15-11.

Tourist services
The **Tourist Office**, at Calle 5A, 14-45 provides excellent service.

Open Tues.-Sat., 8:30am-12:30pm and 1:30-5:30pm; in tourist season only, also Sun. 9am-noon and 1-5pm. The personnel are friendly and helpful, speak English, and are eager to help in whatever way they can. Excellent regional maps, and up to date lists of hotels and restaurants are available.

Attractions in the San Agustín area, such as the archaeological park, are best toured on foot. Places further out can be reached by rented jeep or on horseback. Jeeps can take up to eight passengers. The rentals are fixed, and depend on where you want to go. The price list can be obtained at the tourist office. If you want a guide for the park, the tourist office can provide one who will be happy to offer you a comprehensive survey of the archaeological sites.

The Archaeological park

The most important of the sites around San Agustín is the archaeological park, where most of the Agustín graves and statues are found. It is about 3 km from town, open daily 8am-4pm. A thorough visit takes about three hours.

The administrative offices at the entrance to the park house a small museum with a small exhibit of local archaeological findings. Most of the pottery and gold artifacts found in the area are on display at the National Museum and in the Gold Museum, both in Bogotá. The admission fee for the museum includes entrance to the park.

The archaeological finds are grouped in *mesitas*, or "tables". These are mounds that the Agustíns raised over the graves of the most eminent members of the community. There are four *mesitas* in the park; one of them houses the museum at the entrance. On these mounds are the sarcophagi and statues that served as gravemarkers.

The largest tomb of all is in *Mesita B*, which also has two other tombs and a sarcophagus. *Mesita C* has two statues with carved backs — a rare phenomenon among the statues in the park. A little beyond Mesita C is the large rocky area known as *Fuente de Lavapatas*. Here many figures of monkeys, salamanders, lizards, and human figures were carved into the rockface. The figures are surrounded by tiny channels and many small pools. The water that used to flow through these channels created a picture of total harmony. Today, in order to preserve the rockface, the channels are kept dry. Just the same, these splendid remains — once the Agustíns' most important local shrine — are still extremely impressive.

Further up the hill is the area known as **Alto de Lavapatas**. A number of large statues stand at the top of the hill, enjoying the fine view. It encompasses two mountain ranges (the central and the eastern), the entire archaeological park, and the valley in which San Agustín nestles.

After leaving the park, visit the **Bosque de las Estatuas** (Forest of Statues), a beautiful area set in an enchanting natural forest. Along the path that winds through the thick vegetation, 35 statues — transported here from their original setting — have been erected. They represent the various motifs of the San Agustín statues.

Alto de los Idolos

The second most important place in San Agustín is known as the *Alto de los Idolos* (the Heights of the Idols). There are three ways of getting there: by jeep, approximately an hour's journey along a terrible road; two and a half hours on horseback along a beautiful route that crosses the Magdalena canyon; or a half day hike which includes a visit to the site. The *colectivo* from Pitalito to San José de Isnos picks up passengers at the San Agustín junction (San José has an interesting market on Saturdays). Alto de los Idolos is about a two hour walk from San José. Return to San Agustín by continuing along the same route — a three hour hike leads through a landscape of green mountains and waterfalls plunging into the Magdalena canyon.

Alto de los Idolos was discovered and studied only in the 1970's. Many tombs, sarcophagi and statues were found here, as well as San Agustín's largest statue, about 7 m high and only partially uncovered. The structure of the burial chambers here is clear — statues guard the entrance to the tombs. Open daily 8am-6pm.

Those traveling by rented jeep can stop en route at **Salto del Mortino** — a large waterfall on the Mortino River. Also worth visiting is **Alto de las Piedras**, which has a number of statues, and **Salto de los Borbones**, Colombia's highest and most impressive waterfall.

El Estrecho

El Estrecho is an impressive, natural narrow channel 2.2 m wide, through which the waters of the Rio Magdalena flow. The best way to reach the area is on horseback, which takes about two hours. On the way, one can turn on to the path leading to **El Tablón**, with its five statues of moon gods. Also worth visiting is **La Chaquira**, where more statues crown the bluff that rises from the Magdalena canyon.

Pasto

The capital of Nariño province bordering Ecuador, Pasto lies 2534 m above sea level.

The city was one of the first Spanish settlements in Colombia, but it has long since lost its colonial character. During the War of Independence, Pasto served as a stronghold for supporters of the Spanish crown, and was the last town to fall to the patriots. The inhabitants of Nariño province wanted to become part of Ecuador when it seceded in 1830 from the confederation of "Greater Colombia", but their wish was thwarted by Colombian troops in a bloody struggle.

Today Pasto is the center of the area's agricultural industry. With a population of about 200,000, it is the last major city before Ecuador.

West of Pasto, the Galeras Volcano towers to a height of 4276 m above sea level. It last erupted in the 1950's. Make the ascent by car (app. 30 minutes) for a splendid view of the city and its environs.

In the town itself, visit the **Church of San Juan**, on Calle 18 between Carreras 25 and 26. The inside of the church is richly decorated. Although rebuilt in 1969, the colonial building, one of the oldest in the town, has been repeatedly damaged in earthquakes.

A two day carnival is held here at the beginning of January. The first day (January 5) is known as the *Día de los Negros* (black day), for then the celebrants paint each other's faces with black grease. The next day is the *Día de los Blancos* (white day), when the revelers throw flour at each other. Sometimes the merriment gets out of hand and takes a violent turn.

Even here, beware of the local thieves!

On to Ecuador

The usual crossing to Ecuador is near the border town of Ipiales, about two hours south of Pasto. But there are two other alternative routes; both are jungle trails, difficult and off the beaten track. The first is via the road that turns southeast from Pasto, to the lower reaches of the Amazon basin and Putumayo

Santuario de la Lajas

province; the second runs west to Tumaco, on the Pacific coast.
Both routes are described below.

Ipiales
The road from Pasto to Ipiales (pop. 30,000) is paved and
comfortable; and the trip through beautiful scenery takes about
two hours. A colorful market is held in Ipiales on Saturdays.

Change dollars and traveler's checks into pesos and sucres (Ecuadoran currency) in the modern *Banco de la República*. In the same building is a small branch of the Gold Museum, with a modest collection of gold artifacts and archaeological finds from Nariño province.

Be sure to visit the famous **Santuario de las Lajas**, an ornate Gothic church atop a bridge spanning the canyon. On Sundays, the church is visited by Quechuan Indians from Ecuador, who believe the canyon waters have special properties. Las Lajas is about a ten minute ride east from Ipiales. Taxis to Las Lajas leave Ipiales frequently from the station near the main square.

Many inexpensive hotels are situated near the central plaza of Ipiales. Of these, we recommend the *Nueva York*. There are no first-class hotels; the closest approximation is the *Central*, also near the central plaza.

The Ecuadoran border, only a few kilometers from Ipiales, runs along the canyon of the Rio Carchi. A natural bridge links the two sides of the border. Taxis, which reach the border in a few minutes, set out frequently from the market in Ipiales. The crossing is open daily 8am-6pm, though it may be closed during *siesta*. Have your passport stamped at the DAS office in Colombia, and at the Ecuadoran border police office. You may have to prove to the Ecuadoran immigration officials that you have sufficient means to finance your stay. A tourist visa is valid for 30 days. Vehicles must be fumigated against diseases affecting coffee trees. This is done at the border itself.

Via Putumayo province
Trans Ipiales runs several buses a day from Pasto to the town of **Puerto Asís**, in Putumayo province, on the edges of the tropical Amazon jungle. The trip takes about 11 hours. The road first passes through green, pastoral scenery, near Laguna Cocha. It then climbs a steep mountain range, and crosses it to the east. The eastern slopes of this range are covered with exotic mountainous jungle. The narrow, tortuous road winds through thick vegetation, and crosses many rivers and waterfalls, and terrifying abysses, before descending to the extremely hot and humid jungle plains.

Cargo boats sail down the Río Putumayo from Puerto Asís on their way to Puerto Leguizamo (two days' journey) and Leticia (a week). The cruise begins on a fairly narrow channel of the river, which winds through beautiful thick jungle vegetation. Although this is jungle territory, do not expect to encounter a wide variety of wildlife en route.

Although the Ecuadoran border is not far from Puerto Asís, it is a 5 hours journey. Local transportation is typically a truck that has been converted to carry passengers, packed to bursting point with people and goods. The Colombian border village is called San Miguel. From there, travel by canoe down the Río San Miguel, half an hour from the Ecuadoran border, from which a vehicle leaves every hour for the town of **Lago Agrio**. This can be a convenient starting point for a jungle safari of several days through the eastern part of Ecuador (see "Ecuador — El Oriente").

Remember to have your passport stamped before leaving Colombia at the DAS office in Puerto Asís! Entry stamps for Ecuador are arranged at the police station in Lago Agrio.

Warning: Putumayo province is full of coca plantations; in fact, it is the starting point of the cocaine smuggling route to the West. The residents of Puerto Asís are active in the drug trade, making this a particularly violent area! Frequent and thorough checks are carried out by the army and police. Think carefully before undertaking this route. Consider, too, that the area is infested with malaria; take the appropriate medication.

Via Tumaco

About 250 km west of Pasto lies the city of Tumaco. The road to Tumaco is unpaved and extremely difficult to negotiate; the trip takes about 12 hours. Part of the road runs along the trans-Andean oil pipeline, which starts in Putumayo. Cattle ranches and rice and cocoa plantations are frequent sights along the road. Most of the people here are black, and they live in two-storey wood houses. The remains of the pre-Columbian civilization which lent the province its name have been discovered in the Tumaco area.

Tumaco (pop. 100,000 inhabitants) is rife with unemployment and poverty. It's nonetheless an interesting place to visit. Houses are built on piles over the water. A nocturnal visit is bound to be dangerous and is not advised! Neither should one drink water which is polluted here. The coastal area is marshy, with lots of mangroves. Many streams cross the marshes, and it is worth renting a boat at Tumaco to cruise through the area.

Ecuador is reached by water only — partly along beautiful streams, and partly by sea, which is usually fairly stormy. A canoe leaves Tumaco each day for **San Lorenzo**, Ecuador. Passports are stamped on the Colombian side at the DAS offices in Pasto or Cali. The Ecuadoran entry visa is affixed in the Ecuadoran coastal town (see "Ecuador — San Lorenzo").

COLOMBIA

The Amazon Basin and the Llanos

Though most of the mighty Amazon basin is in Brazil, it also extends into the neighboring Andean countries, including Colombia. All of southeast Colombia is one vast green plain, of which little has been explored by white men. The primeval nature of this zone has therefore been preserved, and both the thick tropical vegetation and wildlife continue to exist here undisturbed. The climate is of course tropical, and extremely hot. Annual rainfall is about 4000 mm (4 m!) . The area is almost entirely unpopulated, and the handful of isolated houses are scattered along the rivers. There are no overland roads, and the only means of transport are boat, ship or plane. The two tributaries that carry most of the river traffic are the Putumayo and the Caqueta. Most of the local population are Indians or *mestizos*.

The best starting point for a jungle safari is **Leticia**, the southernmost point in Colombia. There are organized tourist services here, and one should have no trouble finding a travel agent or local guide. After a short boat ride, the local guides will lead you into the heart of the tropical jungle.

Much less touristy is the area around **Mitú**, a village on the banks of the Rio Vaupes near the Brazilian border. It is a good base for visiting interesting Indian villages, which are a subject of anthropological research.

The options for interesting treks through the unexplored jungle are almost infinite. All one needs is an adventurous spirit, and plenty of time, money and patience. There is no regular transport, since the local population lives at a very leisurely pace.

Special instructions
Leticia has a good exchange rate for dollars; buy enough local currency here for the entire jungle trip. Elsewhere in the jungle, the dollar rate is extremely low, if foreign currency is accepted at all.

Bring anti-malaria pills, and purify drinking water with chlorine tablets. Important, too, are mosquito repellents and mosquito netting. When setting off down the river, remember to include enough food and fuel, and, of course, a first aid kit.

Leticia

Leticia was founded in 1867 by the Peruvian Captain Bustamante. It is situated 3200 km from the mouth of the Amazon River, at the border point shared by Colombia, Brazil, and Peru. An agreement among the three countries in 1922 awarded a narrow strip of jungle to Colombia. Leticia lies at the southern tip of this strip, on the northern bank of the Amazon.

The 30,000 inhabitants are of mixed Indian, Asian, and European descent; their language is a blend of Spanish and Portuguese. The old wooden houses are increasingly giving way to modern buildings, and the town is expanding and developing all the time. The harbor, on the main trade route with neighboring Brazil and Peru, teems with life.

Leticia is the starting point for many tourists who take the lengthy cruise down the Amazon River. The cruise ends in Brazil, at Manaus or Belem, where the Amazon empties into the Atlantic Ocean. But Leticia is also a tourist attraction in its own right. Many tourists prefer to take short and relatively uncomplicated trips into the country around the city. These can provide a good idea of the nature of the jungle, and a glimpse of the secrets of the fascinating Amazon world.

When to visit

It's always hot in Leticia, with an average temperature of 30°C (86°F). Getting around is hard during the rainy season (December-March) and when the rivers rise several meters (May-June). The best time for a visit is during the dry season — from July to November.

Transportation (to Colombia and other countries)

By air: *Avianca* and *Satena* cover the route to Bogotá several times a week, a close to two hours flight. *Aeropesca* and *Aerotal* have many cargo flights. Try to get on to these by speaking to the pilot at the airport.

The Brazilian airline *Cruzeiro* has three weekly return flights along the route Manaus-Tabatinga-Iquitos (in Peru). (Tabatinga is Leticia's Brazilian neighbor). One of these flights continues from Iquitos to Pucallpa (in Peru).

By boat: Puerto Asís is the furthest departure point upstream for boats to Leticia. The trip takes about a week. Boats leave Puerto Asís fairly infrequently, but one can sail to Puerto Leguizamo, where boats sail more frequently to Leticia.

There are only a few boats from Leticia to Manaus (Brazil), but boat service from adjacent Tabatinga is more frequent. The trip takes about five days. Private cabins are available on the boat, but this is quite expensive. First class (upper deck) is easier on the budget. Second class is not recommended, since it is in the cargo hold below deck. The price of the cruise includes meals. It is advisable to bring your own food (at least fruit) since meals are awful. Buy provisions in Leticia, which has a larger selection than Tabatinga.

Boats leave Ramón Castilla, on the Peruvian side of the river, for Iquitos and Pucallpa. These boats have no fixed timetables. At each border point, remember to request an exit and entry stamp in your passport. The Brazilian immigration office is located at Tabatinga, the Peruvian one in Ramón Castilla, and the Colombian one in Leticia.

Food and lodging
Generally speaking, a stay in the jungle towns is far more expensive than one in the center of the country, because most goods have to be freighted in.

Parador Ticuna: Calle 17, 5-43, Tel. 27-243, reservations in Bogotá, Tel. 342-8648. A first class hotel with all the facilities, including pool and restaurant.
Anaconda: Carrera 11, 7-34, Tel. 27-119, Fax. 27-005, reservations in Bogotá, Tel. 218-0125. Popular and fairly expensive, air condition, pool.
Residencia Familiar: Calle 8. Basic, economic and recommended.

The main restaurant fare is excellent fresh water fish. Inexpensive local food, such as fried bananas or yucca, is sold in the market near the port, but hygienic conditions are not the best. Good tropical fruit can also be bought here at low prices.

Tourist services
The **Tourist Office** is situated at Calle 10, 9-86. Various tourist agencies organize jungle trips. The most highly recommended of these agencies is *Turamazonas*, on Parador Ticuna. The agency offers a variety of tours; service is good, and the staff are reliable professionals. It is the most expensive agency, but the service justifies the price. Another good company is *Amatours*, in the *Hotel Anaconda*. Other agencies are not reliable; tourists are forced to haggle, and to make sure the necessary equipment is really available. The least costly way of touring is on one's own, hiring a local guide with a canoe.

Always make sure the guide is reliable and responsible, since anyone who is not totally familiar with the area is liable to cause a disaster.

Change money at the cambio opposite the *Hotel Anaconda*, where the rates are better than at the banks.

Tourist sites
Isla de los Micos (Monkey Island) is one of the most popular tourist attractions. The island is about 90 minutes out of town, upriver by canoe. It was purchased in the early 1950's by an American who established a monkey reserve there. Today, the monkey community is very large; don't be suprised if the bolder specimens welcome you ashore. Walk through the forest to the center of the island, and imbibe the jungle atmosphere. The pools hidden beneath the undergrowth are the habitat of the *Victoria Regia*, a gigantic water plant with a circumference of 2 m! The island has a hostel.

Another 90 minutes upstream is **Taraporto**, the lake district. Here, too, the gigantic water plant flourishes, as do a myriad of fish.

You may come across a few Indian villages here and there. The Indians are used to tourists, indeed, it is somewhat sad to think that they have turned into tourist attractions.

Ticuna Indians live in the village of **Arara**, on the river of the same name, only a few kilometers from Leticia. The cruise to the village is extremely enjoyable and passes through dense, luxuriant jungle. The *Yaguas* live on the Rio Atucuarí. They are isolated and inaccessible, which makes this trip more expensive. The *Caciques* of Peru can be visited as well.

Crossing to the Brazilian side of the border one reaches **Benjamín Constant**, where one can see rubber trees. When the bark is punctured this tree secretes a white liquid, which hardens after a few seconds, and is latter processed into rubber.

Los Llanos — the Savanna
The savanna stretches between the slopes of the Cordillera Oriental and the Orinoco jungle. Here the population is very sparse, and there are few roads. Until the Spaniash arrived in 1531, the area was inhabited by primitive Indian tribes. Over the years, they intermingled with the Spanish settlers; most of the current population of 500,000 are mestizos. They raise livestock on the grassy plains, and fish in of the Orinoco tributaries that cross the area.

To tour the savanna, one must first get to **Villavicencio**, at the foot of the Cordillera Oriental. Frequent buses travel the lovely route from Bogotá in about 3 hours (Tourist Office on Plaza Santander). From here, the possibilities are almost endless. Continue along a paved road to **San Martín**, or visit **Sierra de la Macarena**, a park with a huge variety of wildlife. Take a canoe trip from **Puerto López**, or drive across the endless stretches of plains extending east and south. The best time for this is December-March, when the dirt trails are passable by jeep. Remember to bring food, water, anti-malaria pills, and plenty of spare fuel. Thus equipped, one can enter this wasteland and escape from civilization for a while.

Maps and further details about road conditions and attractions can be obtained in Bogotá, at the offices of the *Gobernación del Departamento de Metá*, Calle 34 at Carrera 14, or at the National Tourist Office (see "Bogotá — Important Addresses").

V *ENEZUELA*

Upon reaching Caracas' modern and luxurious airport, you will sense the qualities that characterize the entire country — plenitude, prosperity and modern construction — all a result of the economic boom Venezuela has enjoyed since the development of its oilfields.

For centuries Venezuela was a poor, forgotten country carved up by mountain ranges and giant rivers, on the northern periphery of South America. When the Spanish arrived in the early 16th century, their main quest was gold. When that proved an empty dream, they abandoned Venezuela to its fate, and channelled their energies elsewhere. The fact that "black gold" was discovered under Venezuelan soil four hundred years later, certainly seems like fate's last laugh.

Venezuela has bloomed since the turn of the century; cities built, roads paved, dams constructed and vast stretches of territory settled. Today Venezuela is among the wealthiest of South America's nations — some say the wealthiest — and is one of the world's leading oil exporters.

Caracas' grand streets, munificently-stocked stores and high-rise neighborhoods faithfully reflect the Venezuelans' energetic spirit — but hide the dire poverty on the outskirts of the cities. Like much of South America, in recent years, Venezuela has been afflicted by severe economic and social crisis, stemming from governmental corruption and unequal distribution of wealth.

History

Although Columbus discovered Venezuela as early as 1498 on his third voyage to America, it was only about thirty years later that the first Spanish settlement, Cumana, was founded. The Spanish, with the help of the peaceful native tribes, who had submissively welcomed them, spent several years searching for gold spurred on by the example of the discoverers and conquerors of Peru. Some tried to locate the legendary city of El Dorado on Venezuelan soil, while others prospected for ore. All suffered bitter disappointment, however, as Venezuela yielded no gold. It did give forth a respectable agricultural crop but only after great efforts had been invested in burning jungles and preparing the land.

Only those Spaniards who decided to stick to agriculture

remained in Venezuela and were assimilated into the sparse Indian population. It was not until the mid-16th century that settlement activity began in earnest. Its nature and location were dictated largely by the country's geography. These first settlers laid the foundation of urban organization that continues to dominate Venezuela to this very day.

Since its founding in 1567, Caracas, Venezuela's heart and capital, has served as the focus of national identity. Through the centuries and under all governments, Caracas has enjoyed the support and recognition of the entire population, its supremacy unchallenged.

The country's fractured geography led to the development of separate regional identities, which on several occasions refused to bow to outside control, and ignored dictates issued from the capital. It also served as the background for the anti-Spanish uprisings, which took place as early as the 18th century. However, it was not until 1806, and then in 1811, that a rebellion of substance erupted. The Venezuelans, led by Francisco de Miranda and Simón Bolívar, broke away from Spain and established an independent Republic. Venezuela independence was first declared on July 5, 1811, but no fewer than twenty years of struggle and bloodshed were to pass, before it was established de facto.

Simón Bolívar was the first and greatest of Venezuela's revolutionary leaders, responsible for the liberation of Colombia, Ecuador, Peru and Bolivia. Bolívar, for whom Bolivia is named, was born in Caracas in 1783 to one of the city's wealthiest and most prestigious families. He spent long periods of his youth in Europe, where he was influenced by the current ideas of liberalism and progress. He brought these ideas when he returned to Latin America, steadfast in his desire to liberate the local peoples from the Spanish yoke and to give them the right to an independent and secure existence. His great dream was to found a "Greater Colombia" consisting of Ecuador, Colombia, Panama and Venezuela, an end to which he labored greatly. However, "Greater Colombia" did not survive long after Bolívar's death in 1830, because of the separatist ambitions of the leaders of each country.

Throughout the 19th century, as a unified national identity struggled to be born, Venezuela was plagued by severe internal strife which at times reached a state of civil war. Indian roots, Spanish heritage and Western ideas combined into a mass of contradictions that could hardly coexist. The difficulty of integrating these disparate entities ultimately led to an economic and social stagnation which has left its marks to this day. The Federal War, 1859-1863, was the most devastating of these series of internal struggles.

The constitution of 1864 established a federal system with

VENEZUELA

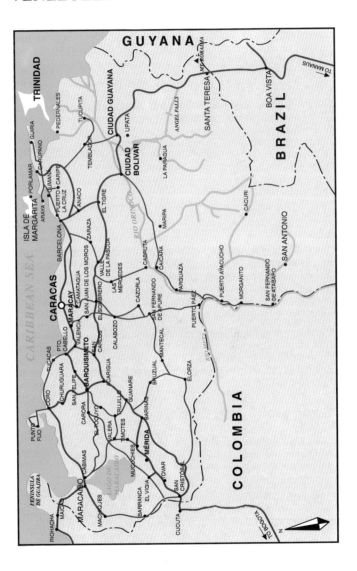

provincial autonomy, but the reforms did not bring the expected political stability.

Juan Gómez seized power in 1908 and his twenty-six years of rule which followed were characterized by terror, violence and repression. It was during this period, just when the first flames of World War I began to flicker in Europe, that oil was discovered in the Maracaibo area. By 1928, Venezuela had become the world's second largest oil producer and exporter.

"Black gold" put Venezuela on the world economic map and Caracas became a major capital. The growing purchasing power of the Venezuelans and their government attracted businessmen from all over the world, who flocked to the country with goods of every sort. Venezuela's near-total lack of industry and its limited and low-quality agricultural output, forced the country to rely on imports for just about everything — from automobiles and technological instruments to matches. During this time, the oil boom eased social tensions and helped stabilize the political structure.

A democratic regime, one of the most stable in Latin America to this day, was established after the overthrow of the old regime in 1958 and the election of Rómulo Betancourt as president. Betancourt served until 1964. He initiated national development program and an agrarian reform, and he improved the standard of living, particularly the health and educational systems. He also contributed to the stabilization of Venezuela's political system.

In the last decades power has alternated between the country's two major parties. In 1974 Carlos Andrés Pérez was elected president, and served until 1979. In 1989 he was elected once again, but this term is unstable, and until the end of 1992 he had to confront twice unsuccesful revolts.

Geography and climate

Venezuela, with an area of 912,050 sq/km, is bordered by Guayana to the east, Brazil to the south and Colombia to the west. The Atlantic Ocean and the Caribbean wash the long coastline (some 3000 km) to the north.

Venezuela is divided into twenty-one administrative districts. Geographically there are only five major sections. The first is the western plains region around Lake Maracaibo. The second is the mountain range that borders the plains to the east — the Sierra Nevada de Mérida — an extension of the Colombian Andes. The third, the Orinoco Basin, is located in the center; the fourth, to the east, Guayana Highlands, covering half of Venezuela's territory; and finally, the central and eastern coastal zone, a narrow strip with almost half the population of the country.

The Orinoco River flows for 2575 km from the mountain slopes through the jungles to the Atlantic Ocean. About 80% of the country's water drains into the river and emptying through a vast delta opposite the islands of Trinidad and Tobago.

A considerable area of Venezuela is covered with virgin forest where travel is difficult and complicated. Entire districts of the Orinoco Basin and the Guyana Highlands are nearly uninhabited. Only in recent years have trails been blazed and new settlements founded, chiefly in those areas with economic potential.

Venezuela enjoys a tropical climate: it is uniformly hot and humid the year round. The dry season, when temperatures are slightly lower, runs from December to April. The mountain regions are cooler than along the coast.

Population and government

The population of Venezuela numbers 20 million, of which 40% are under 15. The natural increase is 2.3%. A significant percentage of native Venezuelans are of mixed Spanish-Indian blood, with only 20% of European descent. However, since World War II, hundreds of thousands of Europeans have immigrated to enjoy the economic boom.

Venezuela is a highly urbanized country due to its topography; with some 80% of its population as city-dwellers. The flight from farm to city has created severe social and economic problems. The cities cannot provide sufficient employment and housing, and tens of thousands live in slums that surround every city's downtown area. Close to half the population of Caracas live in these shanty-towns called *barrios*, raising their children amid rife unemployment and crime.

Though the country's educational system is growing constantly, over 10% of the population is still illiterate. About 500,000 of all Venezuelans acquire a university education.

Presidential elections are held in Venezuela every five years; the minimum voting age is 18. Election campaigns are intense, and the public is very politically active. Apart from the President, senators and representatives are elected from constituencies.

Spanish is the dominant language in Venezuela, though other European languages are also widely spoken. The dominant faith in Venezuela is Roman Catholicism.

Economy

The economy of Venezuela is complex and problematic. Since the economic boom commenced, vast resources have been diverted to developing cities, roads, energy projects, and the expansion of public services. The national economy has come to rely on oil revenues, which account for more than 83%

of exports and is the 6th largest producer in the world. Until recently, industrial and agricultural diversification have been neglected.

In the eighties Venezuela faced an economic crisis because of the fluctuations in the oil markets. A sharp fall in petroleum sales, together with a huge foreign debt and a government unable to restrain its expenses, have caused an unprecedented flight of capital — estimated at billions of dollars a year! Most of that money has found its way to banks in the United States and Europe, where Venezuela's wealthy have bank deposits and properties. The country itself has had to plead with its creditor-banks for special extensions while scraping the funds for loan repayments. It threatens not only the economic stability but also its democratic regime: an attempt of coup took place in 1992, and unrest was evident for a time.

Nonetheles, the Venezuelan currency, the *Bolívar*, is considered one of the most stable in Latin America and was once among the soundest in the world. In view of the difficulties of the mid 1980's, however, the Caracas government was compelled, for the first time in more than twenty years, to institute foreign-currency controls and to devalue the *Bolívar* by about 100%. A system of multi-level exchange rates was introduced aimed at restraining imports, a step which caused the private sector considerable difficulties in paying off debts to non-Venezuelan creditors. As a result, external credit has also been reduced. The inflation rate was decreased to a little more than 30% in 1990.

In Venezuela itself, the crisis is more evident in the social sphere than in the economic sphere. Unemployment runs at about 15% and the civil service — a tangled bureaucracy that employs about 25% of the workforce — has become less tolerant and more corrupt.

In an effort to restore economic equilibrium, billions of dollars have been invested to encourage agriculture, which at present employs only 16% of the workforce and provides less than half of Venezuela's food needs (only 6% of the gross domestic production). Among other steps, special incentives are offered for building and developing factories in remote areas, especially in Guayana. All this, has not been enough and the import of food and essential goods still imposes a heavy burden on the economy. On January 1, 1976, all oil wells were nationalized and are now run by a special corporation established for that purpose, PDVSA. In the late 1980's and early 1990's the government developped alternative industries mainly in eastern Venezuela, around Ciudad Guayana. This area has become a bustling provincial center, for iron, steel and aluminium industries.

VENEZUELA

General information
How to get there
By air: Most airlines fly to Caracas from Europe. *Air France*, *Alitalia*, *Iberia*, *KLM* and *Lufthansa* all fly from their respective capitals. *Viasa*, the Venezuelan national airline, flies to destinations in all major European countries.

From the United States, *Delta*, *Varig* and *Viasa* all have daily direct flights to Caracas. At times, it may be cheaper to use certain South American carriers to reach Colombia even though they are routed through their respective capitals. The flight takes a little more than four hours from New York and about two and a half hours from Miami.

South and Central American countries and the Caribbean Islands are serviced daily by *Viasa* or other national airlines. *BWIA* and *Aeropostal* fly to Trinidad. Flights between the United States and Buenos Aires or Rio de Janeiro stop over in Caracas en route. You must pay a departure tax when leaving Venezuela; passengers in transit for less than seventy-two hours are exempt.

By land: The most convenient overland route to Venezuela from Colombia is via the coastal highway from Barranquilla. To reach San Cristóbal in Venezuela (for those coming from Bogotá), pass through Cordillera Oriental from the Colombian city of Cúcuta. From Brazil, a more difficult, complicated route passes from Manaus via Boa Vista to Santa Elena (see "Ciudad Guayana: Southward to Brazil").

Documents
Most tourists are required to obtain a visa prior to arriving in Venezuela at any Venezuelan consulate. Upon arrival at the border, a tourist card will be issued. A tourist card is good for a sixty-day stay in Venezuela and may be extended for another sixty days in the Immigration Office in Caracas. If you come by car, you'll need to present a permit from a Venezuelan consulate, registration and title papers, and a valid driver's license. Be sure to carry your passport at all times! Due to massive illegal immigration, the local police are strict and conduct searches.

When to visit: holidays and festivals
The weather is stable most of the year with the dry season running from December through April. The national holidays are January 1, May 1, July 5 (Independence Day), July 24 (Bolívar's Birthday), October 12 (Colombus Day), November 1 (All-Saints' Day), December 24-25 and December 31. There are additional bank holidays.

Accommodation
Hotels in Venezuela are clean, tidy and safe — but expensive.

VENEZUELA

There are almost no cheap hotels or pensions and visitors arriving from the Andean countries are certainly in for a shock. Big city hotels are of no lower quality than their American or European counterparts, though service is not always top-grade. Camping is acceptable **only** in uninhabited areas. The coastal strip offers a long series of luxury hotels and rather expensive resorts. Most hotels accept credit cards.

Food and drink

The economic boom gave rise to hundreds of excellent restaurants with international menus. Venezuelan restaurants are by no means inexpensive; add a 10% service charge to the bill along with a tip of equal size. Most restaurants accept credit cards and all, by law, must display a menu and price list outside their door. Inexpensive meals are available at *fuentes de soda*, kiosks found on every street corner. The most popular foods, Italian and Spanish, are available at stands and local eateries.

Breakfast and lunch are generally served at the usual hours, while dinner is late — between 9pm and 11pm. Most restaurants are closed on Sundays or Mondays. Due to the proliferation and diversity of restaurants you'll have little trouble in finding something that appeals to your taste, but we recommend that you try a number of the local specialties. These may be found at local food stands and in the Creole restaurants. Beef comes first. Venezuelans are used to the same cuts of meat as those of Argentina and to similar sized portions. Almost every restaurant serves the popular *lomito* and *parrilla*, beef with rice or with French fries. The *parrilla* sold at stands consists of pieces of grilled beef served shish kebab style and is excellent. Most restaurants serve instead of, or in addition to bread, *arepas* — a popular local cornflour roll, crisp on the outside and incredibly soft on the inside. At the stands, you can order *arepas tostadas* — cornflour rolls filled with meat, vegetables and more — superb! *Hervido* is a local meat-and-vegetable soup and *sancocho* is a ragout of meat and local vegetables (including *yuka*, a type of sweet potato). *Hallaca* is another popular dish — a mixture of beef or chicken with onion, vegetables and spices, wrapped in banana leaves and steamed.

To all this, add the mouth-watering *empanada* — filled with cheese or meat, vegetables, and spices. And don't forget the pizza, pasta, cake, ice cream, and wonderful and exotic fruits — pineapple, papaya, strawberries, and others.

Currency

The local currency is the *Bolívar*, marked *Bs*. and called by the locals with its slang name "bolos". Common banknotes are ten, twenty, fifty, one hundred, five hundred and one thousand *Bolívares*.

VENEZUELA

Until early 1982, Venezuela was one of the most expensive tourist countries. However, since the devaluation, it has become far more attractive to visitors. Today the "free rate" and the official one are unified. You can change your money at the banks or at a casa de cambio, where there is less red tape. Travelers' checks and credit cards are very common and are eagerly accepted. As usual in South America, out of the capital it can be difficult to change currency other than American dollars.

Business hours

Banks are open from 8:30am-4:30pm, with a siesta from noon till 2pm. Government offices are open to the public at irregular hours, but always only in the mornings. Shops and offices are open from 8am-6pm with a short midday siesta.

Domestic transportation

Aeropostal and *Avensa* fly between all of Venezuela's large cities. Though the flights are short and convenient, they are generally full. We recommend that you make reservations as early as possible and confirm them 24 hours before departure time. It's best to reach the airport two hours before your planned departure. The timetables are not reliable, so check by phone whether your flight has been delayed.

Students are entitled to a discount on internal flights through the *ONTEJ* student organization (see "Caracas: Tourist services").

Comfortable buses ply the modern highways which link the large cities and destinations can be reached speedily and more cheaply than by air. Some lines, especially the coastal ones, run modern buses. Others, especially in the mountain areas and the Guyana Highland industrial cities, use old and uncomfortable buses. In addition, taxis, known as *por puesto*, are available — these are faster but costlier.

Avis, Hertz and local companies rent cars — all late-model Fords — at the Caracas airport, in Caracas itself or in other cities. Although the intercity speed limit is only 80 kph and most of these roads are of high quality (dirt roads are not lacking), road trouble is commonplace. Stealings from cars is quite frequent.

Measurements, electricity, and time

The metric system is used. Electricity is 110 volts. The local time is GMT -4.

Caracas

Caracas (pop. approximately 2.7 million) accurately reflects the results of the great boom. A modern, bustling downtown area is packed with skyscrapers, plazas, parks and public buildings. A superb road system, one of the most advanced in South America, serves the city and its suburbs, and thousands of cars crowd them day and night. Shopping centers, giant stores and sport and entertainment centers all adorn the city.

Elsewhere in Caracas poverty, want, unemployment and crime abound — the seamier side of life in the gleaming metropolis. There is a constant stream of people from the rural countryside to the urban centers — all moving toward the city in search of a better future. This has given birth to slums where hundreds of thousands live in unbearable conditions in the shadow of all the opulence which is beyond their reach.

Generally, Caracas is not a pleasant city. The atmosphere is cold and estranged. Local residents, the *Caraqueños*, will usually treat you as nicely as they have to, but no better. The rising crime rate has led most *Caraqueños* to sequester themselves in their homes by early evening, and in the residential quarters it's rare to see anyone strolling about after dark. By contrast, downtown, in **Sabana Grande** and the entertainment centers, the city remains alive and bubbling well into the small hours of the night.

Climate
Almost 1000 m above sea level, Caracas enjoys a temperate climate. Its elevation and distance from the coast (20-45 km) contribute to its coolness and moderate the influence of the harsh tropical climate. Average temperatures range from 30°C (86°F) in summer (July-August) to 9°C (48°F) in winter (January-February). Warm rain falls mainly in the summer, and wet clothes can become sticky and unpleasant. Due to the heat, clothing begins to "give off steam" but dries within minutes after the rain has stoped. Synthetic fabrics will prove unpleasant; light cotton clothing is best.

How to get there
By air: Caracas's modern **Simón Bolívar Airport** is 30 km out of town. Immigration, customs and currency exchange procedures are quick and easy. The airport Tourist Information Office will provide you with information, maps, and even assist

in making hotel reservations. The international car-rental firms have airport offices. The facility does not offer a baggage-checking service — a considerable inconvenience, particularly for transit passengers. Next to the Simón Bolívar Airport is Caracas's old airfield, **Maiquetía**, used for domestic flights. A special bus leaves every half hour from the airports to Parque Central, the bus terminal at the foot of the downtown Caracas Hilton. Parque Central is rather isolated and can be unpleasant after dark, and from there we recommend taking a taxi straight to your hotel. A taxi from the airport into Caracas costs more than $20 and the trip on the Autopista (freeway) la Guaira, takes close to an hour depending on traffic. Buses marked **Catia la Mar** head for the airport from Parque Central every half hour. Arrive early.

By land: Buses to and from Colombia, Guyana, and various Venezuelan cities generally use the Nuevo Circo Central Bus Terminal, where a Tourist Information office is located. It's advisable to make reservations several days before departure, particularly if you intend to travel on a holiday or weekend. When booking an intercity trip, you must present a passport. Taxi service also runs between cities.

Where to stay

Most Caracas hotels are rather expensive in comparison to those in the United States or Europe, and much more so than those elsewhere in Latin America. Caracas, unlike other South American cities, has almost no cheap pensions or hostels and the simplest of hotels, where rooms are very hard to find, are costly. For intermediate class hotels we highly recommend reservations. Make them at the airport if not from your country of departure. Wandering through Caracas with your luggage, especially after nightfall, is liable to be exhausting and unpleasant.

A concentration of relatively inexpensive hotels along Avenida Las Acacias in Sabana Grande allows you to go from one to another in search of a room. This is the best area to stay in, both in terms of price and location.

Tamanaco Intercontinental: Av. Principal de las Mercedes, Tel. 914-555, Fax 208-7116. In Las Mercedes quarter, away from downtown. The most expensive in town, very elegant, with restaurants, art galleries, a swimming pool, offices and more. Make reservation in advance.

Caracas Hilton: Plaza Morelos, Av. Sur 25, El Conde, Tel. 574-1122, Fax 575-0024. Much more convenient location than the Tamanaco, and the usual Hilton facilities.

Crillón: Av. Libertador, Las Acacias, Tel. 714-411, Fax 716-911. Less expensive, recommended. It is off the Plaza Venezuela metro station.

Tampa: Av. Francisco Solano López. Spacious rooms, good service.

Myriam: Las Acacias in Sabana Grande. Perhaps the most suitable for those with a tight budget — clean, very centrally located, comfortable.

A final tip — an association of inexpensive hotels and hostelries gives information about inexpensive places to stay in Caracas and elsewhere in the country (Tel. 782-8433, Fax 782-4407).

Where to eat

As in Buenos Aires, here too we abandon any pretentions of compiling a list of the best restaurants. Unlike other South American cities, where the best eateries could be chosen with no great difficulty, the Venezuelan and Argentinian capitals have such high standards and offer such a large variety, that to try to list them all would be futile. Changes are so frequent that an "in" place would be "out" and a superbly grilled steak would become steak tartare before ink had dried.

Here are a number of hints to help you choose, what, where, and how expensively to eat. First, all hotels (intermediate and upwards) have at least one restaurant, while the genuinely elegant offer two or three. A number of Caracas hotel restaurants are certainly recommendable, though not as bargain selections. For more economical eating it's best to stroll through Sabana Grande, especially the main boulevard shopping centers where you'll find cafeterias, hamburger stands, kiosks and cafes. Prices at the latter are liable to be very high since they are considered more prestigious. Elsewhere you can eat in a much less elegant, though no less satisfying, atmosphere. The Sabana Grande area is full of diverse places to eat, and it's a nice place to explore at any hour.

You'll find Chinese restaurants around Avenida Naiguata, most of which are relatively inexpensive. Most good restaurants charge lower prices in the afternoons, when a standard three-course fixed-price meal called *menú* or *cubierto* is served.

Transportation

The modern subway with 2 lines is the fastest, quietest, most convenient and pleasant alternative to surface transit. The latter consists chiefly of noisy, crowded, buses, moving slowly, with poorly marked stops and irregular "schedules". Most buses depart from the Nuevo Circo Terminal. The taxis, which will stop at a wave of a hand, are faster and less problematic for finding your way around the city.

Taxi fares are metered; add 20% after 10pm and on Sundays and holidays. Taxis are hard to find in the downtown area and it's best to get one at the stands.

Car rental

Driving in Caracas is not recommended. The city's tangled traffic, congestion and complicated street system — the bright signs don't elucidate it sufficiently for a foreigner — all combine to make driving a harrowing experience. Nonetheless, one learns the rules of the road here within a day or two, after several wasted kilometers, getting off at the wrong interchanges, etc. Rental cars, not for those on a limited budget, are available at the following agencies:

Avis: Centro Altamira, Av. San Juan Bosco, Tel. 316-420.
Budget: Qta. Los Irunes 50, Av. Luis Roche, Altamira, Tel. 283-4333.
National: Edif. Sterno, Av. Papal, Los Ruices, Tel. 239-1134.
Hertz: Edif. Pichincha, Av. Papal, corner with Av. Solano, Chacaíto, Tel. 952-1603.

All have airport branches (the above addresses and phone numbers are for their city offices). They can also be arranged through the major hotels.

Due to problems of the congestion, all cars are forbidden to enter Caracas one day a week, according to the final license plate digit. When renting a car, remember to verify the day on which its movement is restricted.

Tourist services

The central Tourist Office, *Corpoturismo*, is located in Torre Oeste, Parque Central (Tel. 507-8726). It has a great deal of explanatory material and information, and a hotel reservation service for other Venezuelan cities. *Corpoturismo* has branches at the airport and the bus terminal.

Good maps may be purchased at gasoline stations. *Adónde Vamos*, a magazine available free of charge at the hotels, has information on shopping, entertainment, restaurants as well as maps. The English-language *Caracas Daily Journal* is a good reference source for up-to-date information on entertainment and restaurants.

A reservation service for inexpensive hotels and pensions is now available (see "Where to stay"). For other tourist services, contact Caracas' various travel agencies, some of which are located around Plaza Venezuela. The *Viasa* offices are not far from Plaza Venezuela, near the Tourist Office.

ONTEJ, the local students' organization, offers tourist services to holders of valid student cards, is located at Parque Central in the Catuche Building (Tel. 573-3722 or 572-7621). They'll help you with thrifty tourism options, and offer significant discounts (up to 50%) on flights within Venezuela and occasionally to the surrounding countries. *ONTEJ* offers holiday and tourist packages to the Carribbean and elsewhere.

CARACAS

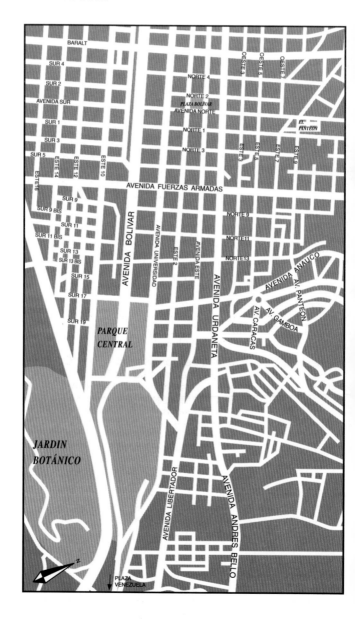

VENEZUELA

Venezuela's auto club — *Touring y Automóvil Club de Venezuela* — is located in Centro Integral Santa Rosa, Calle A, Av. Principal, Tel. 914-879. Maps and information concerning recommended travel routes and service stations, are available here.

Tourist sites

Little remains of the Caracas built by Diego de Losada and his fellow founding fathers in 1567, or of the city built by the Spaniards who followed. The city center, in the Plaza Bolívar area, has been redone into a packed agglomeration of office and commercial towers. Traces of the past in Caracas are hard to find; the compulsive drive for "progress" seems to dominate. Visitors will find a humming cosmopolitan city which displays the whole gamut of urban ailments — slums, filth, air pollution and traffic jams. It is however, at the same time, a fascinating city. New buildings were designed by creative architects who enjoyed free artistic rein and innovative construction methods that would have certainly been rejected by many a city council were encouraged and supported here. The results speak for themselves: dozens of imposing ultra-modern buildings made of concrete, steel and glass.

Enormous sums were invested in Caracas' magnificent and showy buildings, new streets, multi-lane expressways, well-developed plazas, parks and more. The latest grandiose urban renewal plan was the building of the subway during the 1980's. The results are visible in the lovely Plaza Venezuela, the revitalized Sabana Grande and elsewhere.

The best vantage point for an encompassing view of Caracas, trapped in the Muarnac Valley between Monte Avila to the north and the gentler slopes to the south, is atop **Monte Avila**. The cablecar (*teleférico*) from the Mariperez station has not been in operation for some years, so the only way to reach the summit is to climb it. From up here you have a totally different view of Caracas: a homogeneous concrete block of impressive proportions, with clusters of buildings protruding from its center.

To the left, notice the grand El Este residential quarter, home to only the very wealthy. It abounds with multi-story residences, green boulevards and prestigious shopping centers. Straight ahead is the downtown area, between Sabana Grande to the east and Plaza Bolívar to the west. To the right, Catia, the city's industrial zone can vaguely be seen. Rich tropical vegetation covers Monte Avila and on the summit a restaurant, a roller-skating rink and sports facilities are found.

Most of the interesting sites in Caracas itself are concentrated in the center of the valley, laid out one after another like a spinal column. We shall survey downtown Caracas from east to west, one attraction after another, straying only briefly in other directions. Remember that distances are great and that one site may at times be separated from another not only by several kilometers but also by several main traffic arteries that are difficult, if not impossible, to cross on foot. Most museums and national shrines are closed on Mondays.

We shall begin from the eastern end of the Sabana Grande, an entertainment center which, due to the subway project, has been given a new image.

Sabana Grande
Until the late 1970's, Sabana Grande suffered the plagues of bustling commercial centers; traffic congestion, air pollution, peeling plaster and so on. The subway and urban renewal program changed the area entirely. Sabana Grande's main boulevard became a pedestrian mall (repaved and tastefully illuminated), lined with dozens of coffee houses, restaurants, shops, movie theaters, ice cream parlors, and more. At the mall's eastern end is the **Chacaíto Commercial Center**, one of Caracas' largest. Hundreds of magnificent, well designed shops on several floors offer a wealth of products imported from all over the world. This is also the end of subway Line 1 and thousands of people flock out of its tunnel onto the promenade and disappear into surrounding offices and businesses.

A stroll through Sabana Grande is one of the best-loved *Caraqueño* pastimes, and the boulevard is packed day and night. The coffee houses are crowded at almost any hour with people engrossed in conversation over coffee, beer, or milk shakes. Stroll down the mall to the western end to **Plaza Venezuela**. The impressive plaza (one of the city's loveliest), with its central fountain illuminated at night by colored spotlights, is surrounded by a number of high-rise office buildings, the first skyscrapers built in Caracas. The Tourist Office and the Aeropostal offices are located here.

Before proceeding westward to Parque Los Caobos, turn left for a moment to the modern Ciudad Universitario — University City. Note that all the crowded freeways are hard to cross; so access to the university is easier through the park.

Ciudad Universitaria
"University City" is a prime example of modern architectural development, with acre upon acre of unusual concrete buildings interspersed with works of modern art that serve both ornamental and practical needs. Tens of thousands of students, lecturers, workers and staff members — throng the enormous campus every day. Nearby, a bit to the west, are the huge **Botanical Gardens**, boasting a large collection of plant species from all over the world.

Los Caobos Park

One of Caracas' jewels, a green enclave amidst the mountains of concrete, is the Los Caobos (mahogany tree) Park. It lies sandwiched between Plaza Venezuela and the giant Parque Central building complex. The concrete walkways, stone buildings and paved plazas in its midst, fail to mar the vitality of the exquisite park, which is also graced by the Ateneo de Caracas, a cultural center with a theater complex, art gallery and a bookstore.

At the park's western end is the **Museo de Bellas Artes** (Fine Arts Museum), one of the loveliest of its kind in Latin America (second to the one in Buenos Aires). The museum, housed in an impressive building, has a rich collection of European and Oriental art, alongside a wide range of Venezuelan art works from various periods. The spacious exhibition halls and the ramps between the floors add to the quiet and serene atmosphere which envelops its visitors. Highly recommended. Open Tues.-Fri. 9am-noon and 3-5:30pm, Sat.-Sun. 10am-5pm. Closed Mondays. Tel. 571-0176.

Stop by next door at the **Museo de Ciencias Naturales** (Museum of Natural History) for a look at it's collection of stuffed animals and archaeological finds. Open Tues.-Fri., 9am-noon and 2-5pm, Sat.-Sun., 10am-5pm. Closed Mondays.

Across from the museums, but still within the park, is the **Teresa Carreno Cultural Complex,** housing theaters, concert halls and the like. From here we cross a special pedestrian bridge to our next destination.

Parque Central

Perhaps the most impressive structure in Caracas is Parque Central, at the end of Avenida Bolívar and across the street from Parque Los Caobos. Construction of this complex, whose towers soar 56 stories skyward, began in the mid-1960's at the peak of the "boom". Plans call for its ultimate development into one of the world's largest residential complexes (designed for some 10,000 people). It not only houses hundreds of offices and shops but also a luxurious convention center, museums, the *Anauco Hilton Apartment Hotel* and much more. While strolling along the various floors of the giant building and wandering about its hundreds of corridors, staircases, elevators, gardens and so on, you'll feel its city-within-a-city atmosphere. Everything seems to be at arm's reach — there's no need to abandon the air-conditioning for the noisy, sweaty city.

Parque Central has four museums — **Museo de los Niños** (children), **Museo de Instrumentos del Teclado** (music), which are in the same building, **Museo Audiovisual** and **Museo de Arte Contemporáneo** (modern art). The latter displays an exhaustive collection of primarily 20th-century Venezuelan and foreign artists. Recommended. Open Tues.-Sun., 10am-6pm.

Centro Simón Bolívar

Continuing from Parque Central westward, along the broad Avenida Bolívar or on one of the parallel streets, we pass the Nuevo Circo Bus Terminal and arrive at the twin towers of Centro Simón Bolívar.

Centro Bolívar was erected in the 1950's and reflects the prosperity which then reigned in Caracas. Avenida Bolívar lined with parking lots, restaurants, stores and offices on either side passes under the thirty-story towers. The center is surrounded by important public buildings: to the left (looking from Parque Central) is the **Basílica de San Pedro,** followed by the **National Theater** and one block further, the **Municipal Theater** and **Plaza Miranda.** To the right (the north) is the **Church of San Francisco,** one of the few buildings surviving from the 16th century, worth noting for its design and impressive wood carvings. Beside it is the **National Library,** housed in what was once the University. The National Library, which faces the Capitol, contains hundreds of thousands of volumes, some of them centuries old.

We now turn right onto Calle San Francisco, and two blocks up we reach the historical center of Caracas — Plaza Bolívar.

Plaza Bolívar

Handsome trees shade the equestrian statue of the liberator in the heart of the attractive square bearing his name. Although the nerve center of Caracas has shifted elsewhere, Plaza Bolívar is still the heart of town in the eyes of many, and Venezuelans look upon it with great affection. In its eastern corner is the **Municipal Cathedral**, built in 1595 but restored about a hundred years ago after having been destroyed in an earthquake. The cathedral has a wooden altar, impressive carvings and several paintings by Rubens. Across the way is a reconstruction of Bolívar's birthplace — **Casa Natal de Simón Bolívar** — displaying many belongings from his youth, military service and personal life. The Colonial-style house reflects the appearance of Caracas about two hundred years ago, and gives an idea of the interior layout, furniture and other items typical of the local aristocracy of the time. The **Museo Bolívar** next door has an exhibit of artifacts and documents from the period of struggle for independence. Both the house and museum are open Tues.-Fri., 9am-noon and 2.30-5pm, and on Sun. and holidays 10am-5pm.

Still on the Plaza, we come to the city hall — **Concejo Municipal**, which houses a museum of Caracas' history on its ground floor. The city's past is depicted here through miniature houses and streets. Various artifacts dating from the earliest period, maps, flags and more are also on display. Across the square is **Casa Amarilla**, site of the Foreign Ministry and of a Venezuelan art exhibition. The museums open Tues.-Fri., 9.30am-noon and 3-6pm, weekends 9.30am-6pm.

At Plaza Bolívar's southwest corner is the Congress Building, **El Capitolio**, which was built in 1873 — in only 114 days! Its golden dome shelters a beautiful tropical garden along with the offices. Dozens of portraits of national heroes are on display in **Salon Elíptico**. Look at the ceiling which has scenes from the War of Independence depicting battles against the Spanish painted by Venezuelan artist Martín Tovar y Tovar. Open for visitors Tues.-Sun., 9am-noon and 3-6pm. Bring along your passport.

Additional sites

In addition to the sites surveyed thus far (in geographical order), a number of other important and recommended places to visit, dispersed throughout Caracas, must not be overlooked.

Heading north up Avenida Norte from Plaza Bolívar to the old La Pastora quarter, we reach the **National Pantheon** (El Panteon Nacional). It was founded in 1874 in memory of Venezuela's heroes and fallen soldiers, and Simón Bolívar is buried here. Open for visitors Tues.-Sun., 9am-1pm and 2-5pm.

The Museum of Colonial Art is located on Avenida Panteón in San Bernardino, a placid residential quarter in Caracas's north between Avenida Urdaneta and the slopes of Monte Avila. The gorgeous colonial-era building, dating from 1720, houses a fascinating collection of paintings, furniture, books and other displays from the Colonial period. All are attractively arranged and reflect the spirit of the period. Open for visitors Tues.-Sat., 9am-noon and 2-5pm; Sun., 10am-5.30pm. Highly recommended.

Cuadra Bolívar is a reconstruction of the house in which Simón Bolívar spent his youth. It is located six blocks south of Centro Bolívar. Open Tues.-Sat., 9am-1pm and 2.30-5pm; Sun., 9am-5pm.

Miraflores is the President's Palace where the affairs of state are conducted. The lovely 19th-century building, four blocks west of Plaza Bolívar and parallel to Avenida Urdaneta, is open to visitors on Sundays only by previous arrangement.

Parque del Este, an expansive park at Caracas' eastern extremity offers playgrounds, artificial lakes, lawns, sports fields and more. Closed Monday.

Parque Los Proceres is located on Avenida Los Próceres in Santa Mónica. Dedicated to Caracas's and Venezuela's founding fathers, it boasts well-tended gardens, benches, statues, fountains and more. Impressive and interesting.

Entertainment

Caracas center blossoms at night throughout the week but even more so on weekends. Cinemas are open around the clock. The Municipal Theater, south of Centro Bolívar, has performances (in Spanish) almost every evening as well as ballet, opera and concerts by local and foreign artists. Sunday morning concerts are often held at the Municipal Theater and in Plaza Bolívar.

The liveliest after-dark activities take place in nightclubs, bars and discotheques. Just walk around the Sabana Grande pedestrian mall for a taste of drinking, eating and talking in the coffee houses. A bit farther on, toward Plaza Venezuela, you'll find a popular discotheque. Avenida Venezuela in El Rosal has a "strip" of clubs, bars and discotheques. There's another "strip" around Plaza Altamira Sur. Recommended.

Sports

Caracas offers a selection of sports events which are exceptional in South America. There are numerous sports facilities for almost every imaginable sport — soccer, tennis, golf, boxing, and more. Soccer matches are held in the university stadium. **La Rinconada**, Caracas's elegant racetrack, has exciting photo-finish races. *Caraqueños* are sports-minded and many are members in a variety of private sport and recreation clubs.

The seashore abounds in water-sports clubs — fishing, sailing, diving and more. Equipment may be rented at the *Macuto Sheraton*. Many beaches are privately owned and used by the city's wealthy for weekend recreation.

Banking and currency exchange

Caracas's many banks (branches can be found around town) have morning and afternoon hours and exchange money at a fluctuating rate (see Introduction "General information"). The exchange process is somewhat exhausting and can be handled far more simply at private moneychangers, along the Sabana Grande pedestrian mall.

Postal and telephone service

The Venezuelan mail and telephone services, like most government services, are slow and complicated. A letter sent to Venezuela from Europe or the United States (and vice versa), takes a few weeks (sometimes more than a month) to reach its destination. Mail your letters from a post office, and not from a mailbox in town.

Parcels up to 10 kilos can be mailed from post offices. There is usually no problem sending parcels from Venezuela by surface mail.

The international telephone service is operated by the *CANTV* government corporation in Centro Simón Bolívar (facing Plaza Caracas). It's very expensive to call from Venezuela. Discount rates to certain countries, the United States among them, are in effect evenings and Sundays.

From a private phone one can call abroad using the 122 exchange. Dial 109 for "directory assistance".

Shopping
Caracas is not the best place to shop for two reasons: prices are high and there is nothing special to buy. Most goods are imported and few justify the expense.

If you're on the way to other South American countries, save time and money and shop there. If you're returning from those countries, you've certainly bought everything you can possibly carry. If you are visiting only Venezuela and find it hard to go home empty-handed, you'll have to shell out for some rather kitsch souvenirs. Except for gold jewelry, Venezuela as a country offers a tourist little that is worthwhile or unique.

Nevertheless, take the time to walk through Caracas's modern shopping centers. There are hundreds of shops offering an abundance of goods of every type, imported from all over the world, and all expensive.

Important addresses and phone numbers
First aid: Tel. 283-9733.
Ambulance: Tel. 454-545.
Police: Tel. 169.
Tourist Office (*Corpoturismo*): Tel. 507-8726.
Hotel Reservations (Fairmont): Torre Capriles, Plaza Venezuela, Tel. 782-8433.
Touring y Automóvil Club de Venezuela: Centro Integral Santa Rosa, Calle A, Av. Principal, Tel. 914-879.

Airlines
Viasa: Torre Viasa, Plaza Morelos, Av. Sur 25, Los Caobos, Tel. 576-0411.
Avensa: Torre El Chorro, Av. Universidad, Tel. 509-3666.
Air France: Edif. Parque Cristal, Torre Oeste, Av. Francisco. de Miranda, Los Palos Grandes, Tel. 285-2311.
British Airways: Torre Británica, Av. José Félix Sosa, Altamira Sur, Tel. 261-0768.
Iberia: Edificio Iberia, Av. Urdaneta, Tel. 562-6444.

Swissair. Torre Europa, Av. Francisco de Miranda, Campo Alegre, Tel. 951-1211.
Lufthansa: Torre Bayer, Av. Tamanaco, El Rosal, Tel. 951-0044.
TWA: Torre El Chorro, Av. Universidad, Tel. 564-1822.

Embassies
U.S.A.: Av. Principal La Floresta, Tel. 285-3111.
United Kingdom: Edif. Torre Las Mercedes, Av. La Estancia, Chuao, Tel. 751-1022.
Germany: Edif. Panaven, Av. San Juan Bosco, Altamira, Tel. 261-2229.
Australia: Qta. Yolanda, Av. Luis Riche, Altamira, Tel. 263-4033.
Canada: Torre Europa, Av. Francisco de Miranda, Campo Alegre, Tel. 951-6166.
Spain: Qta. Embajada de España, Av. Mohedano, Tel. 263-2855.
France: Edif. Parque Cristal, Torre Oeste, Av. Francisco. de Miranda, Los Palos Grandes, Tel. 285-3455.
Italy: Edif. Atrium, Calle Sorocalma, El Rosal, Tel. 952-7311.
Switzerland: Torre Europa, Av. Francisco de Miranda, Chacaíto, Tel. 951-4606.

Excursions

The beaches
Given Caracas's summer weather, ocean bathing is the most popular weekend activity. On those days it seems that the entire city empties into the blue waters. **El Litoral**, past Monte Avila, offers a handsome strip of shore although its most beautiful sections are closed to the public. Located here are the exclusive private clubs, among them the famous **Playa Azul**, **Playa Grande** and **Camuri Chico**. The area may be reached by bus or taxi (*por puestos*). Both depart every few minutes from every part of town.

The beach at **Macuto** is one of the most popular, but neglect and dirt have turned this town, once the favorite stamping ground of Caracas's wealthy, into a graceless place. Rental equipment for sailing, fishing and diving are available at the *Macuto Sheraton*. Continuing eastward, we come to **Naiguata**, where the beach is also rather dirty.

A few hours on the road heading west from Caracas will bring you to far more tranquil cities which have clean and enchanting beaches. North of Maracay are two beautiful and popular beaches, **Ocumara de la Costa** and **Cata.** From Maracay you may set out for nearby **Lake Valencia**. About 100 km west of Caracas is the industrial port town of Puerto Cabello. Several of Venezuela's most beautiful and well-tended beaches lie to its west.

VENEZUELA

Isla Margarita

Isla Margarita, east of Caracas, is a popular resort. Its 90,000 inhabitants make a living chiefly from the sea and from tourism. Most devote their weekends and holidays to serving the thousands of tourists who flood **Porlamar**, the largest town (pop. 25,000) on the island.

Isla Margarita has kilometer after kilometer of pristine beach, wonderful weather, good restaurants, comfortable hotels and great bargains. As a duty-free zone, luxury goods are available at attractive prices. The most popular beach is palm-shaded **El Agua**, north of Porlamar and easy to reach by bus or hitchhiking. On the island's west side is **Golfo de Juan Griego**, famous for its gorgeous sunsets. Tourism on Isla Margarita has developed rapidly in recent years. New hotels have been built, beaches developed and roads paved — all to create a tourist resort similar to the nearby Caribbean Islands.

A one-hour flight and $100 separate Margarita from Caracas, and *Aeropostal* and *Avensa* will be glad to help you overcome the former in exchange for the latter. If you intend to fly on weekends or during holiday periods, reservations should be made several weeks in advance. A less expensive way of reaching the islands is via the ferries which ply the sea lanes from the coastal cities of Puerto la Cruz (about 4 hours) and Cumana (about 3 hours) every day. They may be reached by bus or *por puesto* (7-8 hours). It's a wonderful place, with a taste of the Caribbean. Be sure to bring a sun-screen lotion to prevent sunburn and money to get the best in this duty-free zone.

Colonia Tovar

In 1843, a group of Bavarian emigrants founded a small town on the mountain slopes, 60 km from Caracas. Colonia Tovar has remained isolated from the rest of Venezuela and its descendants have preserved their Bavarian origins — language, dress, customs, food and architecture. Tovar, at 2000 m above sea level, enjoys wonderful weather. Its people, who speak the Black Forest German of their ancestors, are warm and friendly.

This picturesque town, which has a number of souvenir shops, good Bavarian restaurants, and quiet hotels, is recommended for a short visit. But stay away on weekends when it can be very crowded and the trip may take hours. Regular public transportation to Colonia Tovar is not available from Caracas, though *por puestos* do set out from time to time. The most convenient way to go is either to rent a car or to organize a small group and hire a taxi. Tovar is easier to reach from the town of El Junquito either by public transit or hitchhiking.

San Juan de los Morros

Only 150 km southwest of Caracas, on the edge of a broad plain covering hundreds of thousands of square kilometers between the Andes and the Orinoco are the **Llanos** ("plains"). This is the birthplace of Venezuelan folklore, folk music, song and dance. The cattle-raising **llaneros** ride their horses barefoot, leading their large herds over vast pasturelands. This flood-prone stretch of territory is totally submerged for months every year, driving cattle and cowboys to higher, drier ground.

The *llaneros* live exactly as their forebears did, decades or centuries ago. Cattle raising is a full-time job and the only recreation is quiet singing and joyous dancing. Most of the songs tell of village life and the nomadic cowboy's life on horseback. Lyre and *cuatro* (similar to a small guitar) provide the accompaniment.

San Juan de los Morros is the *llaneros*' town. Here they gather to rest and recuperate. They bathe up in the nearby hot springs, revel in the stormy *joropo* dance, and compete in rodeos. The atmosphere is almost like the set of an old movie, where the scent of bygone days delicately lingers on.

Buses set out for San Juan every day, via Maracay. The town has small hotels, restaurants and pleasant taverns.

Western Venezuela

Venezuela's western section is dominated to a great extent by Lake Maracaibo and the surrounding plains — the country's oil center. The other attraction is the picturesque mountain town of Merida which has integrated old and new to preserve a disappearing old-time charm. It also boasts a large university.

Maracaibo

It was only about seventy years ago that Maracaibo was a small provincial town of little importance. 20,000 people scraped out a living in the hot, humid climate from the export of coffee and other crops. Today Maracaibo is the second-largest city in Venezuela, (pop. 1.3 million) and is the heart of the country's oil industry.

Maracaibo rests on the northwestern shore of Lake Maracaibo, the largest lake in South America. It is 150 km in length, and stretches more than 100 km at its widest point, with a total surface area of 14,347 km^2. A canal links it to the Gulf of Venezuela which empties into the Atlantic Ocean. Using this route, tens of thousands of barrels of petroleum set forth worldwide every day, accounting for about 75% of Venezuela's total exports.

Lake Maracaibo, surrounded by broad plains, is pinned between mountain spurs to the east and west — both extensions of the eastern Andes (Cordillera Oriental) of Colombia. Its shores are pocked with thousands of oil derricks.

Maracaibo, approached by the enormous Ordante Bridge, is a busy city. Apart from the port area and the adjacent streets, where one may still find old houses, it is no different from any other industrial city.

As an important economic center, Maracaibo enjoys convenient transportation to and from Caracas both by air (1 hour) and by bus (12 hours). Good connections are available to most of Venezuela's other large cities as well as to the Caribbean Islands, Miami and New York.

Where to stay
Hotels in Maracaibo are rather expensive, and reservations are recommended the year round in the upper categories.

Intercontinental del Lago: Av. 2, El Milagro, Tel. 912-022, Fax 914-551. The best and most expensive, on the lakeshore itself; it has a swimming pool, restaurant, etc.
Kristoff: Av. 8, Tel. 72-911, Fax 61-369. Not quite as expensive, nonetheless far from being moderate.

Roma: Calle 86, Tel. 220-868. Moderate prices, good Italian food. Recommended.

Yacambú: Av. Libertador, inexpensive, well located.

As for food, the city offers good restaurants, usually expensive ones, and less costly ones which serve light meals and snacks, which are good values. They are easily spotted on Av. 4.

Excursions in the area

The Lake Maracaibo area offers much more than drilling towns and oil rigs. North and west of the city itself live two Indian tribes, one southwest of Maracaibo and the second north of the city, mostly in Colombia.

The Motilones Tribe

A little more than three hours south of Maracaibo, on the expressway to San Cristóbal, is the town of Machiques. This is the departure point for a visit to the Motilones Indian-settlements.

From the arrival of the Spanish, until the end of the 1950's, there was little cooperation between these Indians and the new settlers. All offers of friendship were aggressively rejected. Had it not been for Venezuelans' urgent need to enter Indian territories in search of new drilling sites, these Indians might have been left alone to this day. However, after several years of bloody conflict, an agreement was reached and the Motilones are now a tranquil and friendly tribe.

The Motilones' villages are situated amidst the swamps, a good distance from Machiques. It can be reached on foot from one of the local monasteries.

Guajira Peninsula

North of Maracaibo, on the other side of the Gulf of Venezuela, lies the Guajira Peninsula. Here authentic Indian life can still be seen. Though most of the peninsula lies in Colombia, the close tribal relations on either side of the border make for simple and speedy crossing procedures.

There are buses from Maracaibo to various places on the peninsula and to Maicao, the Colombian border town. From Maicao you can continue to the peninsula villages (see "Personal security" in our Introduction to Colombia!).

Here, in the Guajira villages, you'll encounter a vanishing world. The women, who dress in colorful canvas dresses called *manta*, keep house and support the family. The locals live in structures almost straight from Indian tales set at the onset of the Spanish conquest. Both men and women paint their faces and wear their traditional dress. A fascinating place to visit. From here you may proceed to Colombia.

From Maracaibo to Mérida

The Maracaibo-Mérida expressway — the Pan American Highway — runs first along Lake Maracaibo at the base of the mountains and then climbs steeply towards the city. There's an alternate route between the cities passing through the towns and villages located in the mountains themselves. On this route, be sure to visit Valera and Boconó (where the garden-enveloped houses are built on the steep mountainside), as well as the village of Timotes and the resort towns of La Mesa and La Puerta.

About 50 km past Timotes, the road passes through the Aguilar Gap. This is the very place where Simón Bolívar and his army crossed the mountains during their famous campaign to liberate Colombia in 1819. An eagle-capped monument commemorates the historic trek. Continuing, you descend toward Apartaderos, a valley of Indian houses and stone terraces, which are still plowed by oxen. The road then forks; one branch continues to Santo Domingo (and from there to the Llanos Plains and eastward to the Venezuelan heartland), the other heads south to the town of Mucuchíes and Mérida.

The stretch between Apartaderos and Mucuchies abounds in small lakes and shady groves, all accessible by foot (preferably early in the morning). It's a lovely route through the lesser known and more enchanting parts of the country, winding through scenery and flora of rare beauty. The green-gold hues of the *frailejón* plant intermingle with the Indians' blue-red clothing to create a matchless mosaic.

Mérida

At the foot of Monte Bolívar in the middle of the Sierra Nevada de Mérida, 1640 m above sea level, lies Venezuela's highest city and one of the most enchanting in the country — Mérida. Almost 25% of its 140,000 residents are students at the local university, one of South America's oldest. The city itself was founded in 1558 and has always been noteworthy for its enchanting scenery — snow capped peaks in the distance and gorgeous vegetation all around as well as its tranquil way of life.

Mérida has been damaged more than once by earthquakes and only a few pre-Independence buildings have survived. The central plaza is graced with a cathedral, rebuilt in colonial style, while modern buildings have sprung up elsewhere in town.

Transportation

Aeropostal and *Avensa* airlines fly daily to Merida from Caracas. Buses link the city with Caracas (15 hours), Maracaibo (about 8 hours) and San Cristóbal (6 hours), from which you can cross into Colombia. Merida has a wealth of hotels and restaurants. A Tourist Information Office is located next to the Hotel Mucubají.

Where to stay

Pedregosa: on Av. Panamericana, edge of town; best and most expensive.

Prado Río Hotel, at the end of Av. Universidad, Hoyada de Milla, Tel. 520-633, Fax 525-152. On the foothills of the Sierra Nevada. Medium prices.

Panamá: On calle 17, inexpensive, popular with backpackers.

Tourist sites

The temperate climate and suitable geographic conditions have created a garden city. It boasts more than twenty public parks and gardens, where natives and visitors spend afternoons and weekends. **Parque Los Chorros de Milla**, rather far from downtown, is the best developed and has a zoo, flowing streams and more (closed Mondays). On Third Avenue, next to Plaza Bolívar, are the **Museums of Colonial** and **Modern Art.**

Mérida's main attraction, however, is actually overhead: the world's highest cablecar, reaching a height of 4765 m on **Pico Espejo**. This point offers a spectacular view of mountains and glaciers. The cablecar does not run every day and mechanical breakdowns are frequent. When the service does operate, lines are long and it is advisable to arrive early, preferably before 7am. The last trip up starts at noon. The trip itself takes more than an hour each way.

At the top, there are various hiking trails, some of several days' duration. These include a trek to the ice cave in the **Timoncitos Glacier** and a hike to **Los Nevados** — Venezuela's highest village. Details and guidance are available at Club Andino de Mérida. Don't forget that it's very cold up there and, except at the cablecar terminal, food is not available. Accurate maps, reliable equipment are a must. Hiking permits must be obtained from the Parks Authority and Police.

On to Colombia

From Mérida, the road continues on to San Cristóbal, about 80 km from the Colombian border. From here you can go on to San Antonio, the Venezuelan frontier town and cross the bridge into Colombia after completing border-crossing procedures. Final immigration procedures are handled in Cúcuta, Colombia. Bogota may be reached from here by land or air.

Currency exchange here is not simple and only cash dollars are accepted. All exchanges should be made on the Venezuelan side.

It's important to mention that there's no border station on the bridge. Immigration procedures must be made in the cities **before** you cross the border.

Southeast Venezuela

One of the more interesting and lesser known of Venezuela's regions runs along the length of the Orinoco Basin, across the 2575 km between its sources somewhere in the heart of the jungle, to the Atlantic Ocean, into which it empties through a tremendous delta.

The Orinoco Basin covers more than half of Venezuela's total area. It is sparsely settled, chiefly by indigenous Indians and by prospectors in search of buried treasures — gold, diamonds, oil, aluminium and copper.

Venezuelan governments have worked for decades to develop and promote the Orinoco Basin. Aware of its economic potential, they are fighting to overcome the tremendous financial burden involved in opening up the region. Roads have been paved, cities built, dams constructed and several industrial projects established. This is only the beginning.

Few roads lead to the Guayana Plateau, to the Gran Sabana and to the Amazon Basin, and even fewer are suitable for passenger cars without front-wheel drive. Few airplanes serve the remote towns whose inhabitants seldom leave in favor of the crowded, noisy Venezuelan heartland. Two cities, Ciudad Bolívar and Ciudad Guayana, are the largest in this part of Venezuela. From these cities one can penetrate deep into the tangles of a lost world of arid plateaus, bald mountains and dense jungles.

Ciudad Bolívar

Four hundred km up the Orinoco, on the river's southern bank, is Ciudad Bolívar, the city of Simón Bolívar. He declared it his capital in 1817, and from here, organized his army and set out on the famous campaign across the Andes en route to the battle of Boyacá (Colombia). There, by defeating the Spanish loyalists, he reached a turning point in Venezuela's War of Independence.

A little of the spirit of those days is still preserved in Ciudad Bolívar, which today is the home to approximately 200,000. Colonial buildings line its streets and the atmosphere is pleasant and easygoing. Along the riverbank are Indian peddlers who engage in lively commerce.

The city was originally called *Angostura* because of its location on the Orinoco's narrowest stretch, but today only the large suspension bridge over the river still bears the old name. Ciudad Bolívar, once a trading center for gold and diamonds, preserves a quiet, restrained character. It's worthwhile to buy gold and gold jewelry here, and is one of the few places in Venezuela where locally produced *objets d'art* have artistic merit.

The climate here is hot and warm, though it eases a bit in the afternoons and evenings.

Transportation
Ciudad Bolívar is easy to reach from Caracas. Follow the coast east, 350 km, as far as Puerto La Cruz and then another 300 km via Barcelona and El Tigre. If coming from San Juan de los Morros, the Llanos road is preferable, via El Tigre (467 km) and another 130 km to Ciudad Bolívar. A number of buses set out daily to Caracas (8-10 hours) and many more to Ciudad Guayana, close to El Dorado. *Aeropostal* and *Onesa* link Ciudad Bolívar with important cities in Venezuela and Santa Elena, on the Brazilian border.

Food and lodging
Ciudad Bolívar has several hotels and restaurants.

Orinoco: out of town, the best and most expensive.
Gran Hotel Bolívar: on Paseo Orinoco, corner with Dalla Costa, is pleasantly situated on the banks of the river, with a good restaurant.
Caracas: Paseo Orinoco, inexpensive, good value.
Italia: also on the banks of the river, inexpensive and friendly; good restaurant.

On Av. Táchira you will find a number of reasonable hotels, while the cheaper ones are on the eastern end of Paseo Orinoco.

Also on the east end, you will find the local market where you can buy cheap local foodstuff.

Excursions in the area
The road south from Ciudad Bolívar leads to **La Paragua**, a primitive mining town where most of its inhabitants prospect for diamonds and gold (not without considerable success). It's a 200 km trip on a difficult route which passes near Cerro Bolívar — the massive "iron mountain" whose ore fuels one of Venezuela's most important industries — iron production. From La Paragua you can set out for nearby villages where the main employment is diamond-hunting.

Energetic tourists who wish to visit Angel Falls economy-style can leave from La Paragua on a combined river cruise and hike toward Canaima, — the tourists' camp near the falls. It's a difficult, complicated route which requires not only superb physical condition but also navigation and jungle skills, suitable equipment, food and lots of time and perseverance. There are also flights to Angel Falls (see "Angel Falls").

Ciudad Guayana

Like Manaus and Iquitos, which blossomed almost overnight into centers of international economic importance with the discovery of rubber, so did the graceless industrial city of Ciudad Guayana. It has been developing at an astonishing pace — thanks to the growth of the iron and steel industries in the vicinity. Mining and processing metals rank second only to oil in the Venezuelan economy. In recent decades, the government has made great effort to develop these industries and increase their share in the national product. Ciudad Guayana was established as the center of the mining and metal processing industries. A large harbor, an airport and a rail link to the important mines were constructed to accommodate the growing industries. Some of Venezuela's largest factories producing steel, aluminium and iron were built in and around the city.

The Venezuelan government plans to settle a million people in the heart of the Guayana Plateau by the early 2000, despite the hot, harsh climate and unfavorable geographic conditions. The population of Ciudad Guayana and its surroundings has reached the 500,000 and is increasing at an astonishing pace, being encouraged by the central government. Ciudad Guayana is situated on the Orinoco, about 100 km from the beginning of the delta and an equal distance from Ciudad Bolívar, at the confluence of the Orinoco and Caroni Rivers.

Ciudad Guayana's Puerto Ordaz Airport has daily flights to and from Caracas and stopovers en route to Angel Falls (see below). Buses head south to El Dorado and northwest to Caracas. The city has hotels and restaurants and serves as point of departure for interesting excursions: east to the Orinoco Delta and south to Sabana and the Brazilian border.

Where to stay

Intercontinental Guayana: Parque Punta Vista. High standards and prices.
El Rasil: Centro Cívico. Somewhat less expensive and offers good services.
Turista: Av. Caracas. Inexpensive, friendly.

Reasonably priced hotels are found in San Félix, the historical town, but they are crowded with the workers which are building the new projected parts of town, making quite difficult the finding of cheap lodging.

Excursions in the area

The first three routes surveyed are loops, with Ciudad Guayana at their beginning and end. The last two — east to the delta and south to Sabana — may be taken either separately or en route to the coast (in the first case) or Brazil (in the second).

VENEZUELA

Guri Dam

Several dozen kilometers up the Caroni River we come to Guri which is destined, upon completion, to be the world's fourth-largest dam and the third-largest hydroelectric facility. In the early nineties, when most of it was already finished, it provided close to half the power consumption of the country.

The trip takes upwards of an hour and half by taxi and you must get there before 9am, when the guided tour begins. Upon completion, the dam will soar to 272 m at its highest point, create a lake 70,762 sq/km and will help generate eight million kilowatts of electricity! One of the world's great construction projects, Guri is an exceptionally interesting place to visit.

Cerro Bolívar

Venezuela's largest iron mine (annual output: two million tons of ore) is 134 km south of Ciudad Guayana near the town of Ciudad Piar. A new railroad leads from Ciudad Guayana to the area and brings the ore back into town — where it's loaded onto freighters for export to many countries.

The government corporation that runs the mine, *Ferrominera Orinoco*, organizes guided tours almost every day from its Ciudad Guyana offices. You can visit the site yourself by going directly to Ciudad Piar, near the mountain, though it's harder to enter that way and guides are not always available.

Angel Falls

When Jimmy Angel flew over the falls in 1935, he didn't know he'd discovered the world's highest waterfall (980 m). Returning two years later, Angel tried to land atop the mountain (from which the mighty waters descend) in hope of finding gold there. Though the mountaintop looks rather flat from the air, Angel and his party barely survived the rough landing. The falls have borne his name ever since, and their great height — seventeen times that of Niagara — has attracted many tourists and visitors.

Angel Falls are about 250 km south of Ciudad Guayana and there's no road or proper land access to them. The conventional method of getting there is with *Avensa*, which flies every day to the Canaima camp from which one sets off to the falls.

Canaima has two visitors' centers, one belonging to *Avensa* and the other to Rudy ("Jungle") Truffino, Canaima's founder and veteran director. The flights from Caracas are rather expensive and include lodging, food and a tour of the falls. You can economize by reserving only a flight and foregoing the accommodation, but then you'll need food and camping gear unless you decide to stay at the hotel (if there's room) and pay separately. The *Avensa* flights stop over at Puerto Ordaz Airport in Ciudad Guayana, so you can board there at far less expense. Planes fly to Canaima from Ciudad Bolívar from time to time as well, but they are usually private or chartered and are not always willing to take on passengers. A difficult route — a combined river voyage and hike — leads from Ciudad Bolívar to Canaima and Angel Falls (see "Ciudad Bolívar: Excursions in the area").

The Orinoco Delta
One of the most interesting ways of returning to the coastal plain from Ciudad Guayana is to trek down the Orinoco and visit the villages on the shores of the gigantic Orinoco Delta. Take the paved highway from Ciudad Guayana to **Tucupita**, a town of some 30,000 Indians who lost their lands upstream in the wake of the Guri Dam project and were resettled here. Automobile and *por puesto* travel between the two cities is frequent, as is river freight and passenger traffic (inquire about boats and directions along the river in Ciudad Guayana). *Aeropostal* flies here several times weekly from Ciudad Bolívar with a stopover in Maturin (by way of which one may continue afterward to the coastal area and Caracas).

Tucupita is a good point of departure for a small boat cruise among the riverside villages, where you can form an impression of the local Indians and view their way of life, work, and dress. Another interesting possibility is to head about 60 km upstream to the village of Barrancas. From Tucupita you can also set out by boat to Curiapo Island, right in the middle of the river, where there's a large and impressive Indian village. It is here, a little before the river splits into thousands of branches in the delta region, that the Orinoco reaches its greatest width — more than 18 km.

South to Brazil
From Ciudad Guayana a road leads south to Santa Elena — the Venezuelan town on the Brazilian border. From here you can go on to Manaus. This difficult route requires either a dependable vehicle or the patience and persistence necessary for slow progress by bus, truck and hitchhiking. Bring food (although there are enough restaurants on the way, it's hard to know where you'll get stuck), camping gear and enough local currency. Public transportation, fuel, lodging and food are very expensive here.

You'll pass through gorgeous scenery, thick vegetation and flat-topped mountains called *tapuies* (table mountains). These mountains, among South America's strangest and oldest geological structures, jut out with surprising steepness. At times the gradient is 90 degrees — and is nearly impossible to climb. The road passes between the mountains, crosses the Gran Sabana and descends to Santa Elena.

The paved road leads south from Ciudad Guayana for 285 km, skirting the town of Upata and the pleasant little jungle village of El Callao. It continues to Tumeremo and finally pulls into El Dorado.

El Dorado came into existence when hordes of prospectors began to pan for gold in the vicinity. Since the great hunt ground to a halt due to lack of success, the town appears to have kept running by sheer inertia. It is quiet, passive, and uninspiring. Buses come from Caracas, Ciudad Guayana and Ciudad Bolivar. There are several hotels and places to eat and you can organize river outings here to various villages and even to Canaima and Angel Falls.

From El Dorado, the road continues to **Kilometer 88**, a half-settlement half-crossroads, the starting point for the climb to Gran Sabana. It's a lovely trip amid lush vegetation, streams, lakes, waterfalls and table mountains.

The road used to end here and was pushed through to **Santa Elena** only in the mid-1970's. It is full of ruts and pot holes and the climb over La Escalera is exhausting and lengthy. The road continues on through Gran Sabana, crossing rivulets and streams until it reaches Santa Elena. This border town came into being in the early 20th century as a by-product of the diamond hunt and has since become a center for diamond miners and traders. Its several hundred inhabitants live in simple houses and are almost totally out of touch with the modern world.

Santa Elena is also accessible by *Aeropostal* flights, but reservations must be made well in advance. Daily buses run the routes between Santa Elena and Ciudad Bolívar (13-16 hours).

From Santa Elena you can head for the countryside — to Monte Roraima and the Indian village of Peraitepuí (difficult and complicated trip invlolves 10-14 days hike), or to the mining camps in the vicinity.

The border station is open until evening on weekdays and sometimes on weekends as well. If you're going on to Brazil, complete the crossing procedures in Santa Elena and cross the border at the nearby checkpoint. From here it's 220 km to Boa Vista, Brazil (approximately 6 hours by bus). Buses travel the route almost every day. From Boa Vista there are plane and bus connections to Manaus (760 km, around 24 hours) and from there, to the rest of Brazil.

Vocabulary

English	Spanish
good morning	*buenos días*
hello/good bye	*hola, adiós*
good evening	*buenas tardes*
good night	*buenas noches*
please	*por favor*
thank you	*gracias*
pardon, excuse	*perdón*
yes	*sí*
non	*no*
what...?	*qué...?*
when...?	*cuándo...?*
where...?	*dónde...?*
there is...	*hay...*
there is not...	*no hay...*
what is the time?	*Qué hora es?*
how are you?	*Cómo está?*
far	*lejos*
near	*cerca*
big/large	*grande*
small	*pequeño*
new	*nuevo*
old	*antiguo/viejo*
left	*izquierda*
right	*derecha*
first	*primero*
last	*último*
open	*abierto*
closed	*cerrado*
entrance	*entrada*
exit	*salida*
train	*tren*
ticket	*billete*
taxi	*taxi*
car	*coche*
plane	*avión*
airport	*aeropuerto*

English	Spanish
boat/ship	*barco*
port/wharf	*puerto/muelle*
gas-gasolina	
hotel	*hotel*
hostel	*albergue*
room	*habitación*
toilets	*servicios*
bath/shower	*baño/ducha*
restaurant	*restaurante*
café	*café/bar*
table	*mesa*
chair	*silla*
breakfast-desayuno	
lunch	*almuerzo*
dinner	*cena*
waiter	*camarero*
water	*agua*
bread	*pan*
drink	*bebida*
menu	*menú*
hot	*caliente*
cold	*frio*
bill	*cuenta*
receipt	*recibo*
cinema	*cine*
theatre	*teatro*
pharmacy	*farmacia*
shop, store	*tienda*
post office	*correos*
hospital	*hospital*
police	*policia*
embassy	*embajada*
market, bazaar	*mercado*
how much does it cost?	*cuánto cuesta?*

English	Spanish		English	Spanish
expensive	caro		October	Octubre
cheap	barato		November	Noviembre
			December	Diciembre
road, highway	carretera, autopista		1	uno/una
street	calle		2	dos
avenue	avenida		3	tres
square	plaza		4	cuatro
alley	callejuela		5	cinco
esplanade	paseo		6	seis
bridge	puente		7	siete
monument	monumento		8	ocho
fountain	fuente		9	nueve
church	iglesia		10	diez
palace	palacio		11	once
fort/castle	castillo		12	doce
town/city	ciudad		13	trece
village	pueblo		14	catorce
museum	museo		15	quince
			16	dieciseis
east	este		17	diecisiete
north	norte		18	dieciocho
west	oeste		19	diecinueve
south	sur		20	veinte
valley	valle		21	veintiuno
mountain	montaña		30	trenta
range	cordillera		31	trentiuno
hill	colina		40	cuarenta
forest	bosque		50	cincuenta
river	rio		60	sesenta
			70	setenta
Sunday	Domingo		80	ochenta
Monday	Lunes		90	noventa
Tuesday	Martes		100	cien
Wednesday	Miércoles		101	ciento uno
Thursday	Jueves		110	ciento diez
Friday	Viernes		200	doscientos
Saturday	Sábado		300	trescientos
			400	quatrocientos
January	Enero		500	quinientos
February	Febrero		600	seiscientos
March	Marzo		700	setecientos
April	Abril		800	ochocientos
May	Mayo		900	nuevecientos
June	Junio		1000	mil
July	Julio		2000	dos mil
August	Agosto		million	un millón
September	Septiembre			

*I*NDEX

QUESTIONNAIRE

In our efforts to keep up with the pace and pulse of South America, we kindly ask your cooperation in sharing with us any information which you may have as well as your comments. We would greatly appreciate your completing and returning the following questionnaire. Feel free to add additional pages.

Our many thanks!

_____

To: Inbal Travel Information (1983) Ltd.
18 Hayetzira Street
Ramat Gan 52521
Israel

Name: _____

Address: _____

_____

Occupation: _____

Date of visit: _____

_____

Purpose of trip (vacation, business, etc.): _____

_____

_____

Comments/Information: _____

_____

_____

_____

_____

_____

_____

_____

_____

_____

_____

_____

_____

_____

_____

_____

INBAL Travel Information Ltd.
P.O.B. 39090 Tel Aviv
ISRAEL 61390